ALBERT SLOSMAN

THE GREAT HYPOTHESIS

*Outline of a history of monotheism
from the origin to the end of the world*

ALBERT SLOSMAN (1925-1981)

THE GREAT HYPOTHESIS
*Outline of a history of monotheism
from the origin to the end of the world*

THE GREAT HYPOTHESIS
Outline of a history of monotheism
from the origin to the end of the world
First edition Robert Laffont, Paris, 1982

Translated and published by
OMNIA VERITAS LTD

www.omnia-veritas.com

Omnia Veritas Limited - 2025

All rights reserved. No part of this publication may be reproduced by any means without the prior permission of the publisher. The intellectual property code prohibits copies or reproductions for collective use. Any representation or reproduction in whole or in part by any means whatsoever, without the consent of the publisher, the author or their successors, is unlawful and constitutes an infringement punishable by articles of the Code of Intellectual Property.

1. 13
    DOES CHANCE EXIST? 13
2. 28
    WITH GENERAL VON STÜLPNAGEL 28
3. 39
    IS DESTINY ALSO WRITTEN? 39
4. 52
    THE GREAT CATACLYSM 52
5. 66
    THE ATLANTEAN SOUL IS NOT LOST! 66
6. 81
    THE SURVIVORS OF THE AHÂ-MEN-PTAH 81
7. 99
    THE RESURRECTION OF PTAH AT DENDERAH 99
8. 116
    DISCOVERING THE GREAT LABYRINTH 116
        Note on the original by Diodorus of Sicily *132*
        (with additions by A.-J. Letronne) *132*
9. 135
    THE GOLDEN CIRCLE 135
10. 153
    DISCOVERING DENDERAH 153
        Note on the burning of a book by Champollion *170*
11. 174
    THE AGE OF TAURUS IN ATH-KÂ-PTAH 174
12. 186
    THE AGE OF ARIES: MOSES THE REBEL 186
13. 203

GOD FORGOT EGYPT: 203
CAMBYSES THE MADMAN... 203
14 .... **220**
THE AGE OF PISCES : JESUS THE CHRIST 220
Restitution of the Hebrew calendar (4726-4744) *239*
15 .... **240**
WHAT I SAW AND UNDERSTOOD 240
16 .... **254**
ETERNITY BELONGS TO GOD ALONE 254
IN CONCLUSION... **269**
FOR OUR TIME 269
Celestial harmonic pulses *275*
List of the 36 "Egyptian" decans *278*
NOTE NUMBER 1 282
CHRONOLOGICAL DATES ACCORDING TO SIRIUS 282
NOTE N° 2 285
THEON OF ALEXANDRIA AND SIRIUS 285
BIBLIOGRAPHY... **291**
A) AT THE TIME OF ORIGIN.. *291*
B) IN THE TIME OF MOSES *294*
C) IN THE TIME OF JESUS... *297*
ON THE WORK OF ALBERT SLOSMAN 300
OTHER TITLES **301**

Publisher's note

In order to preserve authenticity, and given the simplicity of the language, we have chosen to keep certain tables and names in their original language. This should not present any difficulty to the experienced reader, and may encourage him to take a more active interest in Albert Slosman's research.

This book is dedicated to the memory of the woman who first taught me about kindness and fraternity above all other considerations, and who died as a result, even though she was awarded the Légion d'honneur.

To Madame Odette Micheli, President of the Swiss Red Cross in France during the Occupation, whose courage and self-sacrifice saved almost 100,000 children from hunger, despair and death.

A.S.

The Temple of Denderah, while showing us that at the time it was built the spirit of old Egypt was still alive, also proves that in the two centuries that preceded and followed the advent of Christianity, the foreign seeds that were to so profoundly modify that spirit were already deposited there.

These remarks only add to the interest of the revelations that the temple itself will provide us with about its own antiquity. The temple was still being built when Jesus Christ was preaching in Palestine. But it is with profound astonishment that we follow the traces of temples predating the present temple in the most distant past that the history of mankind has so far been able to reach. A temple erected to the Hathor of Denderah did indeed exist under Ramses II and Thutmes III; remains can be found under the XIIth, VIth and IVth dynasties, the dynasty contemporary with the Pyramids. What's more, the dogma that forms the basis of the temple, i.e. the philosophical belief in beauty represented and symbolised by Hathor, is already present beyond anything that can be imagined as far back history, beyond Menes and the founder of the Egyptian monarchy. If the remains of monuments predating Menes are ever found in Egypt, it is clear that nothing will be discovered that recalls the brilliant culture of the time of Ramses or even the time of Cheops. But it is nonetheless worth noting as a considerable fact that by this remote period Egypt had already seen God, and that, consequently, it had already been born to civilisation. At a time when the science of prehistoric studies is turning its attention with such commendable ardour to the origins of the civilised world, it is curious to see Egypt pushing back further and further into the past the point at which man ceased to be precisely a savage.

Auguste Mariette

(End of the foreword to the important five-volume work entitled *Denderah*, four of which are devoted to the plates drawn copying all the hieroglyphic texts of the Great Temple of Hathor .¹ First published in 1875).

---

[1] Hathor, or Heart of Horus. This is Horus' mother, Isis, whose goddess name Hathor idealises mother and child. Denderah is therefore the temple of the Divine Triad: Osiris, Isis and their son Horus. (A.S.)

1

DOES CHANCE EXIST?

> *There is not a moment when God creates, and a moment when second causes develop. There is only ever one creative action that continually lifts creatures towards greater well-being through their second activity and their previous improvements.*
>
> Pierre Teilhard de Chardin (*How I believe*)

— You are sitting on what was once God's abode, Albert. Your gaze dominates the eternity of the Great Architect of the Universe...

— The house of God? I don't understand?

— You can't understand, because today only the last children of the ancient Fakos tribe know this truth, which represents the first page in the history of humanity.

I had to strain my ears in the din to catch all the words of my old companion. So I preferred to wait for the rest without asking unnecessary questions. And it didn't take long.

— This mountain, on whose summit we stand today, is around four thousand metres high. But a long time ago, it was more than twice that height: it was the only place in the world that could boast of touching the sky! "Fako", the name of this summit in the Douala dialect, means "sorcerer". It was over ten thousand metres high and it was from here that God dispensed His justice. He was the Creator of all things and He punished or rewarded His creatures without distinction, depending on whether they obeyed or broke His Laws!

— But God wasn't a sorcerer, was he?

— Of course not! But one day, in a holy anger of which he has the secret, God decided to punish all humans who had become impious and the worst of the foolish unbelievers.

— What did he do?

— The whole earth shook, and there was a great, great cataclysm, which almost completely engulfed an immense continent to the northwest of where we are now. Your eyes could have imagined the golden roofs of its cities at the end of the horizon, if this sea of raging clouds didn't limit our view to this natural splendour alone.

— But it's not written anywhere!...

— No! Because destiny cannot be written down: it has to be told. It is passed down from generation to generation in every part of the world, becoming legends born of the Truth that I have just told you and that constitutes the past.

— What happens next, since there are always humans?

— God, in his mercy, decided to give the survivors of the disaster another chance by allowing them to survive in another environment where the sun was no longer in the same place. But to show that he still refused to forgive, he blew up his Abode, which in turn sank, but only partially, so that no one would forget that God is God! That's why this mountain is only four thousand metres high today. But you know that just opposite it is the island of Fernando Poo. It rose out of the sea at that very moment, raising a single mountain to over three thousand metres! And God went back to heaven to await the day of final judgement: the day when mankind will have to give account to him!

— It's fascinating! A few years ago, Mrs Micheli, president of the Swiss Red Cross for which I worked, told me about similar events. But they related to stories told on Egyptian papyrus.

— Egypt was once a very great nation, a long time ago, Albert. No doubt the survivors of the cataclysm I told you about made it there. I didn't have time to study this religion during my school years Germany and France, and now I'm far too old! But you will! I burst out laughing.

— It would have to be so fortuitous for that to happen that I don't think there's a chance in a million...

— You're very young. Your future lies ahead of you, not behind. As for chance, I'll prove to you another day that it doesn't exist.

This sentence left me wondering, because in my very early years I had already asked myself the agonising question: "Does chance exist? As if in answer, the voice of my old companion came to me, mingled with the wind:

— Do you realise that it wasn't mere chance that drew you to this country, Albert?

— Not very well, and the misfortunes I've had so far don't do much to clear my head on this thorny issue. Yet it was I who freely chose to come to this side of the world, rather than go to America or Asia.

— There was a specific reason for this.

— Which one?

— You'll discover it yourself when you get there, but probably after a lot of searching and disappointment.

— I hope not! However, I remember that when I chose to come to Cameroon, I devoured all the books about it, including Hannon's journey.

— Who is it?

— He was a Carthaginian navigator who travelled six centuries before Christ. He wrote an account of his journey, in which he tells of the eruption of a gigantic volcano at the bottom of a gulf that is believed to be the very one on which Douala is built.

— I haven't heard of it, but it's interesting. When we get back down, don't forget to ask the mission library for me. It's bound to be there.

— I will; but if I read this text in Paris, it was purely by chance. It had no influence on my decision to come here. I remain sceptical.

— So the time has not yet come, son. There's no such thing as chance, you'll understand when the time comes, because you have a mission to fulfil here on earth.

— In Cameroon?

— Only God could say, and He is no longer in this Abode...

— How difficult it is to acquire some knowledge!

— It takes time, a lot of patience, and even more openness to wisdom. For if the world is to remain our world, humanity must become wiser.

— If not?

— Otherwise, it will be doomed. And it has already begun, because the war that has just ended is only the essential prelude to the one that will follow!

A great sigh escaped me, carried away by the furious wind that swept across the place where we were huddled together, wrapped in blankets. We were chatting serenely, despite the raging elements, waiting for nightfall. I gazed down at the sea of clouds that made this extravagant scene even more unreal than nature had created it. I asked myself so many questions: was I ready to become a superman, or just an underachiever? I felt incapable of answering.

At that distant time, which had been one of the high points of my life, I was twenty-two years old, and my companion was of an indefinable age, probably closer to *four times* mine. We more 4,000 metres above sea level, right on the African equator! Admittedly, this situation may seem quite banal in 1981, but it certainly wasn't in 1948 on the summit of the Fako, culminating at 4,170 metres, in what was then still English Cameroon.

The old man was a native pastor who had been retired for a number of years. He had done all his studies in Germany before 1900, because Cameroon, which had become partly French and partly English after the 1914-1918 war, had previously been a German colony. Then he started all over again, valiantly, in order to regain his place in the French Protestant missions, where he remained until the Second World War.

Having arrived in this country with what seemed to me to be a kind of halo, both of a saint and of a twenty-year-old martyr, I realise today that for some people I must have seemed gifted above all with immeasurable stupidity! But others, like this extraordinary being who kept me company, saw beyond my ridiculousness a predestination to play an important role in the vital phases of a future, still undetermined at the time, in which I would be involved. I didn't know anything yet, and my sigh was somehow a sign of my exasperation and sadness at being faced with an imprecise fact that no longer constituted a simple alternative. I was already aware, however, that the events of the past, those that had so severely marked my young life, were not due to simple coincidences, more or less fortunate. But I was still asking myself the question: "Does chance exist? And this terminology of 'chance' took on the form of a concrete entity.

The unfolding and sequencing of my actions had occurred without me being able to do anything to weigh on one or other of the scales forming the actions of destiny. So the 'coincidences' had taken on a disturbing weight in my soul. I could no longer describe as such the continuous sequence of events that had led me to find myself at the age of twenty-two on the summit the highest mountain in Cameroon! Was it just chance? The old pastor was by no means convinced... and I was beginning to seriously .

With the benefit of hindsight, since thirty-five years have gone by since that memorable ascent, I realise that personal experience is a sham, since I subsequently changed my lifestyle three more times, against my better judgement, before being led to undertake my current work, in almost unbearable physical conditions, since I am, alas, more than 80% disabled. In other words, I *can* only move around with the assistance of another person.

The fierce need to achieve the goal I've set myself from now on depends solely on my will to get there before death catches up with me. I know that this race against time sounds very melodramatic. I'm still reluctant to use that very graphic description. But it's clear that my willpower currently exceeds the framework of my life, pushing my remaining strength towards achieving what I've set out to do, in parallel with a weak physical constitution that I refuse to worry about.

Before reaching this resolution, I had two serious accidents, for which chance can hardly be blamed. The first, in 1970, left me in a coma for four months, during which time I was totally paralysed, followed by twenty-two months in hospital. The other was in 1956, when I was clinically declared dead and had to spend almost three years in bed. If we add to this the fact that before going to Cameroon I had an extraordinary life from 1942 to 1945, which led me directly to the Gestapo in Dole, in the Jura, where I was tortured, then saved almost miraculously to be taken to a clinic in Lausanne, where I spent many months regaining a human appearance, the retrospective will also begin to take shape. But it's still very incomplete, because there were far more horrific moments, interspersed with episodes that were almost fabulous because they carried me so high î But that didn't stop my human carcass, or at least its current appearance, from remaining the most anonymous among the others!

So it's easiest to go back in time to 1942, to start at the beginning, and let Cameroon arrive in its own chronological time...

As far as I can remember, the second year of the German occupation of Paris was even more grim than the previous ones. March 1942 stretched on interminably in the Siberian cold, weighed down by a snow that nothing and nobody could keep off the Parisian pavements. I'd just turned seventeen, and for three days I'd been living alone in a flat next to the Boulevard Bonne-Nouvelle, close to the big *Rex* cinema, which had become the most luxurious of the *Soldatenkino* for the occasion. My parents were no longer there, and I had escaped arrest by the Gestapo because of my absence at the time. The German occupation was having a heavy impact on everyone, but particularly on foreigners and Jews. My mother was Russian and my father of Israeli-German origin. Having fought in the 1914 war for France, against Germany, he had easily obtained French nationality afterwards. So I was born a fully-fledged French citizen in Paris in 1925. But under the Occupation, the whole family was automatically condemned by Hitler.

A brother of my mother's living in Geneva, Switzerland, had informed my parents several months previously that if there were any problems concerning us, they should contact him through the Swiss Chancellery in Paris. So, after some natural hesitation, I went to the legation on rue de Grenelle. I was extremely well received and asked to telephone three days later to find out the result of the steps I had taken.

When the time came, I called back and was given a name and address in Paris by my uncle, "in order to regain confidence in the future", I was told. It was the president of the Swiss Red Cross in occupied France, Mrs Odette Micheli, who was looking after children who had been victims of the war, and who might be able to help me in some way. The offices of this charity occupied an entire floor of the Ministry for the Family, in the Rue de Tilsit, which had been graciously lent to them by the French government. But it was an unheard-of 'coincidence' that I had met this lady the day before, under astonishing circumstances, during an alert at a children's home! From that first contact, there was a kind of current that, although not electric, galvanised me in a matter of seconds. Mrs Micheli, with her very special voice, instilled dynamism and optimism in me, and enabled me to see the future in a different light, whatever the negative events that had brought me to meet her.

So the next day, when I got her name and address, I felt a strange shock at this 'coincidence' and the double chain of events that were now leading me to her. It was such a twist of fate that I found it very funny! But I made no attempt to investigate the event, content to accept the fact.

After that, I noticed on many occasions the almost hypnotic attraction that the President exerted on the desperate people who came to see her, and who left her office with a soothing balm in their hearts and a smile on their faces; I thought that I too had been simply charmed. On that famous day of our first meeting, when she judged me by my potential for the future, Odette Micheli hired me without hesitation to assist her in the various tasks directly related to the administration of her presidential post.

Although she had a large number of secretaries, in fact she only had two deputies and one Swiss assistant in management positions, where they were clearly overworked. The President was on her own to make her many official visits. In addition, she lacked help in organising the reception centres for French children from all over the country, where they were awaiting their departure for Switzerland for a period of three or six months, renewable in serious cases. The Swiss Red Cross was in a privileged position to act in this way, not only because Switzerland's neutrality was recognised by the Germans, but also because the Swiss had signed an agreement with Hitler's government stipulating that for every French child leaving for the land of William Tell, as many German children would also go there under the same conditions and for the same reasons.

This unexpected and unhoped-for situation not only protected me from prosecution, but also provided me with interesting work that gave me a new zest for life. For the first time, I learned from Mrs Micheli that this social life could quickly open the way to an understanding that would make me a wise man, endowed with many powers. Although I didn't immediately understand the meaning of this prophetic phrase, I remembered it often afterwards...

Naturally, new Swiss papers gave me a different identity and a higher age, which made it much easier for me to become fully integrated into the workings of the organisation. I barely had time to familiarise myself with the various departments when the President asked me to travel with her to Vichy to assist her at an important meeting she was to have with Marshal Pétain.

To fully understand what follows, we need to go back to May 1942, when the Germans had their tentacles in almost every corner of France, thanks to an effective fifth column in every field. However, a charity like the Swiss Red Cross was not involved in their espionage, as it was also doing Germany a huge favour by taking in children who had fallen victim to the British bombing raids across the Rhine. This did not prevent the occupying authorities in France from "watching" the Red Cross offices.

With the aid service expanding enormously, the small reception centres were no longer sufficient, and the President was looking for a much larger building capable of accommodating a thousand children at once. However, despite all the enquiries made in Paris and the inner suburbs, there was only one possible location: a disused barracks near Boulevard Henri I. Other organisations were also involved in the search: the French Red Cross, Secours national, Entraide d'hiver and others. This explains why so many people were aware of the need expressed by the Swiss Red Cross. So, one morning, a man came to Rue de Tilsit to see Mrs Micheli, and the President had taken a very big risk by seeing him. That's what she told me on the train that was taking us both to Vichy that same night.

The man was a captain in the Second French Bureau expatriated to Lyon, still in the free zone, and who had risked his life to come and inform her of a very delicate situation, which could nonetheless enable her to obtain a reception centre in Paris commensurate with her hopes. The centre was the École Polytechnique itself, near the Panthéon, which had been empty since the Armistice because the Polytechniques had moved back to Lyon.

This officer was obviously not making this proposal just to do the Swiss Red Cross a favour, but because General von Stülpnagel, the Chief of Staff of the German armies in France, had set his sights on the École Polytechnique as the site for his main headquarters.

However, all the trophies from past wars were still in the Paris premises, at the mercy of Nazi looting, with no way of recovering them beforehand. The only hope was that the Swiss Red Cross would be able to use them as a reception centre before the arrival of General von

Stülpnagel, scheduled for the following Monday. The captain had come on Thursday morning to explain to us that Marshal Pétain had agreed to sign a valid requisition on condition that we were at his house at eleven o'clock on the following day, when he could interpose our visit to the Hôtel du Parc between two appointments.

The President, hearing only the name of the prestigious school, instantly 'forgot' the other reason given by the officer from Lyon. She immediately booked two seats on the night train to Vichy. As there were no more sleeping cars or couchettes, we had time to discuss and prepare an extremely detailed plan for occupying the premises that had been left completely empty. All night long, I wrote down under his dictation, in spite of the blue light that had been turned on to respond to air raid warnings, the requirements in terms of various equipment, supplies and staff that would be needed to receive between one thousand and eleven hundred children by Sunday evening, in other words before the next three days were up! The head offices of the French Red Cross in Lille, Le Havre and Saint-Nazaire, who were responsible for preparing the files of child victims of the war for their respective regions, had already been informed by telephone during the afternoon. Each region would have to send its children home by train on Saturday evening. As for André François-Poncet, President of the French Red Cross at the time, he had put all his departments on alert so that, in agreement with Secours National, all the necessary equipment would be ready for Saturday.

In Vichy, Marshal Pétain, assisted by Dr Ménétrel, had no difficulty in obtaining the requisition. Everything was ready, and not a word was said about the trophies still hidden in the basement of the Grande Ecole. The return to Paris was uneventful, and it was in the heat of the moment that a whole army of volunteers organised the premises, fitting out the dormitories, kitchens, etc., with the help of a team of volunteers.

A book would obviously not be enough to describe this page of history, virtually unknown, but true point by point. I took advantage of my long convalescence in 1958 to write a first draft of this epic, then of those that followed. All this remained buried in the bottom of a trunk until 1969, when I undertook to put the draft on a typewriter myself. And, to keep a record of it, I gave a copy to a well-known

Geneva journalist[2] ... three weeks before my second accident. It then disappeared again for eleven years, before I asked for it back, which I did in the middle of finalising this manuscript, in May 1981.

The nine hundred or so typewritten pages would later become the subject of an autobiography. But among all the still unknown episodes of this important period of my life that I am going to reproduce here, so that everyone can better understand the various steps, high and low, that led me to write *L'Histoire du Monothéisme* and some twenty works published or to be published, is that of the École polytechnique de Paris. So I was seventeen, but my papers made me a Swiss citizen of twenty-three. It was Monday morning, 8 o'clock. Five hundred children were having breakfast in the refectory of the prestigious school: a huge hall with long marble-paved tables.

It was the end of the first shift, and I was about to get up to give the signal to leave, so as not to delay the arrival of the second group, a thousand children who had slept there last night, when the Germans who had come to occupy the school intruded. They came down the few steps leading to the refectory...

Here, copied verbatim, is the part of the manuscript written over twenty years ago about the École Polytechnique and the General-in-Chief of the German occupying armies in France...

... We were surrounded and the machine guns were pointed at us. We were at gunpoint! All the adults were more or less paralysed with fear, and I have to say that it was the same for me. I was certain that at the slightest misunderstanding these people would shoot us without warning! I couldn't even try to reassure them, because the slightest pretext would be good enough to provoke a murderous incident. These soldiers looked so bad, with their bulldog-like appearance and their huge collars around their necks, that it was better to turn into a statue for the time being.

Another order, suddenly shouted, brought all the soldiers to impeccable attention, with an impressive clatter of heels. As if in a well-rehearsed operetta, several pairs of gleaming boots appeared at the top of the refectory entrance steps, followed by grey-green trousers of varying shades, embroidered with long vertical stripes of red or

---

[2] It was Martin Leu, a former reporter for *La Suisse* newspaper, to whom I would like to express my sincere gratitude.

carmine, and topped by tunics studded with gold and decorations. The heads at the end of these bodies proved, if proof were needed, that these were senior officers. Their caps, however, told me nothing about their respective ranks.

At the bottom of the slowly descending steps, these gentlemen stepped aside to let an officer pass who, by his appearance, must have been an even higher ranking officer. He was dressed in trousers, not booted, with a haughty air, well-furnished eyebrows and moustache, but the general appearance was rather disillusioned.

There were seven officers in all. They came to meet us, beautifully framed between the machine guns of two soldiers who were standing, legs spread, in front of our table. I felt like I was looking at a life-size photograph, or a scene from a war film I'd been involved in! The one walking alone in front was clearly a general, as I finally realised from his epaulettes. The others followed at a respectful distance, copying their movements left and right to those of their superior. I saw the Iron Cross of the leading man who, unlike his escort, wore no other decoration. The man's grey moustache, his aristocratic appearance and his high forehead under his cap did not remind me of anything! I had no idea who this general was...

This smashing entrance would have been interesting, even entertaining, if we hadn't been guarded by the military, and if frightened children hadn't been in danger of retaining traces of it later. clatter of the boots earlier, and the soldiers who had frozen in rigorous immobility, had calmed the children. They were now silently watching the group make their way down the central aisle towards us, as was I, who was anxiously wondering what was going to happen next!

We were only a few metres apart when I recognised Colonel Oberg in the man directly behind the General. I'd bumped into him at the Majestic Hotel on several occasions, and he was very identifiable, given his appearance. Suddenly I was startled! I realised that if he was standing *behind* the general, and if everyone was acting deferentially, it was because the senior officer could only be *von Stülpnagel!... Der Militärbefelhshaber in Frankreich!...* In other words, the general commanding the occupying troops in France was marching right up to me!

My face paled even more! I certainly hadn't expected, and neither had the President, such an invasion. The occupation was there, omnipotent, personified by its leader in France. I no longer felt up to the task of taking responsibility for the meeting that was about to take place. But as the final steps were being taken, I realised that no one else could take my place. It wasn't Mr Grandjean or Mrs Robelin who would get us out of this mess. If I had known what to do, or how to invoke God in that last second, I would have said a prayer! But there wasn't enough time... even to try and invoke God.

The general had just stopped, gazing majestically at our table. The group of six following him also stopped a few paces behind. Only one officer detached himself to slip past the occupant and come up to us. The soldiers guarding us moved aside, while in a haughty voice, in mincing words, the officer questioned us in correct but hesitant French:

— Who... is... in charge... here?

This ridiculous request restored my composure. I replied in a firm voice, which I hoped would be calm:

— No one is in charge! This is no longer the École Polytechnique. As you can see, there are only children around you. What is the meaning of this armed intrusion, which is a real scandal?

— Who lives here then? How dare you... talk... like that in front of General *Herr von Stülpnagel?*...

— You're in an *official* Swiss Red Cross reception centre, under the protection of the neutrality treaty that links your country to ours: Switzerland!

The man was obviously stunned. He murmured:

— *Schweizerisches Rotes Kreuz!... Mein Gott!*

The guttural pronunciation of his statement that this was the Swiss Red Cross and his involuntary invocation of God were worth their weight in gold! But I didn't linger to smile at his catastrophic expression. I continued loud enough for all the officers to hear me, for I had seen the general wink when I had spoken in French, and I suspected that he understood perfectly well:

— Your brutal entrance forced the nurses, who could be recognised by their uniforms by anyone, to calm down hundreds of children whom you had terrified and possibly made ill... What need is there here for all these soldiers with their guns pointed at us? Do you think we're terrorists up to no good?

In an uncertain, less confident voice, the officer replied with an apology:

— I... I am... an interpreter, only...

— Well, tell your superiors that I am here as a representative of the Swiss Red Cross, myself a citizen of this country.

— But... I... we...

The man stammered and did not finish his sentence. He turned to the general, stood to attention again and faithfully translated our short dialogue. The occupant calmly replied to him in a low voice, which I could not understand, but which the interpreter, turning another half-turn, immediately translated for me:

- General von Stülpnagel... has come to take... delivery of the École... polytechnique... in the name of the *Führer!*... He asks what... you do and why... you are here?

I was back on my game, this kind of question being one I'd been thinking about for a long time. The only difference was who was asking them. I answered, straightening up:

— We take in children who are victims of the British bombing raids, and we send them to Switzerland. But before answering any more questions, ask the Commander-in-Chief to remove all the soldiers, as they are terrorising the children. With regard to the Swiss Red Cross, a neutral organisation on two counts, there is no justification for such an act of hostility, which constitutes an unspeakable abuse of power for which I will have to report to our President.

— But... But... I don't...

— No! I don't want to hear anything as long as there are these... armed soldiers in the mess hall. Please translate my words for the General.

Distraught, the interpreter didn't know what to do, because it was obvious that he feared his boss would be furious when he heard the translation! With a heavy heart, after looking at me once more and realising that I wasn't going to change my mind, he turned again to explain what I had just said. But there was no denying that the General had understood. I saw him bat his eyelashes at the same time as his interpreter during my tirade. He then flashed a quickly concealed smile when I said I wanted to get the soldiers out, which was not the case for the poor man who was trying to arrange my sentences in a less bellicose way. The general, who had had time to prepare his reply, remained silent, however, frowning very conspicuously with his bushy eyebrows. I wondered anxiously how he took my desire. In any case, he gave no answer to his subordinate, who just stood there, at attention, like a picket in a thunderstorm. And yet the cyclone didn't come: there was complete calm and total silence in the huge room, apart from a few sniffles from the kids.

After a fairly long time, the general finally turned his head slightly towards those behind him, who hadn't flinched at all and had turned pale at the translation of my request. I thought I had signed my death warrant when I saw the big soldier's mouth open. It appeared that he was speaking calmly and only to call his chief of staff:

— *Oberg!*

The colonel stepped forward quickly.

— *Ya, Herr General!*

— *Macht dass alles heraus kommt (Get everyone out.)*

Visibly stunned by this order, the colonel stammered:

— *Aber... Herr General... (But... my General...)*

Von Stülpnagel frowned even more, before chanting:

— *Al -les -he -raus ! (All -of -the -outside!)*

As Colonel Oberg clicked his heels and bowed under the repetition of the order, the General added:

— *Warten Sie in meinem Wagen* (Wait for me in my car).

— *Zu Befehl, Herr General!* (At your orders, General!)

As if stunned, Colonel Oberg returned to the other officers in the suite. Even he had been asked to leave, which I had not requested. He gave the order in a subdued voice, trembling with fury. The officers rushed in, realising that they had better hurry. They shouted in vain, because the soldiers had already lowered their weapons when they heard the general speak.

— *Alles heraus! Alles heraus! Schnell!... Schnell!*

This time the shouts were welcome. The soldiers all rushed with the same enthusiasm towards the exit, with the same sound of their boots, followed by the officers and Colonel Oberg. Only the interpreter remained in the same place, undecided and motionless, two steps away from von Stülpnagel.

I breathed a huge sigh of relief. Recovering from this success, I stood up so as not to be rude any longer. To thank him for this simple act of humanity, I pulled a chair over to the corner of the table and invited him, in German, to take a seat. Watching my accent, I added:

— Would you care for a cup of chocolate, General? It's Swiss...

Von Stülpnagel stared at me for a moment, a little surprised by my sudden and, it has to be said, changing position. Perhaps he was also surprised by my German. Then he smiled, bowed his head and took his seat. He replied in the same calm voice, but in French:

— With pleasure, sir!

2

WITH GENERAL VON STÜLPNAGEL

Where they have made a desert, they say they have made peace...
Tacitus (*Annals*)

The General took off his cap, looked at the refectory where five hundred little faces were staring at him in surprise.

Madeleine quickly understood. Smiling, she grabbed a bowl and offered it to the distinguished-looking officer, before going to the kitchen for some hot chocolate.

I asked Mme Robelin, who was losing her colour, to let the children who had just finished lunch out. Grandjean also went out, which was preferable.

Released, the young class scattered. Conversation and noise resumed as they left. The General meditated, lost in thought. The silence became heavy. He stared at me and smiled, saw his interpreter, still like a statue, and curtly asked him to leave:

— *Folgt auch den Kinder, Otto...*

The officer clicked his heels and left. The general began, in French, in the tone of a social conversation:

— It's nice of children, they forget very quickly, fortunately.

Frowning, in a strong German voice, he continued:

— There is no justification for your tone with my interpreter. Your occupation is illegal and arbitrary. It is very unfortunate.

— Why, General?

— I could have done without the diplomatic incident that's about to erupt.

— I'll only complain if there's an incident, as I said.

— You are here illegally. My soldiers have had to leave this room, but they will not leave. We are moving to the Military Academy on the Führer's orders.

— We're here legally, General.

His eyes became two small slits, and he repeated:

— Legally?

I said without reply, and he replied sharply:

— I am the law in France.

— I...

Speechless, I took out my wallet and carefully removed the requisition order signed by Marshal Pétain.

The general looked at me curiously. I was arousing his attention. Remaining calm and impassive, I handed it over.

— Is this legal, General?

He felt the blow. His lips, thin as a line, expressed perplexity and anger.

Madeleine, appearing and seeing the requisition in General's hands, understood. She smiled enticingly. She presented him with the tray, filled with the fresh aroma of cocoa, lightening the mood by saying gently:

— Do you mind?

This question stopped the General in his tracks. He nodded curtly. He contented himself with watching his hostess serve us. Without consulting each other, we ate. He took a whiff and said:

— Switzerland is a lovely country when it exports cocoa! Why thwart our Führer and do something naughty?

He blew on his slightly hot chocolate. As he drank, I replied:

— That's not our intention, as you well know, General.

— This requisition is dated 1st May, and you occupied the premises a few hours before us. Don't play innocent.

— How does the date change our intentions, General?

— Don't you see? Three days before, our file leaves for Berlin and also returns signed on 1 May. Curious, isn't it?

— How can the Swiss Red Cross be responsible for this unfortunate coincidence, General?

He almost choked. He replied, raising his voice:

— But the collusion is obvious! Our enemies didn't want us at Polytechnique.

— Collusion, sir? Is this an attempt at intimidation or a faulty translation from French? Our organisation cannot be associated with your "enemies". What's more, the Swiss are strictly neutral, an essential condition for their action.

The General sighed and stared at me intently. Did he doubt my sincerity? Such a coincidence could really be fortuitous. It was a sad fate for him. I was in the right. Our president saw nothing but a providential windfall for her children. I wasn't lying when I said that.

With a very sceptical pout, the general remarked:

— If you're only here a day early, it's not down to chance.

— General, tomorrow a convoy of a thousand children is leaving for Switzerland.

— A thousand children!

— Tomorrow evening, General, come and count them. There will be one thousand two hundred and eleven exactly.

— We receive our children three days beforehand. Housing them, cleaning them, examining them medically and dressing them all take up this time.

Up until now, our small centre has been sufficient for around a hundred children. It is impossible, General, to use this method for a thousand. The first convoy leaving on 3 May has been planned for two months. That's the truth of the matter.

— It's easy to say, but I'm leaning towards much less.

— General! Is it possible to get a special train of sixteen wagons in just a few days? And the authorisation of the Kommandantur for this formation?

— Exactly when did your Red Cross make the request?

— I think it was in February, three months ago.

— That may be true, but there are other places than this school to welcome you.

— Certainly, but not for a thousand children. We've been looking for premises for weeks. Our president couldn't sleep. *At the last minute*, we had to cancel our first major convoy. At the last minute, she heard about the École Polytechnique. She scrambled to get it in time.

— I would believe it if I weren't so experienced in all the tricks of war.

— My general, the President and I were in Vichy the day before yesterday. The Marshal signed because we were talking about a thousand children who had fallen victim to British bombing. What's more, we were the Swiss Red Cross.

Von Stülpnagel did not surrender.

— That doesn't change my impression, sir.

— But really, General, you're dragging our President into an unspeakable deal!

— Hm!

— Do you think she's engaged in espionage and is aware of your plans?

— Of course not! But what a bizarre coincidence.

— I'm not fighting your prejudice any more, General, but find us a large enough building that meets our needs, with the same advantages. We'll move straight away!

— You know that's impossible.

— I wanted to make that clear. It's impossible and that's the reason for the emergency request, but it's perfectly legal. It's for the children, General, and for nothing else!

He hesitated, finished his chocolate and then made up his mind.

— Your point of view can be accepted. But we're being played, aren't we?

Exasperated, I got angry and, in a vehement tone, I resumed.

— A game, sir! Making this place a refuge for children who no longer have a home and often no parents!

— Don't exaggerate, sir!

— Ask the little people from Le Havre and Dunkirk who are here if I'm being dramatic!

— Is that where they're from?

— Yes, General, you are well placed to know the state of these towns. What is the spirit of these children, if we add that these towns were run by the German administration in Brussels! Whether by chance or not, your Führer preaches so much about European unity. Isn't it better to have children here than a barracks?

— I'm a soldier. I have orders to occupy these premises. I can't do that because you're .

I took the time to calm down, determined not to let myself be intimidated again.

— General, as you know, German children are going to Switzerland under the same conditions. As neutrals, all those we can save, both large and small, must be saved on the same level. They are innocent victims.

— I know all about it. I know what you do for everyone.

— I don't know under what conditions our colleagues in Berlin run their reception centres, what they have to do the same job, but, if I were there, I would fight just as hard to have a centre like this.

Von Stülpnagel heaved a deep sigh. I added:

— Wouldn't you sacrifice a barracks for the same cause?

The General nodded and poured himself some more chocolate to give himself time to think.

Forgetting that I was addressing the general, with the unconsciousness of my age, I continued:

— It's not a game to them. Like us, they do their duty to help all children, while their elders play at war in the name of I don't know what freedom. I was getting hot under the collar and every word led me to air my grievances. I was afraid I'd gone too far. The General abruptly put down his bowl.

— This is war, sir, and personal freedom has nothing to do with it. What counts is the liberation of Europe and the world.

I was filled with bitterness.

— Yes, it's war! Men are mad enough to kill each other in the name of what freedom? That's their business, but... the children. Their land has become hell! Let us save them in peace.

Von Stülpnagel remained silent. I resumed, more persuasively:

— It makes no difference whether they are German or French. These children will be the France and Germany of tomorrow. They will be the ones to reckon with, not the adults of today. Their memories will drive their behaviour. We must keep this centre to save as many children as possible. Later, perhaps they will really live hand in hand.

The red of my cheeks reflected my state of mind. I couldn't stop. Faced with a silence that I felt was less hostile, I continued:

— These children, later, after the war, will be men. They will get married one day, just as I will with mademoiselle...

— Really, congratulations.

— Alas, with the war on, we have to be patient. Do you want our children, to whom Germany refused help, to remember afterwards?

— I repeat, sir, this is war. I am not responsible for it.

— In your mind, General, is that enough to cover up all abuses? The defeated need only shut up and accept, yes, but we are Swiss, neutral, from a country that welcomes your children.

— You're very young to be talking to me like this.

I heaved a sigh, thinking I'd been turned down. I persevered, certain that I would lose:

— I was at school not so long ago. I was studying my classics. I had a weakness for the Greco-Latin authors. That's how I learned about the barbaric behaviour of the Romans 2,000 years ago. Our teacher made us memorise this sentence from Tacitus, in which Galgacus, scourging war, says: "Where they made a desert, they said they made peace".

— I know that phrase!

— Will this title of glory be yours for the next 2,000 years, by replacing Romans with Germans?

I had gone too far. I'd forgotten that I was facing the General-in-Chief of the occupying troops. I sighed...

— I'm sorry, General, but I wasn't supposed to say what was on my mind.

— Why? You're neutral... but too young. How old are you?

— Twenty-three years.

He became pensive again. He murmured in a distant tone:

— *Ubi solitudinem faciunt, pacem appellant...* I met Tacitus at school, in Cologne. How far away that is!

The general seemed to grow older. He looked at me more kindly.

— I'm a soldier, young man. My responsibilities are heavy! I obey orders. The problems of history are not mine. Historians will talk about them.

— But you make history!

— As a military man, worthy of the name above all. I could be referred to as Chief of the General Staff. Who will turn Europe into a desert? History will tell.

— It's true, General, only the present and the children interest me. If posterity knows what is going on here between the occupying forces and the Swiss Red Cross, will you be lauded for chasing away a thousand children when at the same time they are saving your own?

— I don't have orders to throw you out. I have to occupy the École Polytechnique this morning at 8 o'clock, that's all.

— But... here we are with a legal and signed requisition.

— In my report, it's better not to talk about the Marshal and his schemes.

— What do you intend to do, General?

— Oberg wouldn't like asking for instructions. He was delighted to be here.

— Which means, if I understand correctly, that today we're staying?

— I suppose so. And maybe later. We need Switzerland. Beware of Oberg's reactions, he's all-powerful. We in the military don't like him too much.

This reminder lessened my joy, but... we were being left here. I regained my composure. I spoke calmly to challenge Colonel Oberg:

— General, he knew we'd been here for two days.

— Don't you understand? I looked at Madeleine.

— Would you ask Mrs Robelin for the signed list of children that Mrs Micheli gave her?

She agreed, winking to moderate me. That was my intention. The General seemed well disposed. I smiled, determined to talk only about Colonel Oberg.

— I'm surprised, General. Colonel Oberg knew all about it.

— I don't think so. He would have saved me from this ridiculous situation. I don't forgive him anyway. He doesn't use the Gestapo for these things. He didn't . He couldn't have known you were there.

— Very simply, General. Yesterday morning, our president had her sign the list of children leaving. The reception address was written in full. He should have seen it. Mrs Micheli specified that she had obtained this centre at the last minute.

— No !

— Yes, sir. Two copies are in the archives. As usual, everything was done in the open. My secretary will bring you a copy signed by the colonel.

— *Mein Gott* (My God)

— The President was acting in good faith when she came here with the children. If the colonel had signed, it was because he agreed.

Von Stülpnagel was silent. Faced with his silence, I added:

— As far as I was concerned, everything was in order. When I came here, I didn't see any soldiers barring us from entering. How was I supposed to know that you hadn't checked the availability of the premises the day before?

— That's your most judicious comment, sir. I'll ask for an explanation.

The general frowned. There would soon be a storm at headquarters. The colonel would give a few others a hard time. I added innocently:

— Even with the requisition, if there had just been a soldier at the door, we wouldn't have got in.

The General stared at me. He must have seen the mischievous gleam in my eyes. He relaxed and smiled. Just , Madeleine returned. I had time to collect my wits after that Scottish shower. I knew we were staying, that was the main thing. Unaware of the solution, she handed me the list, which I gave to the general. To put her mind at rest I added:

— We're staying, Madeleine, the General agrees.

She remained silent, following the general's movements with her eyes. The last page of the list, covered with Nazi eagle stamps and the colonel's signature, stunned him. He burst out laughing and quietly finished his chocolate.

— Excuse me for making spectacle of myself, but put Colonel Oberg in his place! I'll show him your requisition and above all... his signature, with his visas.

He continued sharply:

— For future convoys, please comply with the regulations. Submit your files to the Lutétia at least 20 days in advance. I don't want you to have to face me directly in another incident. Is that clear?

— Exactly, General.

Having regained his poise, he put his cap back on and beckoned me to come with him. With a sigh, he said:

— Come on, Oberg, let's hear him out. Be careful in the future, he'll be your enemy.

I said nothing. Of course, enemy or not, I had to be wary.

He turned to me and said:

— Compliments, you're an ardent defender of the cause.

— What cause, General?

— Good or bad, the choice is yours.

We set off towards the main gate. The general stiffened and resumed his martial pace, taking measured steps towards a Mercedes. All the soldiers stood at attention as we passed. The driver opened the door. Colonel Oberg was sitting in front. He wanted to get out, but his boss stopped him. The general handed him the papers.

He spoke harshly. Oberg turned crimson, gestured wildly and pointed at me. My shoes were getting tight and my nerves were growing. I was panicking in this courtyard swarming with verdigris uniforms. There were six lorries, four coaches, two caterpillars, three cars and the Mercedes. There were also sidecars and motorbikes everywhere. They were all waiting for orders. The colonel suddenly came out, glowered at me and went towards the other officers. He angrily gave a few orders before taking his place again. The officers, dumbfounded, rushed forward shouting. Everyone jumped into their vehicles, the 'dog collars' getting on their machines.

The children scattered in fear, called back by the nurses. Then the general called me, handed me back the papers and said in a loud voice:

- You're staying here. Never be in default of Colonel Oberg's services, or mine, sir. I bowed. Von Stülpnagel got in and the chauffeur drove off.

The interpreting officer's car, in the lead, started off, followed all the other vehicles. Polytechnique had once again become a reception centre. The surrounding neighbours looked on in bewilderment at this exodus from unconquered Germany.

The children were the masters of the place, and they gave a triple hurrah, in all innocence. They felt victorious... and so did I...

3

IS DESTINY ALSO WRITTEN?

> *There is a great difference between a series of natural causes which, from all eternity, make a future event certain, and the fortuitous knowledge that we can have in advance of the certainty of a fact, without it being linked to an infinite series of natural causes.*
> Cicero (*Treatise on Destiny*, ch. XIV)

The École Polytechnique was saved from the pounding of German boots, and its trophies remained intact in its cellars. What was more, and this was the most important thing, it made it possible to receive and send even more children to Switzerland. As we needed a considerable number of staff, in addition to those provided by the French Red Cross and Secours National (nearly three hundred), we had the opportunity on several occasions to include people who had run afoul of the occupying forces. That's how I met Francis Mazière, among other young people who had come there to seek refuge under the protective wing of the École Polytechnique, which had become an annex of the Swiss Red Cross.

Although I never saw General von Stülpnagel again, the same could be said of Colonel Oberg, who instigated my 'punishment' at the Gestapo in Dole two years later! It seems that an implacable destiny intertwined a multitude of coincidences to bring about this event, which almost led to my death under a variety of beatings and tortures. But in the end, Oberg died as he deserved, and the general met an even more horrible end. He took part in the plot against Hitler on 20 July 1944. In the early hours of the morning, he ordered the arrest of all the Gestapo henchmen in Paris and had them imprisoned. But alas, the Führer escaped. Von Stülpnagel learned of this and set off alone in his Mercedes.

He left the Hotel Meurice, where his headquarters were, secretly, to go to Verdun. In the cemetery of the heroes of the 14-18 war, he shot himself in the head, removing his right eye but not killing himself. He was found unconscious on a grave by the S.S. who had come after him. They took him to Berlin where, like the other conspirators, he was hanged from a butcher's hook on *Potsdammerplatz*. And so ended the commander-in-chief of the German army in France!

Fate is such that you have to wait several years to find out the real ins and outs. When we met at Polytechnique, who could have predicted what would happen to the General and what would happen to me! No one could have predicted either of our respective futures.

As I was only interested in my own, I didn't have much time to look into this problem at the time. The rest of that year, and then 1943, saw an intensive increase in the number of departures, which was natural given the rate of Anglo-American bombing raids on France. The idea of a landing on the French coast was gaining ground in people's minds, changing German strategy in France and even disrupting the social work of the Swiss Red Cross. The Swiss Red Cross was no longer completely *persona grata*, and trips to Lake Geneva were becoming increasingly restricted.

From February 1944 onwards, it was therefore necessary to look for places in France that could accommodate the children who continued to flock to Polytechnique. Two locations were chosen: the departments bordering Switzerland, with a headquarters and reception centre at Saint-Laurent-du-Jura, near Les Rousses, twenty kilometres from the Franco-Swiss border; and Normandy, with Louvigné-du-Désert as the main centre, near... Avranches! It has to be said that no-one could have predicted at the time that the D-Day landings would place on this side of the Channel! Francis Mazière lived through an extraordinary epic, and perhaps one day he will write about it. At the beginning of July 1944, when he and Mrs Micheli were evacuating the children who had taken refuge in Normandy and taking them back to the capital in Parisian buses with huge red crosses painted on the roofs, planes were strafing everything that moved! The buses fell prey to *Spitfires*, which may have thought they were camouflaged German convoys, and *Messerschmitts*, furious at being forced to evacuate strategic positions! One day, without knowing how, they found themselves in the Canadian defences and under the command of General Clark, who couldn't believe his eyes!

As for me, I had set up my headquarters in Saint-Laurent-du-Jura, where links between the various hostels were easier. What's more, the forbidden zone prevented any contact with Paris, so I made frequent trips to Switzerland to bring back supplies and medicines from Geneva, all as officially as possible.

But, at nineteen, youth is carefree, and I paid little attention to the growing danger that threatened me. Our centre in Saint-Laurent was run by a French couple, one of whom had become the leader of the maquis in the area. His secure official position provided ideal cover. This man felt all the more at ease because he knew that I had smuggled myself into Switzerland several times through the forest, not to hide anything, but because it was much quicker than going down the main road to Geneva. You had to go over the Col de la Faucille, fortified by the Germans, and there were always endless queues to cross the border at La Cure.

Last but not least, at the age of nineteen, with the mentality that the President had instilled in me, I couldn't accept that this director was taking advantage of his double position to black-market meat obtained by 'requisitioning' from neighbouring farms, and obviously without paying for it! A very lucrative business, to be sure, but one that I didn't like to see carried out in a Swiss Red Cross hostel. That's why I got into a heated argument with him, and told him I was going to tell the president everything the next time I was in Switzerland.

This opportunity came with the visit of a man wanted by the Gestapo and who wanted to cross the border as a matter of urgency. I took him the same day and left a message for Mme Micheli before returning with some medicines I'd been asked to deliver to an F.T.P. maquis in Savoie. I often transported parcels of pharmaceutical products for one or other of these Resistance troops. It was a way of helping the Resistance while continuing my work. Crossing the border at Le Brassus, four kilometres from La Cure, I was intercepted by an alert SS patrol and taken to the fort at Les Rousses before being evacuated to the Gestapo headquarters at the sub-prefecture in Dole.

The first tragic episode took place on the night that the S.S. set fire to Les Rousses-en-bas, and a hundred or so hostages were arrested and imprisoned in the Fort des Rousses, following an attack that claimed the lives of two German motorcyclists.

By the time I arrived at the fort, the mayor, the priest, the dentist and other members of the town council had vouched for the release of the hostages, and at dawn the next morning they were hanged from the ski jump in the town, which is still a famous ski resort in the Jura.

Transferred that same morning to the Gestapo in Dole on the orders of Colonel Oberg for more serious questioning, I was held there for six days! Naturally, the director of the Saint-Laurent centre, whom I had been able to get to warn, did nothing to warn Mrs Micheli. But another kind soul did, and I was released. The president had gone to see General von Stülpnagel and told him that, if I wasn't released immediately, all the convoys of children leaving Germany would be stopped, just when the Germans needed this help so badly. She also asked that I be taken to the border at La Cure, where a Swiss ambulance would be waiting. I had to spend four months in a clinic in Lausanne to recover from this more than painful "interrogation" by Oberg's telephone orders, as I later found out.

With the Liberation in the meantime, I no longer wanted to use my false papers. So I decided to go back to France, clandestinely, to return to Paris and resume my old identity. I was arrested again, but by the French Second Bureau stationed in the Jura, who didn't want to admit my version of events. This was made all the easier by the fact that they found a card from a maquis "commander" describing me as a "deserter in the face of the enemy". This was the former director of the centre who had become the leader of his maquis. As much out of fear of me as in retaliation for my report on him to the president, he had found a way of putting me out of action.

Did he do it before he knew that the Germans had tortured me, or afterwards? In fact, that's the only point I still wonder about, because I never heard from him again. That time, however, I had my first real misfortune, because Mrs Micheli was no longer there to testify. She had suffered a serious breakdown and was in a specialist clinic, where she forced to take it easy.

When you're twenty, you form your own idea of your moral rectitude and conscience. I never defended myself against this accusation of desertion, even though I never wore a uniform and could never be called up. Here too, my autobiography will tell of my ordeal in Dijon prison awaiting court martial! It was following this judgement that I moved Cameroon. But I must add that military justice being the strength of armies, I received a year later, in Douala where I was, and without having made any complaint, a magnificent military booklet gratifying me with eighteen months of active combat as a "volunteer enlisted in the French army". It was accompanied by an impressive warrant for the time, totalling eighteen months' voluntary enlistment pay, demobilisation bonus and several other bonuses! To put an end to this first lamentable episode, I left for Cameroon to do another job, where the company of the missionaries did me a great deal of moral good. I momentarily regained a balance that was already very disturbed. It was in this way that I made friends with this old retired Cameroonian pastor. He was fascinated by my youth and my adventures, of which I had made no secret! It was he who introduced me to the Fako sect of sorcerers, who later taught me the beginnings of what would later serve me in Egypt. But I had no idea at the time.

The seven years I spent in Cameroon will be included in one of the volumes of my biography. The only difference is that it takes place in sub-Saharan Africa instead of the former Indochina, where the hero, in this case me, loses his wife in dramatic circumstances, because I had married little Madeleine from the École Polytechnique, and we had both left, drunk on our Cameroonian adventure.

To conclude this episode, when I learned of Marshal Pétain's trial over there, I couldn't do anything to testify about Polytechnique because, as Mrs Micheli had died in the meantime, I didn't want to talk about myself or what had happened. In fact, the death of this great lady followed on from the above, since fatigue and the great pressures of all the events of the war had taken their toll on her strong personality and dynamism. She had disappeared, virtually ignored by everyone.

For the same reasons as above, I'm going to skip other important episodes in my life for the moment, because it would take several hundred pages of explanation to fully understand them and place them in the exact time frame in which 'destiny' brought them about.

So let's skip ahead several years to the secret camp where I was working for the Americans on a radar assembly base. I was simply in charge of civil security: protection of workers, fire safety, etc. I was in charge of the department with the rank of captain. I was in charge of the department with the rank captain, and I had just turned thirty-one, which brings us to 1956.

Receiving important military personnel at the base's airport, the helicopter's blades separated fifty metres from the ground. The aircraft fell like a sledgehammer and exploded when it hit the ground. It was a *Sikorski*, not a small *Alouette*, so the damage to both equipment and personnel was extensive. I was badly burned, as were many of those waiting on the ground, and above all I swallowed a lot of the toxic extinguishing products that flooded the scene of the disaster. So it was the inside of my body that suffered the most serious after-effects, from which I am still suffering today, having just undergone two eye operations as a result of these burns and carbon tetrachloride splashes.

From hospital to hospital, I ended up in Paris, in the tuberculosis ward at Bichat, which, although already renowned, was still one of the most archaic hospital establishments. At the time, there was no ward for patients with severe burns. As I was, after all, only a 'civilian', I had to be admitted somewhere, and in totally hygienic and aseptic conditions. The only place was near the ward that received thirty lung patients, a small glassed-in area with two beds, appropriately named the *aquarium*. I was laid there alone, like a mummy, so tightly was I wrapped in bandages. Perpetual fever, injections of all kinds, including morphine, as I was supposed to be at death's door and to be relieved.

It was 1956, I recall, and a major event occurred with the announcement of the use of cortisone as a flesh restorer. I was used as a guinea pig for high doses of this still natural ointment. Today, it is produced synthetically without the drawbacks it had in its natural state.

So, two days later, I was declared dead without remission at two o'clock in the morning! As the hospital morgue was unable to receive me immediately, it was early in the morning that they came to collect me. Fortunately, the intern on duty that morning, who was doing a traineeship at the hospital but was normally at Val-de-Grâce, was curious enough to lift the sheet covering me to look at this "civilian" who had worked for the American army. And he raised my left arm... only to find that it was not stiff and that my wrist was still warm, with an almost normal pulse. So, was it the effect of the cortisone on the drugs? No one will the cause of the heart failure, or even if there was one!

An initial stay of eleven months got me out this dangerous impasse, after which I was sent for a detox cure at Divonne-les-Bains where, along with my nerves, I rediscovered a more normal life since, instead of drugs, I came under the influence of palfium, a newcomer to the field and administered in pills. I went from taking six a day to just one a day after four months. I then went back to Bichat Hospital, where I had the same 'room' for fifteen months! My whole body had to be rebuilt, and that took time.

When I got out, after a short convalescence, the situation had changed a lot, as General de Gaulle, the head of the government, had sent back the O.T.A.N. troops and the American bases that could have employed me again. As I had no desire to go to Belgium or Germany,

I asked to be retrained in a particular field that I had learned about at the radar base where my unfortunate accident had taken place. In fact, this particular camp was the first to receive a *computer*, even though this machine was not yet on the market and was experimental.

As head of security, I was able to follow the astonishing progress, in 1955, of this computer, which, in binary language, carried out 100,000 operations per second thanks to a whole apparatus made up of electrical wires and light bulbs, in a rattling assembly of eight to ten cubic metres!... Today's specialists will easily understand, and readers will be able to tell the difference, knowing that a small box measuring just half a cubic metre is now capable of performing twelve billion operations a second in an ultra-fast and more sophisticated language.

At the time, however, I admired the speed of the calculations, which meant that certain scrambling parts could be modified in the space of three hours, whereas before the arrival of the huge calculator it took twenty engineers almost four months to do the same job!

So it was to this promising field that I turned without hesitation. But I needed a doctorate to complete my studies and get a teaching post in Geneva. And there was no French university teaching computer science. My path was simple, of course, but here again it depended on a kind of predestination that brought back a reminiscence. To understand it, we need to go back for a moment to Mme Micheli, who lived in rue Bonaparte and to whose house I often went. There was a large library in this elegantly furnished house, where most of the books were translations of ancient Greek authors dealing with philosophy and religion. The rare moments of leisure were filled with lively discussion and relaxation. It was there that I used to devour everything to do with Pythagoras, before delving into Egypt.

That's how, twelve years later, I remembered the famous quote engraved on the pediment of the Crotone philosophical school by Pythagoras himself: *God drew the Earth from nothing, just as he drew the one from the zero to create the many.*

Now, in the binary system of the computer programming language in use at the time, only the one and the zero symbolically represented the current that was flowing or not flowing. This representation inspired not only the start of my thesis, but the whole of it, since with these simple numbers any calculation could be carried out quickly and easily. To complete my writing, I went to Egypt for the first time, to find out where Pythagoras had been initiated, and what it was about that country that had inspired him so much! I explained this at length in *The Extraordinary Life of Pythagoras* .[3]

So I began a new path in IT, which apparently put me back in a normal condition, because none of the after-effects of my accident were visible on the outside. But morally, I was still waiting for some new 'chance' to change the course of my destiny.

And what had to happen happened one Saturday afternoon, as I was returning from Geneva to my French home. On the road to Bonneville, alone in my car, and overtaking a lorry that was going fast, holding up the middle of the road, I accelerated my pace. As I passed it, I honked angrily to get it to move back to the right... and I was wrong! The driver was asleep at the wheel and I woke him up. Surprised, instead of steering to the right, he turned the wheel to the left in a sudden reflex, and hit me head-on, sending me into the ditch five metres below... My spine was shattered between the fourth and fifth cervical vertebrae.

When, five months later, the police were able to come and see me at the hospital to get me to sign a complaint, they told me that the breathalyser test had produced nothing and that the driver had admitted having fallen asleep at the wheel. If I hadn't woken him up and passed him without honking, he would have ended up in the ditch instead of me! His driving licence had been withdrawn and his boss fined heavily, notwithstanding the court case concerning the accident, since there should have been two drivers in that lorry, which had come from Paris without stopping. But that obviously wouldn't give me back the use of my left side, or three lost years...

Fortunately, the firemen who pulled me from the rubble of my car were used to this kind of accident, and they laid me on a board without moving me, realising that I was paralysed but not quite dead! As soon as I arrived at the hospital, the complete hemiplegia was obvious and they saw that my heart was still beating a little. Nothing could make me move, not even my eyelashes! Four holes were made in my skull, without putting me to sleep as I felt nothing, in order to hang four weights of one kilo each on me, which were supposed to straighten me out and keep my spine in an ideal line. A month of this treatment was

---

[3] Published by R. Laffont in 1979, followed by the *Book of Moral and Political Laws*, the famous *Biblion*, translated into French for the first time and published by the same publisher in 1980.

supposed to allow me to be put in a temporary cast. If I hadn't died by then, they would look into how to make a permanent plaster cast from the waist down. It was only after more than four months that one fine morning I opened my eyes, moved my right arm and said to the nurse, who nearly fainted: "I'm hungry!

By the time the doctors realised that my contact with everyday life was definitive, it was too late to restore the spine to its original state. The temporary plaster cast had allowed the fourth and fifth vertebrae to weld together, flattening the intermediate disc and, above all, pinching the spinal cord, which prevented my entire left side from regaining its elasticity.

What can you do when you're bedridden with a huge plaster cast that goes down to your waist, with only your right arm free, and it's impossible to leave the hospital? Nothing but eat... and write! Which I did. First of all, I wrote a detailed account of my life under the Occupation. It took me several months of work to create, in a kind of apprenticeship in the art of filling in a few hundred pages, these two manuscripts which form an interesting whole, which I entrusted at the time to this journalist from *La Suisse*, well known for a daily column, and which I recently recovered.

Then, talking to several friends who had come to visit me about my studies on Pythagoras and my discovery of Egypt, I gradually came up with the idea of writing a fresco on the history of Egyptian religions and their gods. I began to work towards a general plan for the whole thing. I blacked out page after page with no end in sight! Weeks went by, then months, reserving every moment for planning the various books I planned to write on this history of Egyptian religions.

Thus was born in my mind the need to compile all the knowledge I had acquired in my life to date. If I had retained full use of my right arm, as well as all my mental faculties, including my memory, it was solely with a view to this writing. No similar work had ever been done, and it was up to me to do it. I had everything I needed to succeed in this undertaking, which was imposed on me by events. Having travelled to Egypt at every opportunity, I suspected that the hieroglyphics were not translated as clearly as Egyptologists would have you believe, and this made me hesitate about what to do in the composition of my texts.

I had also confirmed the 'vagueness' of our understanding of the pharaonic papyri by looking through the various Franco-Hieroglyphic 'dictionaries' of the pioneers who deciphered the sacred texts at the Jesuit College of the Holy Family in Cairo. However, none of these gave an identical meaning for the same ideogram.

Often they were in total opposition. So I thought I'd do my own research into the subject that fascinated me and, a subject I'd had a splendid introduction to when I visited Denderah, eight hundred kilometres south of Cairo: astronomy and the mathematical combinations that go with it. But as this work progressed, I realised that it was taking me far from the goal I had in mind, since originally there was only one monotheistic religion on the banks of the Nile and an idolatrous schism emanating from Osiris' younger brother, Set.

I was passionate about this research and sent several books to the hospital, including J. Vandier's ten-volume *Manuel d'Archéologie* and Stéphane Gsell's *Histoire ancienne de l'Afrique du Nord*. These works were a revelation, because they confirmed for me that the ancestors of the first pharaohs came from elsewhere, and probably from the Atlantic, in other words from the West. This idea had already occurred to me unconsciously through reminders of dialogues from my stay in Cameroon. The God of Origin lived there to watch over his creatures living in the place where today only the ocean remains, and not in the countries of the East where the sun rises. So it became necessary for me to go and see certain places in Morocco, where the place names bore a strange resemblance to those used in the hieroglyphics of the *Book of the Dead*: the Douat, Ta Mana, and so many others that keep recurring.

"Coincidence, chance or a new predestination, after finishing with my plaster cast and another short stay at the Hôpital Bichat to see if there was any way of re-educating the limbs on my left side, which were lagging behind in their reactions to my wishes for the smallest movements, I had the opportunity to spend my convalescence in... Morocco! Morocco! I recharged my batteries the magnificent sunshine of this welcoming country, while taking part in computer seminars and carrying out the research necessary for the project I had set myself.

From then on, everything came together to make my task easier, as if fate were beckoning me to continue along this path. Moroccan geologists took me south of Erfoud, in the Sahara, to see the geodesic location of the old North Pole, which proved that at some point the Earth had tilted. What's more, the geological texture of the telltales all around represented glaciers that had literally burst open as a result of the sudden heat that had hit them. It was in this same region, at Taouz, that I made the most impressive discovery, in the middle of a very strange sacred burial site. Some Berbers who had befriended me explained to me that this holy site was where a "giant" son of the One God had died, along with all the soldiers who had defended him against a giant who was his blood brother but a traitor to the Father, and who had murdered him with a spear.

If Ta Mana, in hieroglyphic texts, means the "place of the Sunset" and, by extension, the "place of the Blessed", Ta Ouz means "place of Usir", and therefore the place consecrated to Osiris. Tamanar is sixty kilometres north of Agadir, as we shall see in one of the following chapters; and Ta Ouz, at the entrance to the Saharan desert, was finally before my eyes! I had stumbled upon this historic site quite providentially. For years, this place had remained off the tourist map. Situated almost at the border between Algeria and Morocco, it was considered unsafe. Today, it is even in a prohibited zone, with the Polisario of ex-Spanish Morocco making frequent incursions.

It was at this point that the idea germinated in me that there was basically only one God in Egypt and that what I had to write was a "History of Monotheism". All my work should have this one fixed point as its goal: the survival of God's creatures.

The story the Berbers told me about their own origins strengthened me in this opinion, as they told themselves, generation after generation, about their 'divine' origins. They came from an "idyllic elsewhere", lost in the mists of time, while they believed in this just and good God who commanded them, but who had punished them for their disobedience.

So this trip, fruitful from every point of view, made me revise the order and content of the books I had planned to write as soon as I got back. But how could I go about coordinating all the pieces? How could I make sense of this hieroglyphics, which was murky to say the least? It was another trip to Egypt that gave me the answers. I obtained the mathematical papyri known as the Rhind papyri, and my computer training enabled me to see the major gaps, the veritable chasms of incomprehension contained in the dictionaries in use. All of this is detailed in a book that will be published at a later date.[4] From reaction

---

[4] *La Mathématique selon les Égyptiens* (*Mathematics according to the Egyptians*), which will follow on from *L'Astronomie selon les Égyptiens* (*Astronomy according to the Egyptians*), forthcoming.

to reaction, on my return I was taken to the major Jesuit centre in France, at Chantilly. There I continued my convalescence, still incomplete and even disrupted by my efforts in Morocco, while working assiduously in the largest private library in Europe. It contains nearly eight hundred thousand religious, philosophical, scientific and... archaeological volumes! This enabled me to make the most of my wide-ranging research into the original monotheism.

Those were three exciting years, in the sense that the fever to read and write hardly left me during all that time. Short trips to Egypt or Israel barely interrupted my studies. What's more, some of the fathers had taken an interest in my research, and they helped me a great deal to make progress, even though they often disagreed with the meaning I gave to certain vital events affecting Christianity.

In fact, what I was really writing was a 'History of Monotheism from the Origins to the End of the World', with the aim of demonstrating that the God of Christians was the same as the original Creator. The Eternal was Yahweh, but also Ptah. God was the God of Jesus, of Moses, of Abraham, but also of Osiris. And this One God had already the sole Creator of Creation, the One who inspired his creatures with the Law! *Each celestial era had its own Son of God: a Messiah.* This was the result of my work.

So, in 1975, the first book was ready, the crease was set; the press was running, despite all the black holes that dotted its blossoming. Will it always be so dark in human obscurantism? Will it always be this dark in my heart, which cries out in pessimism?

Will it become apocalyptic when the Sun enters Aquarius in 2016?... The whole of the *History of Monotheism* will help us to answer this distressing question.

Three trilogies will form the core of this work under the generic title: "Eternity belongs only to God". In order to facilitate subsequent explanations and avoid tedious reminders or notes, each of the books cited will be referred to in the text itself by one of the notations below:

A) THE ORIGINS TRILOGY :

1. *The Great Cataclysm* -(published in 1976) : book A-1
2. *The Survivors of Atlantis* -(published in 1978) : book A-2
3. *Et Dieu ressuscita à Dendérah* -(published in 1980) : book A-3

B) *THE PAST TRILOGY:*
1. *Moses the Egyptian* (published in 1981): book B-1
2. *Akhenaten the Divine Mortal* -(forthcoming) : book B-2
3. *Et Dieu oublilia l'Égypte* -(forthcoming): book B-3

C) *THE FUTURE TRILOGY:*
1. *Jesus the Christ* -(forthcoming): book C-1
2. *The Apocalypse of the 8th* vision-(forthcoming): book C-2
3. *L'Éternité n'appartient qu'à* Dieu-(): book C-3

D) *THE TETRALOGY OF KNOWLEDGE:*
1. *Astronomy according to the Egyptians* -(forthcoming) : book D-1
2. *Mathematics according to the Egyptians* -(forthcoming) : book D-2
3. *Medicine according to the Egyptians* -(forthcoming) : book D-3
4. *The Gospel according to the Egyptians* -(forthcoming): book D-4

4

THE GREAT CATACLYSM

It dealt with the greatest exploit of all, and one that would rightly have deserved to be the most illustrious of all those that this city has ever accomplished. But due to the passage of time and the death of the actors, the story has not reached us.
                                                            Plato (*The Critias*)

Perhaps you have heard the name Atlas spoken, and that of the race that descended from him in many generations? It is also said that the many families that make up our race descended from him.

Alas! It was once a happy nation, cherished by the gods for as long as it honoured the heavens.
                            Jérôme Frascator (Syphilidis, song III)

Hundreds, not to say thousands, of books have dealt with Atlantis in a more or less serious way, in an attempt to shed light on its reality or myth. *The History of Monotheism*, which I have undertaken to write, details the content of specific texts. It refers to a continent that sank as a result of a cataclysmic upheaval .[5] So there's no question here of arguing about its existence. What could be more natural than to call this land "Atlantis" in French, just as Plato had done following the sage Solon, whom he was trying to translate into prose!

Its hieroglyphic name, Ahâ-Men-Ptah, or "Elder-Bed-God", gave rise to a late contraction in the texts attached to the work improperly called the Book of the Dead: the Amenta. However, this name has retained its original meaning, that of "Land of the Dead", "Land of the Blessed", "Land of the Beyond".

This continent, before it disappeared and its name became Atlantis, or Ahâ-Men-Ptah, or Amenta, was representative of the terrestrial

---

[5] A-1 and A-2.

Eden described in the Bible. The successive monarchs of this enchanting and peaceful land were traditionally the Ptah-Ahâ, which in hieroglyphic means "Elder of God". In fact, all the monarchs were direct descendants of the first Son of God, the Eldest.

Let's start by phonetising these terms in French, for a logical understanding of what follows: *Ahâ* is read: *Ahan* which by extension became Adam, who thus remains the Elder. *Ptah* is also spelt *Phtah* by a Greek phonetisation, where Pi becomes Phi. So *Phtah-Ahan* was phonetised 'Pharaoh', who went from being the Elder of God to becoming the Son of God. This explains the names Ahâ-Men-Ptah (Elder-Death-of-God) and Ath-Kâ-Ptah (Second-Heart-of-God), which in Greek phonetisation became Aeguyptos, and Egypt in French.

Ahâ-Men-Ptah was therefore the original Eden where the Sons of Light, or Children of God, lived before divine wrath caused the continent to be totally lost and become nothing more than an Amenta. This is why the first volume of the vast historical fresco, the title of which serves as the headline for this chapter, begins with the following words in its introduction n[6] : "The Origin, with a capital O, is the Origin of each of us, of everyone, of everything: of heaven and earth, of their containers and their contents! Whether we are believers or atheists, our thoughts, at least once, have been directed towards this common, unique Origin and its Creator, whether he be called God, or simply 'chance', as anyone who has lived only one part of his life without touching the other might decree. And who could be more qualified to speak of this Origin than those who lived it and recounted it to their descendants, engraving it in stone for all eternity?

To get back to this Origin, we need to go backwards through the analytical chronology of the sunken continent. And while it may seem complex to go back so far into the past, the task is by no means insurmountable! There are many extant writings, dating back to the earliest antiquity, which recount the annals of Ahâ-Men-Ptah, albeit in anaglyphic hieroglyphics.

These texts, the oldest of which are lost in the mists of time, are legion, because all the walls of religious buildings were already covered

---

[6] In A-1.

with their inscriptions before hieroglyphics regained their sacred right. One book alone would not be enough to list all this holy writing!

But they all come together in a single glorification: that of Ptah, or God. And they all end as a warning, to try to prevent future generations from witnessing another great cataclysm.

The metaphysics, so surprising in its clarity, both liturgical and theological, that emerges from this predynastic Egyptian knowledge, makes it perfectly logical to say that their authors represented a superior civilisation. Having arrived there as a result of an exodus, they were descended from an infinitely more ancient people who had lived in a motherland that no longer existed, but where humanity lived happily.

And the survivors of this elsewhere wanted to engrave their past misfortunes in imperishable stone, the better to convince those who would follow them of the consequences that their disobedience would inevitably entail.

This notion of divinity, as it existed in those remote times, undeniably required a cycle of abstract thought that was as dominant as it was decisive, and which consisted of a long accumulation of observations, reflections and meditations, spanning many millennia. This goes some way to explaining why, on the day when this maximum of intense spirituality was reached, a certain very human force of inertia was established, hovering over everything and every act of life repeated daily. The lofty, ancient thoughts that linked the soul to its God were submerged at that very moment, giving way to a purely reasoning, materialistic mind. That, at least, is how I translate the hieroglyphic texts.

To fully understand the essential preoccupation of the survivors of the ancient people of the lost continent, we need to delve not only into the primitive meaning of spirituality, but also into a retrospective analysis of their psychology. Indeed, if we consider that many people today are obsessed, not to say embraced, by the anguish of the arrival of the year 2000, the end of time, or quite simply the end of the world, why not admit that these ancestors, who had themselves lived through a Great Cataclysm , were not using every means in their possession to warn the generations of 'younger' people yet to be born?

Many millennia before us, a whole people lived through a time that was foreseen and predicted to come, if they did not return to a better spiritual way of life. This happened because they failed to recognise a healthier conception of divine ethics. The anaglyphic hieroglyphic texts, which have a double meaning and are hermetic for neophytes, were obviously intended only for the ancient Egyptians, so that they could repeat them day after day, so that they could imbibe them to the depths of their souls and repeat them to their children.

All the texts announce practically the same liturgical formulae. I have chosen those engraved at *Dendera* and grouped them together in *The Gospel according to the Egyptians*. This work will be devoted to what was primitive spirituality. I have also called it Tentyrite theology - from Tentyris, the Greek phonetisation of Denderah - because it parallels the theology developed for the cult of Amun, the solar god.

This site is a temple, the current one being the sixth reconstruction based on the original plans. It was to this very spot that the great-grandsons of those who survived the exodus of the Great Cataclysm first arrived. This will be explained in greater detail in the course of this book, when the time comes. For now, thanks to the texts engraved there, let's relive the beginnings of this people...

"In the beginning, these words taught the Ancestors, the Blessed of the First Earth: Ahâ-Men-Ptah. They lived there in the same way as the Images of the Beloved Heart: the Elder Heart.

"Thus were the first Words: - I am the Most High, the First, the Creator of Heaven and Earth, I am the shaper of fleshly bodies and the provider of Divine Parcels. I have placed the Sun on a new horizon as a sign of benevolence and a pledge of the Alliance. I made the Day Star rise on the horizon of my Heart; but for that to happen, I instituted the Law of Creation that acts on the Parcels of my Heart in order to animate them in those of my Creatures. And it was.

Right from the preamble, a number of fundamental concepts are set out. The Eternal One is God, and he is the Origin of everything. He transmits not only life, but also his way of life through predetermination. This will make it possible to choose between the notions of good and evil, and will thus predetermine the cycles of the earth until evil is eliminated, perhaps along with the creatures that cause it.

These cogs in celestial mechanics have the colourful name of : "Divine-Mathematical-Combinations". These are the main engines, representing the geometric figures and mathematical calculations of celestial movements. Those "of the wandering lights in relation to the fixed luminous ones". Cosmic harmony is achieved through these combinations, which are not supputative but depend on a single law that forms the universe. They form the fundamental basis of celestial action on the Divine Parcels, the souls breathed by God into human carnal envelopes through the intermediary of the "Twelve", who are the Twelve Suns of the twelve celestial equatorial constellations. Their rays reach the Earth at the speed of light (300,000 km/s) to form the fabric of the twelve celestial breaths (the Twelve) that will strike the cortex of the new-born child to imprint in its brain the Divine Parcel, or the human thinking soul, which will be essentially different for each person, thanks to two principles:

A) *When the Twelve arrive on earth, they will have an instantaneous position of their own, given the speed with which they strike. They will form "Mathematical Combinations" which will be the assignment of a native predetermination in a global human destiny planned by the Creator for his creatures.*

B) *These Twelve Breaths, which form the celestial equator in 360 degrees, are referred to in the rest of the text as "The Belt", and this image can be understood without the need for a lengthy dissertation. But from this 'Belt' emerge Four Elders, who are the Four Winds arriving from the cardinal points: the Masters, of whom the Four Sons of Horus are the personifications, and who will be found very often in several verses under their own names. They are the ones who imprint the main living pattern of the soul.*

It was this sacred and secret scholastic preamble that the pontiffs who succeeded one another for millennia in the "House of Life" adjoining the "Temple of the Lady of Heaven" at Denderah dispensed sparingly to the high priests alone.

This ancient "School", whose origins date back to the very arrival of the first survivors, is authenticated not only by texts, but also by burials unearthed under the hill of the Pontiffs, less than three kilometres from the temple. There "rest" the "Sages among the Sages", the Blessed who had Knowledge of the divine will. One of them taught under a "Master" of the 2nd Dynasty in the fourth millennium BC; another under Khufu, the famous Cheops. The royal scribe of this pharaoh reports that the temple was rebuilt by his master according to the data found in the original foundations, written on gazelle-leather scrolls by the "Followers of Horus", i.e. by the Elders themselves, long before the first king of the First Dynasty ascended the throne. And here we go back so far that unfamiliar with Egyptian chronology may become dizzy.

It was therefore through these direct descendants that the divine Law was transmitted, whose "Mathematical Combinations" were to enable humans to direct themselves in Justice and Goodness. To understand these facts, we need to go back well before this second homeland, some twenty thousand years earlier, which brings us back to Ahâ-Men-Ptah and his fatal and tragic disobedience.

The ancestors wrote: "I am Myself, born of Myself to become the Creator of the Images that will be similar to Him after the Chaos has passed away. They are the containers of the Divine Parcels that will make them, eternally, the Blessed of the Rising Sun if they keep the strict obedience of my Law. For I am the Past of Yesterday preparing the Future of the Sun thanks to the Twelve".

For the ancient sages, these influences formed the divine thread that personalised each soul, thread that could be calculated with precision because its basic outline was reproduced exactly according to the same coordinates as those that had impressed the cortex. The human soul could thus be in perpetual liaison with the celestial creative soul, if it did not itself break the agreement pre-established at birth.

So this pithy statement: "I am the Past that prepares the Future" is also a form of ultimatum, not to be taken lightly!

The pontiffs of Ahâ-Men-Ptah had defined the problem very well, while at the same time pinpointing the direct powers they attributed to the various combinatorial solutions, having gone back a long way in time to provide solid support for their observations. Hence this accumulation of details on the powers of the Twelve.

We will therefore start from a time ten millennia before the Great Cataclysm, to explain it succinctly. To do this, we need to imagine this Eden, to visualise it in its immensity within the Atlantic. Let's say that at this remote time in the twenty-fifth millennium, the continent of Ahâ-Men-Ptah was much more temperate in its extreme north than the same regions such as Greenland are today. Thick forests covered this part of the territory, where ice had yet to appear and snow made only timid appearances. The Platonic trilogy already gives many details. Lush vegetation grew all year round, inhabited not only by peaceful humans living in village-like clearings, but also by great apes of a type that has completely disappeared; they were similar in size to today's gorillas, but without the 'spiked' face. There were also, here and there, enormous, peaceful, vegetarian mammoths; four-metre rhinoceroses and, with four fingers: aceroatheria. A few old specimens of a bygone gigantism on the verge of extinction were fighting, just amongst themselves, for the right to survive.

Finally, to the very south of the immense continent, nature had spread out her most precious treasures: mountains, of course, but even more so, plains, fertile countryside, from which spontaneously sprang everything that can delight a tranquil humanity! These vast expanses, ideal for the settlement and meditation of a race eager to ascend towards its Creator, were in return blessed with unrivalled abundance.

On the horizon, the mountain ranges were nothing to fear, and the pyramidal cones of the few volcanoes that mingled with them had been extinguished so long ago that human memory had lost track of them. All the inhabitants could see were slopes covered with evergreen trees, some of which were laden with pulpy, juicy fruit all year round.

The walls were made of barely squared tree trunks, dried mud filled the holes in the wooden barrels, and thick dry foliage made the roof watertight.

Ahâ-Men-Ptah had to endure an initial volcanic upheaval that caused the major land subsidence that formed the North Sea, carving out countless gaps as far as present-day Iceland. A period of severe frost set in over the whole of this part of the world, accumulating ice to form a uniform polar cap. Siberia itself, which was a fairly temperate region at the time, saw its verdant vegetation burn to the ground and the mastodons that had been unable to escape the ice cover in time were wiped out.

After this warning, and from this date onwards, the history of Ahâ-Men-Ptah began in earnest, chronology making very logical use of this upheaval, which human memory has endorsed as such, to mark the annals of a characteristic beginning. The scholars of those early days had a growing understanding of celestial movements and combinations, and of the beneficial and malefic phenomena that resulted from them. From the day that a figurative graphic method was instituted, they carefully observed and meticulously noted the movements of the planets, the Sun and the Moon, their figures and configurations, as well as the more geometric forms of the twelve constellations of the celestial equatorial ecliptic, and the more distant constellations of Orion and Sirius, with their singular characteristics.

The repercussions of the "Combinations" on the Earth flowed from this, both in terms of human behaviour and the evolution of nature.

In the wake of the mini-cataclysm, life had regrouped further south, and villages were quickly re-formed, initially with tree-trunk huts, which were soon replaced by much more comfortable mud-brick huts that were more resistant to the surge of animals that the upheaval had brought to this more hospitable area. Bears suddenly swarmed, as did deer and elephants, not to mention wolves.

Another quadruped made its appearance, and soon became man's noblest conquest: the horse. This gave rise to the idea of domesticating other breeds: those that include reindeer, elk, wolverines and musk oxen.

For hunting, at the same time, throwing flints disappeared to make way for bows and arrows, which were soon fitted with metal points sharpened from flint.

The iron had been found on the ground, brownish, in blistered slabs of varying size, leading to a search for similar materials. This is how the surface haematite really became iron. It came from a mine covering several kilometres of land in the far south, just by the sea.

The discovery of other ores and minerals, and above all their rational use after some trial and error, completely changed the face of life for the inhabitants of this country. A new age began with the use of tools to cut stones and assemble them, as been the custom with bricks. Henceforth, the dwellings, although still rudimentarily assembled from unpolished stone, quickly became very "liveable", and gave rise to the idea of building monumental religious edifices so that God would be pleased and come himself to find shelter there, at least in spirit.

A stretch of fifty centuries passed peacefully by among the people themselves, especially those who lived in the countryside. For them, the Divinity's intentions were obvious: all His bounties were spread out before their very eyes! All you have to do is bend down to harvest and enjoy it. Everyone takes what they need, without worrying if someone else takes more than they do!

When travellers passed through, attracted by the rumours about this land of milk and honey, they quenched their thirst at any fresh spring, without any hang-ups, helped quite the opposite by the locals who offered them jugs full of good wine.

During these long centuries, this gentle nation ignored hatred, war, revenge and, more simply, contempt. They expressed their joy as often as possible through popular festivals, where dancing and singing were at their best. These often followed the huge mountains of fruit and vegetables piled up by the frequent harvests. Everyone came to take what they wanted without having to answer to anyone.

At that blessed moment, the first Ahâ, the Elder, was born: Adam. But how? The texts do not say, probably it was still a long way from the cataclysm that was the subject of all the detailed reports, as well as the causes that triggered it. But it is almost certain that the story of the royal couple of this Edenic land, Nut and Geb, was, in terms of the way in which the last Ahâ, Usir or Osiris, was conceived, an exact reflection of the birth of the first Adam. This is the theme of Book A-1, which explains it in great detail. With prosperity reigning more and more in this country since the coming of the original Ahâ, there was nothing left for men to learn in order to use their intelligence and forge a soul in the image of God. Cereals and crops abounded; metals from the soil such as copper and lead, were mined in the open air; tin and antimony were mined in galleries at ground level; iron, silver and gold were mined rationally at greater depths. Fine stones were already sought after by women, and were artistically cut after being collected in the hollows of easily accessible valleys. As for the stones known as 'precious', they were not sought after for their financial value, but for their beneficial power: they were carriers of influences emanating, for each of these twelve stones, from one of the twelve suns of the zodiacal constellations, whose emanations they alone captured: the breaths. Most of these stones came from oblique veins running vertically through certain characteristic but arid soils, where herds of sheep, aurochs and peaceful bison grazed. Finally, there were some rare minerals, much sought-after for their symbolic properties, such as aurichalcite with its shimmering greenish glints, within which glowed the 'Burning Inferno', the symbol of Ath-Mer, where the eternal rejuvenation of the heart was renewed.

The many forests also provided all the types of wood needed for social life. Carpenters and joiners, cabinet-makers and artists used hardwoods as well as rare species, transforming them into delicately shaped furniture or galleys and boats of all kinds.

Only the sycamore tree, of the 'maple' type, was formally forbidden to be cut down or used for private purposes, except after a very strict ritual of blessings. The sycamore was the sacred tree, the *An-Auhi*, which could only be approached by a priest who was always pure. The priest also had to 'take its life' after a highly complex ritual, in order to extract 'the heart' in its entire length and shape the sixteen Tan-Auhi, which became, by contraction, the Tau, or the Crosses of Life, also known as the 'annealed crosses'. It was common knowledge that the owners of these 'taboos' personifying Life, and owned only by 'right-voiced' people, were endowed with the blessings of Almighty God!

A special territory, delimited by the obliquity and degree of the sun's rays, was dedicated to the growth of the sycamore tree. This sacred enclosure was called the Nahi, and only the Ahâ in title, always the Son, apart from the pure priests, could enter it to converse at his ease, face to face with his Father.

The population, generally lymphatic and at ease, paid little heed to the internal strife pitting Ahâ against his neighbours. In those days, the descendant of God was big enough to restore the situation if it was disturbed, which, incidentally, was hardly the case in everyday life for ordinary mortals! Ordinary people even tended to laugh heartily at this opposition, without realising that they would be the first to suffer when the time came to settle scores.

The situation deteriorated little by little until the one who would become the last sovereign before the Great Cataclysm was born!

This was Geb, the penultimate Ahâ of Eden. The strangeness of his story is strongly reminiscent of that of the Bible on two occasions. The first concerns Eve, punished for her curiosity by biting into the apple, and the second concerns Mary, fathered by God, since Nut, the wife of this Geb, was endowed with his son Usir under conditions similar to those of the young girl we would talk about as Joseph's wife.

When the pontiff set the date for the marriage of Geb and Nut, the land of Ahâ-Men-Ptah had only fifty-one years left to subsist above the sea! But on the eve of the appointed day, Nut, who had already moved into the royal palace and was strolling through the gardens with her attendants, happened to come across the back of the sacred sycamore tree dedicated to the Son's dialogue with the Father. Curious, and thinking that her title as the Son's wife from the following day would protect her from reprisals, the princess went in alone, "to see". A little tired and dizzy from running away, Nut sat down against the bark of the sycamore tree...

The annals that have come down to us through the sacred texts of Denderah, as well as through symbolisations of the event engraved in the temples dedicated to Ptah, tell us:

"Princess Nut leaned her hair against the bark of the magnificent trunk, so old and so welcoming. At the same time, her head rested against the tree, and her whole body and soul were instantly at peace with the outside world; her eyes closed without her realising it!

"Sinking into an unreal sleep, Nut had no time to analyse what was happening, for her astonishment turned to fright as a blinding, radiant light enveloped her, penetrating her from all sides at once. Feeling as if she were being consumed, the most intense fear seized her, but she couldn't open her mouth to scream. She was being reduced to ashes, liquefied, while living in spite of herself the most radiant day that the Earth had known since its Origin!...

"Despite the calm that curiously inhabited her, she tried to open her eyelids; she could not even move her eyelashes. Frightened at being paralysed, she felt herself sinking into unconsciousness, when a voice, deep inside her, very firm, but infinitely gentle and reassuring, said to her "distinctly": "My son Usir is now in your bosom; have no fear about this, for you are the daughter of my first child: you are the one I have chosen to help me save mankind once again in spite of themselves! Usir will be the sign of my Power and Goodness. You, Nut, will be his revered mother; you will teach Usir, through the words you speak, that my Heart is within him, and that my Soul will always be with him so that he can exercise his sovereign power... So be it! ". "

In the meantime, Geb had been warned by God to marry Nut in spite of everything, and to wait until Usir was born before conceiving another son, who would be born "of the earth", after which he would be called Usit. And so the eldest Ousir was born, followed seven months later by Ousit, the youngest. One was the son of God and the other the son of Geb. Hence the obvious antagonism when Usir was declared king, successor to Geb, whereas the real son of the sovereign was Usit, whose name in the ensuing rebellion became Sit, or Seth in Greek. To ensure that the family was perfect and that the main pawns took their place on the chessboard that was about to be turned upside down, the twins Nek-Bet and Iset, in other words Nephthys and Isis, were born.

The latter married Usir for love, as the omens foretold that the son born to them would be the generator of the new multitude born of the survivors of the Great Cataclysm. The child that was born was indeed a boy, and his name was Hor, or Horus.

It was shortly before the latter took over from his father that Usit attacked the capital of Ahâ-Men-Ptah with rebel troops raised for the purpose, thus triggering the process of the continent's engulfment, for, Usir having apparently been killed with a spear by Usit, the wrath of God was unleashed on the creatures and his Creation.

That morning, the star of the day seemed to be absent from the sky... as did the sky itself, for a thick fog of diffuse, reddish light, oppressive in its thickness, smothered everything! It absorbed not only noise, but also daylight and the air, making it suddenly wheezy and difficult to breathe. A bitter, pungent smell, similar to the natrum that embalmed the bodies of the dead, wafted through the air and made all the living tremble as they recognised this fetid atmosphere.

In the capital, where no one had slept a wink during that bloody night, everyone knew that the day had come to settle accounts with God, and that nothing would be given to the credit of this careless and unconscious humanity. The night's fratricidal sacrilege was to be punished by God.

The panic that followed was almost indescribable. The annals recount it at length. In reality, it was similar to any terror engendered by such terrifying circumstances. A large proportion of the able-bodied population ran to the Royal Palace to seek refuge with the "Master" to whom anything was possible. The poor people didn't even remember that just the day before they had been openly mocking the man whose protection they were suddenly seeking, and who a few hours earlier had been trying to persuade them to hasten their preparations for exodus.

The time had come!

In his omnipotence, the God of Eternity was going to punish his creatures for the countless sins they had committed, and he, who had failed to prevent them, would suffer the same fate. Sinister creaks rose from the depths, making the feet tremble and then, growing louder, the whole body! The weeping, the cries for mercy, the screams, the anguish entire crowd trying to implore what they had scorned and denied seemed supremely vain.

Dull creaks created disturbances in the reddish glow that tended to lighten overhead. The vibrations put a strain on the eardrums, some of which burst. Geb appeared at this point, weary and exhausted, but keen to make his presence felt in the absence of his son, the Master, to whom the people were turning for help. Clamour of satisfaction arose at the sight of him, for he appeared once again as a Son of God, and therefore as the Saviour. But he no longer felt equal to taking back an authority that was no longer his, but only that of an angry god. The situation would have seemed improbable if this tragic outcome had not been predicted so often and so long in the making.

In the roadstead of the royal port, thousands of 'mandjit' boats, reputed to be unsinkable, had been stored and rigorously guarded, containing complete survival equipment: barley cakes, quarters of dried and salted meat, changed every year, watertight jugs of water. The old king immediately sent emissaries to the four dockyards, so that the gates could be opened immediately and the soldiers could take up their positions so that the departures could take place in the best possible order.

As for the people, they jostled and ran down the stairs, trying to drag behind them an incredible jumble of utensils! Panic gripped all these poor people, who were suddenly faced with a reality so often ridiculed that it was impossible for them to comprehend its true excess.

A hundred kilometres away, volcanoes that had been dormant for thousands of years suddenly began to contract. The subterranean fires became powerful enough to emerge and their pressure became so great that they hurled a shower of powdered earth high into the sky, combining with the fog and falling as far as Ath-Mer. A solid rain of small rocks and rubbish of all kinds fell on the crowds as they marched towards the ports, crushing some and knocking others unconscious; and all hell broke loose.

There was a stampede towards the harbour, everyone abandoning everything precious to run faster. In the harbour, an animal fear swept away all human feeling; the soldiers, who were resisting only with difficulty their own anguish, were suddenly knocked down, crushed and trampled underfoot by a horde storming the frail papyrus boats, woven extremely tightly, then coated with resin and finally with bitumen to make them rot-proof and indestructible.

The terror that gripped them and the horror of the incredible event that was taking place made this horde lose all sense of security. Instead of boarding with just ten people or, at worst, fifteen, the fugitives stormed the first 'mandjit', fighting to the death so that twenty or thirty of them could pile in. So much so that the first flotilla sank before leaving with all its occupants. Thousands of poor, distraught people perished before they had even left the port of what would not be Ahâ-Men-Ptah for much longer!

The volcanoes, once again active, spewed divine wrath, covering the neighbouring villages in lava. The terrified inhabitants, who had huddled in their homes, were buried in seconds beneath a glowing river.

Thousands of tonnes were spewed out in a matter of seconds from a dozen or so freshly opened craters, carving out a thousand new routes with each tremor. The most solidly seated mountains could no longer withstand the tremors imprinted on the ground; flanks ripped open on all sides, others shattered and vanished into thin air.

The same happened at the royal port. The tumult reached a climax, for it was no longer a few thousand people who were panicked by the terror, but several hundred thousand who were crowding in, choking, struggling and killing each other, with not a single soldier left to protect the public property, in other words the boats.

But the total lack of visibility, which stunned the crowd, nonetheless pushed them towards the edge of the pier. An irresistible surge occurred, throwing the first rows into the water, the "mandjit" on board having sunk from their overflow of passengers. The others, managing to overcome the human tide, embarked away from the bottleneck, taking their time so as not to sink their frail skiffs before untying the mooring ropes. It was the end of everyone and everything. The capital and the entire continent sank rapidly beneath the water!

That day was 27 July 9792, and the date is certain thanks to the sky chart engraved on the ceiling of a room in the temple of Dendera, better known as the 'Zodiac' from the moment it was discovered by scientists accompanying General Desaix and his army of the South during Bonaparte's Egyptian campaign. But let's keep the chronological order, to arrive at the exodus of the survivors of Ahâ-Men-Ptah, the now eternally reclining land of the Elder of God: Amenta, which also became the Platonic Atlantis.

5

THE ATLANTEAN SOUL IS NOT LOST!

Mr Flamand likened the spheroid rams to the Egyptian Amon-Ra, because there is a definite kinship with the engraved figures from the Sahara. But Amon is also the ram-god of water throughout Berberia, where the Berber word for water is "amon", as it is among the Guanches of the Canary Islands.
Raymond Furon (*Manual of general prehistory*)

The absence of material changes is sometimes exaggerated, but the identity of the Berber soul, through all its vicissitudes, is truly a force of nature!
J. Célérier (*History of Morocco*)

I was not a survivor of Ahâ-Men-Ptah and I had not yet made the connection between the Amenta of the so-called Book of the Dead and this engulfed country, when I arrived in Morocco in 1973, recovering from the effects of the long immobilisation caused my accident. Although death had wanted me two years earlier, there was nothing to indicate that I would make discoveries of such importance that they would influence the direction of my Egyptological research. How could I have suspected that I was being 'pushed' towards this marvellous country, only to leave in search of the Survivors of the Great Cataclysm of twelve millennia ago? The content of certain texts from the banks of the Nile referring to the "Place of the Sunset" or Ta Mana in hieroglyphic had led me to suppose that this land was Morocco, since this name was only given to it in French, retaining its Arabic meaning: "Moghreb el-Aqsa" or the "Land of the Sunset".

While I was receiving attentive care and massages for my left side, which was still partially paralysed, I prepared an exhibition on computers for young Moroccans for the Rabat Cultural Centre. At same time, I became a reader in the library of the nearby Ministry of Mines. I had at my disposal all the additional books I had missed during my reading of the Pharaonic texts, both from the point of view of geology and mineralogy and the geophysical structure of certain neighbouring terrains, such as those of the Canary Islands, those famous "Fortunate Isles". On the other hand, hundreds of texts about the Berbers gave me a better understanding of this people, who are very different from the Arabs, so that I could prepare a comparative philology of the Berber language and hieroglyphics, in order to resolve certain semantic difficulties.

It was there that I first heard about the essential characteristics of Tamanar, a village some sixty kilometres north of Agadir, whose very old patriarch and prophet was making it famous throughout Morocco.

Nobody had realised the enormous interest I had in the place where the survivors of Ahâ-Men-Ptah had landed! This village was located some ten kilometres away from the ocean, but as its sandy soil was studded with millions of unfossilised shells, there was no impossibility that, several millennia earlier, this place could have been on the and served as a landing place and shelter for survivors of a shipwreck 10,000 years before our era.

The same was true of Ta Ouz, and the local geologists who explained the place to me literally gave me the key to the most ancient past! Ta Ouz, located on the edge of the Algerian-Moroccan desert, served as the extreme point on the shifting border between the two countries at the time. Not only was the place an exceptional mineralogical site where iron played a major role, and where the state of the soil proved that there had been an enormous geological upheaval, Ta Ouz was also a "sacred place" where hundreds of tells were actually mastabas, or funerary necropolises, whose antiquity was lost in the mists of time. And while Ta Mana had retained its primitive meaning all the way to Egypt, this was not the case with Ta Ouz.

While my search for Ta Mana had been precise from the outset, it was by accident that I heard about Ta Ouz from the geologists! In fact, a team of German adventurers in a van equipped with sophisticated equipment, including a generator, had been intercepted while cutting out a piece of wall covered with rock engravings from a very remote antiquity!... As I read more and more about this place and its surroundings, my interest was aroused and my mind was already racing ahead to these places that everything pointed to as an extraordinary site for my curiosity, and also for meditation.

Naturally, the route to get there was punctuated by other places of interest in more ways than one, such as Midelt, in the Middle Atlas, between Meknes and Ksar-es-Souk, where I was able to realise the vanity of mere 'words' compared to the facts themselves! It's this place that I'll start talking about, because it's indicative of the difference that exists between reality and "myth". I stopped here for a simple reason, explained to me by the geologists. Midelt had always extracted lead and copper from its subsoil in very large quantities. Now, as orichalcum interested me as a metal used by the high priests of Ptah, there could be an additional affinity with Moroccan auricalcite, the current name for this copper derivative, which was found in large quantities in the region's mines. In Midelt, I met several Berber families who traded in these minerals, including one who seemed to know many traditional 'legends'. It took me a long time and a great deal of patience to get to know them. I had to stay with them and live according to their customs for almost two months before I managed to talk about anything other than the commercial value of, for the others, were nothing more than 'pebbles'.

After a year of research along a route with rock engravings and high places, and discussions with specialists and locals who faithfully handed down ancestral traditions, I managed to sketch out a valid route for the exodus of the survivors of Ahâ-Men-Ptah. It seemed logical to me, because it was confirmed by texts and facts, that the country that became Morocco was a kind of Atlantean colony in the remote pre-cataclysmic era. It was the closest land to the lost continent, and became Ta Mana. Here's a rough map to help you visualise:

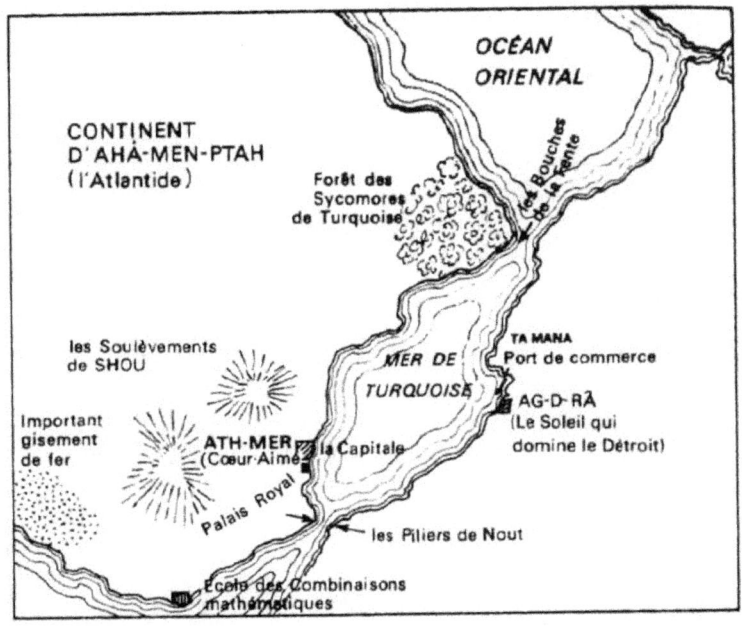

Continent of Ahâ-Men-Ptah (Atlantis)

Metals played a vital role in the life of Ahâ-Men-Ptah, for all the buildings and tools needed for domestic use. Lead and copper, in particular, were sought after in Morocco, as they were almost non-existent in the mother country. The same applied to certain minerals that protected against the evil influences of astral rays during the opposite aspects of the Divine-Mathematical Combinations from the Twelve.

These minerals are also mentioned in the Bible in connection with the breastplate worn by Moses, which enabled him to preserve the unification of the twelve tribes of Israel thanks to the influences it released. But if, at that time, Moses had only been able to recover a few of the original beneficial 'stones' from Egypt, the others being no more than ersatz, the same was not true at the time of Ahâ-Men-Ptah. Each of the twelve minerals really did have a specific influence, the combination of which brought "Long Life, Strength and Health", as all the papyri state when they speak of a pharaoh, adding to his titles this lapidary formula of "Long Life, Strength and Health", which was granted to him by wearing the gems on his breastplate. Not only did those of Ptah retain a religious and political use for them, but those of Ra had accepted them in another form, such as Ramses the Great, thanks to other minerals.

One of these stones was found by me quite by chance, in Midelt, thanks to a perseverance worthy my computer logic, which made me reject any irrational or illogical solution. And that' what kept me going. But this is how it happened, in a context that was certainly hard on my body, which was still partially in plaster at the time.

Midelt is located in the Middle Atlas, on a plateau at an altitude of 1,500 metres, surrounded by very high mountains. Only two passes at over 2,000 metres provide access to the north and south of the region. In winter, snowploughs constantly plough their way through two or three metres of snow, but two or three thousand years ago, to put it mildly, the roads were unusable! Here again is a map showing the location of Midelt between the Atlas ranges, as well as those of the few sites of interest to us:

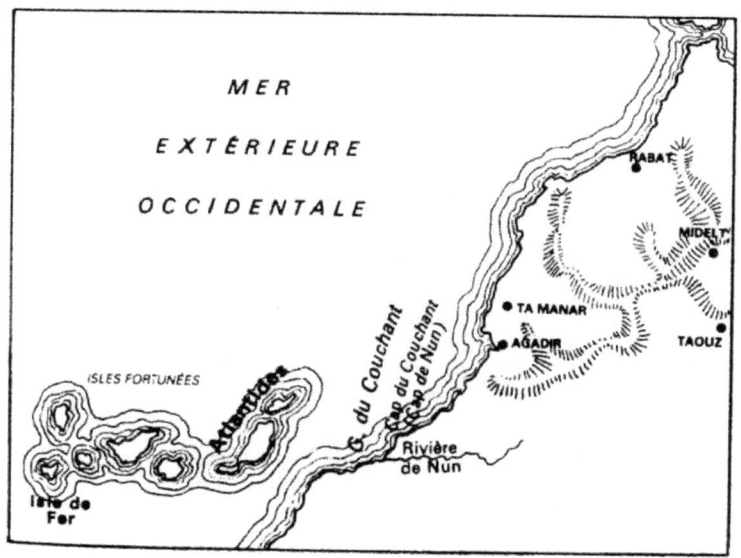

However, when I was finally adopted by the Berber family, I was able to concentrate on my research and ask questions, and I learnt some very interesting things. But it was only little by little, showing with each answer that I was not fooled by a simplicity that was too obvious.

What was it about? To find out where the lead and copper mines came from. The French had drilled the shafts to exploit the ores, but it was clear that in the 19th century the copper and lead miners had not reached this spot, stamping their feet and saying: "This is the place to dig! Clearly, the area had been mined before.

Having accepted this, I was taken to an area not far from the current mines, but hidden behind a mountain. There, other disused and much older shafts proved that the Spaniards had passed through here begin rational lead mining, in particular. However, I had to go back to the same logical analysis as with the French: namely, that the Spanish, and what's more, two centuries earlier, could not have arrived in this desert area and claimed to have found metals precisely in this spot!

A new confidence told me that there had indeed been predecessors, and that they had been Romans!... I then visited some more interesting remains on the road to Meknes, three kilometres from Midelt, well back and totally invisible from the main road. These wells were definitely from the time of the Caesars, both in terms of the design of the vaults and the architecture of the underground galleries. Large deposits of minerals were still piled up there, as if they had no value because they weren't lead. And yet, there was a whole fortune there for contemporary collectors, who would have opened their eyes wide in disbelief at the reality of what they were seeing! But that wasn't the aim of my research, as my concern was always the same: who had led the Romans to this place to extract ore? I had certainly made good progress in my journey back in time, but not enough to be satisfied with my investigations.

It was only after much prevarication, hesitation and an irrational fear of attracting a very serious curse that my Berber friends told me that, originally, well before the Romans, the... Giants to organise the extraction! Hence the name Atlas given to the mountains, because their king was as high as they were! And the myth of Atlas as leader of the Atlanteans reappeared; I had to know!

After more nameless procrastination, often close to a fury that would have ruined everything, I was taken much further, this time on the road to Meknes. About fifteen kilometres from Midelt, the jeep and my two drivers took a road that led us past an enormous plateau that took us two hours to drive around, before arriving at an infernal, lunar landscape: the Mine of the Giants! It was a vast plain riddled with huge holes and small tell-tales, the whole thing just a shade of grey against a black background! I felt as if I'd suddenly changed planets, and I remember shivering in spite of myself! At the bottom of each of these craters, dug out by human hands, people from the earliest times - while others were living in smoke-filled caves in France, eating raw meat and wearing untanned skins - were extracting minerals to make tools and chiselled jewellery! I was in the presence of the remains of an extinct race: the survivors of Ahâ-Men-Ptah! Each heap was palpable proof of this. But were they really "giants"?

I instantly decided to go to the bottom of one of these wells, which was apparently about fifty metres deep. It took me a good week's discussion to overcome my hesitations. But time was running out, because I couldn't wait to get back down to Ta Ouz, where everything was ready for me. And it was only on the last day of my search in Midelt that, in the face of my sadness, the last 'palaver' took away the favourable decision! A sort of wicker basket was woven in less than an hour, and firmly attached to the end of a roll of thick rope! Everything was ready for my descent.

It was easy, but the result was disappointing, in that at the bottom of the shaft there was a gallery about 1.70 metres high, and I had to bend my head down to take a few steps! A giant couldn't have moved more than one leg. Clearly, the creators of these works were not sons of Hercules or Titans, even if their intelligence was far superior to ours: they must have physically resembled us in every way! But this needed to be verified, it had been, and I felt amply satisfied since I could now start from solid foundations: those that gave rise to the theme *of Survivors of Atlantis*.

In Ta Ouz, everything was different because it was in the middle of the desert. Or at least the sand had covered everything with its powdery mantle. A small fortified village, home to an army company, indicated that this was the extreme south-western point of the Algerian-Moroccan border. More or less sandy defiles ran along this invisible line separating the two countries. And as you went further down one of these paths, the landscape changed. Stony at first, it soon revealed blocks of black rock, unmistakably metallic in appearance: pure iron in a variety of mineralised forms: hematite, magnetite, siderite, etc., all of which were found in the rock.

In this place where the compass was beating wildly and was no longer of any use, the atmosphere was very strange. Of course, it was nearly 60°C in the sun, because there was no shade anywhere; of course, the smell was very particular, because all this metal that had been heated for thousands of years was sending its own radiation back to those who walked on it, but there was something else indefinable. Here again, the geologists who accompanied me told me about the burial site at the end of a dried-up wadi running parallel to ours, which led to the place where there were hundreds of rock engravings, right where a military patrol had intercepted the vandals who were cutting up the rock to take it away!

We got there after a great deal of difficulty, and here again I had the impression of entering another world! Here, no more stones, but once again sand covering everything... Hills as far as the eye could see, varying in size and apparently made of agglomerated sand. At the centre of the site, one of them, much higher. The two geologists and our Berber guide had unconsciously lowered their voices.

Like them, I whispered in awe. We were at the burial site, the thrice-holy sacred enclosure that was not to be entered because the time had not yet come. And to show me that each of the hills was a tomb, our guide took a shovel from the jeep and went at random to the foot of one of them. He dug for more than a metre before revealing a pile of rocks and stones joined unmistakably by human hands. He then put the sand back in place and hurried to put the shovel back in our vehicle. It was only then that I became aware of an inexplicable phenomenon that added to my confusion: I was once again swatting away the unwelcome flies, which were swarming in their tens of thousands! And yet, all the time I'd been at the burial site, not a single insect had been there!

The enclosure was bypassed to reach the east of this exceptional panorama, where the survivors of this battle had fled after carving strange drawings and texts into the surrounding rocks. There are hundreds of these engravings everywhere! Even on the ground, where pieces of hard rock are exposed. And it was here that the vandals set about removing whole chunks of this country's most ancient history.

There was no doubt that, if Ta Mana meant the "Land of the Setting Sun", Ta Ouz meant the "Land of Usir"; and the Son of God's name was Osiris in Greek phonetics. Once again, the circle was complete. All that remained was for me to go to Tamanar, north of Agadir, to check whether this really was the ancient Ta Mana of

Egyptian texts, the place where the survivors of the Ahâ-Men-Ptah had landed.

Health problems having arisen during this long journey, I had to rest for a few weeks in Rabat, during which time I set up a mineralogical exhibition with the specimens I had brought back. In order to do things properly, I even brought over from Romania some precious minerals that were very well exploited in that country, whereas they were poorly protected in Morocco, if at all. The exhibition was a great success, with some people showing a mixture of envy and greed, because I was presenting the twelve 'stones' that the ancients said would be beneficial to those who wore them in harmony with their date of birth. However, most of these minerals were not included in the breastplate of Moses, who had revived this ancient Pharaonic custom to ensure divine protection for the wearer.

It was on this subject that I drew the government's attention with a resounding two-page interview published in *Maroc-Soir Hebdo* on Sunday 17 February 1974 and entitled: "Des réserves inépuisables de minéraux précieux dans la région de Midelt" ("Inexhaustible reserves of precious minerals in the Midelt region"). This obviously displeased those who wanted to organise a profitable business there! But I didn't care, because I set off for Tamanar, north of Agadir, without worrying about the possible repercussions for profiteers who were too greedy and uneducated when it came to beneficial minerals. Because there so little information available about the extraction sites, the digs were carried out in the most unexpected places.

Morocco is a wonderful country, where every panorama is different from the one that precedes it. But the coastline has a very special and invigorating charm in this "Land of the Sunset". Agadir became infamous following the earthquake that destroyed almost 100% of the town. But by 1974, it had once again become a pleasant place, where luxury hotels rivalled in opulence those on the best beaches of the Côte d'Azur. Only the flies remained, as the dried fish canneries still attracted them. I stayed for a few days near the new municipality to meet some people to whom I had been introduced. There again, I learned some important facts, before finally being taken to Tamanar, an hour's drive further north.

The reminder of the recent earthquake obviously loosened the tongues of my companions. I also learnt about the 'legends' passed down by the natives. Another terrible earthquake had changed the face of the world thousands of years earlier, and the sun itself, instead of rising in the west, had suddenly set there, only to reappear in the east in the morning. Hence the definition of "Sunset Country" for Morocco, given by the survivors of this adventure, after they had landed "there", such had been the impact of the event on them. This "there" was the entire Agadir region, and more particularly to the north, where Tamanar seemed to be the real focal point.

The astonishing thing is that these old Moroccans told this story, identical to the Egyptian texts, without knowing them, but which their ancestors had perpetuated orally from father to son since time immemorial. So when I decided to leave for Tamanar, one of my new friends whispered to me in particular that I'd better "go up and see the Father of all". In Rabat, I had already heard of a prophet, or a very old patriarch, who knew the past as well as the future, but who was very difficult to approach. Only a few acquaintances or very high personalities like King Hassan II could meet him and talk to him. So I asked for his address, but with a slight smile, the man who had thought he was whispering a revelation to me replied that I needn't worry about that. If I had to meet him, I would.

It was with some trepidation that I approached this enchanting spot, with its rolling hills and exuberant vegetation, which reminded me of a landscape I'd seen before, even though I'd never been here before. Although the village was about ten kilometres from the coast, its air was unmistakably marine and salty. As soon as I left the jeep in the car park on the tarmac road, the fine sand studded with non-fossilised shells treaded pleasantly under my feet. Some of the locals glowered at me, I thought. But the presence of the Moroccan geologists put my mind at rest. There seemed to be very clear opposition from these people to the research I wanted to do there into the origins of the village. It wasn't fear or malevolence that seemed to be present, but a silent, almost palpable animosity that I instantly felt to the depths of my soul! Why was I considered an enemy when I hadn't questioned anyone yet? I was about to find out!

The only person who could tell me anything about the antiquity of this place was the head of a Berber family, whose wrinkles on his forehead showed his advanced age. But he was perfectly aware what he was saying. Unfortunately, he 't speak French, and I had to rely on my young geologist friends to understand what he was saying. His tone, however, allowed all the nuances of the sentences to come through, so that I lost almost none of the essential meaning of the whole conversation.

To simplify things here, since all this was detailed in Volume II of the trilogy, it was indisputable that the Berber tribe were the descendants of those who, millennia earlier, had landed at this spot still by the sea. For obvious reasons, certain families had settled in the area and established themselves there to ensure the back-up of the rest of the survivors who set off in search of "Ta Mér i[7] ", the "Beloved Heart". Metal and supplies to follow. And when it became unnecessary to send all these supplies, a second fixed point having been established much further forward ,[8] those had settled in Ta Mana remained there. Not only because the climate was healthy and cultivation easy, but also because the extraction of metals and minerals had to continue. The third, more spiritual, reason was that the burial site of Ta Ouz should always be protected, until the time came to reveal the Truth before a cataclysm even more radical than the first destroyed the whole Earth!

As my opposite number knew that I had just returned from the thrice-sacred land where the Elder still lay, he wasn't making any revelations, simply confirming everything I already knew. Dozens questions were burning in my mind, but I wasn't sure how to phrase them so that the translation didn't distort them. But the old man took the initiative, telling me that another, more enlightened man than he, a descendant of the 'Great Seers' of his ancestors, would explain to me in great detail what I needed to know to advance my research. He was just one of many lost souls!

After serving us the traditional mint tea and explaining to the geologist-driver how to get to the patriarch, we set off in that direction. My fears were over. There was no longer any doubt that everything had been planned by a higher power to ensure that I continued along the path that lay ahead of me, without any further hiccups. My position as a convalescent from my very serious accident, the after-effects of which were still perfectly visible without the need for a doctor, no doubt made it easier to approach the extraordinary man I was about to

---

[7] Ta Meri, like Ta Mana, is the subject of several quotations in the papyri of the scribes Ani and Nebseni, which have wrongly been included in what has been called the Book of the Dead. This is the Promised Place.

[8] Once again, this settlement became sedentary and gave rise to the great tribe of the Kabyles.

meet, because my terrible pain over more than two years had developed certain mental and spiritual faculties.

Before long we were at the end of the tarmac road, then the dirt track that climbed a hill. I had to walk some more and then climb a path to a knoll where "He" was waiting for us on the doorstep of his house, leaning on a large cane. In perfectly understandable French, he simply said, "Come in", while motioning to my two friends to wait outside. What happened there, for three quarters of an hour, was probably the most extraordinary thing I had ever experienced, my two accidents and the German torture being comparatively banal events!

The start of the interview immediately put me in such a special mood that I felt I was witnessing a scene from twelve millennia ago! Indeed, as soon as I was seated on two low Moroccan-style sofas, the Patriarch, who had not stopped scrutinising me, said to me without any preamble:

— You are standing right here in the place where the Son was raised by his two sisters, with God's help, so that the multitude might be reborn, to live again in obedience to the Law of the Lord. God being God, His wrath alone is to be feared when we try to pierce certain mysteries that only concern the future. Are you ready to pay your tribute to this harsh law of human existence?

— Havent I paid enough?

— The Son was resurrected here 12,000 years ago because he was the Son. That is not your case, whatever task you take on. So it is not for me to answer your question, but for the One whose actions you seek to interpret. It may be worse to reveal the future than to keep it hidden.

— But I'm not trying to read the future! Everything seems to have conspired to make me understand the past life of a people. If this is the case, it is so that I can repeat it to those who would be happy to have this knowledge, which is essential for their survival.

— In this particular case, knowing the past means influencing the future. God alone is the Master of Eternity; and in this capacity, you will attract a great deal of hatred, jealousy and trouble!... Do you feel strong enough to face all that?

— Since you received me, it seems that I must be received, otherwise you'd be wasting your time talking to me.

— The difficulty does not lie there, it lies within you, because the time has not yet come to bring all these revelations. You will have to dose them slowly so that everything is ready when the time comes.

— In this case, there's no problem because I haven't consulted any publishers.

— On the contrary, it will be difficult, because although the beginnings will be slow, and full of uncertainties in relation to the results you will have obtained, when you are halfway there, success will beget success, and it is at this point that you will need to have the willpower and strength necessary to put the brakes on the spread of Knowledge.

— But why?

— Everything must come in its own time: with the cycle that allows it to be in tune with divine harmony. Each era has its own particular rhythm. The age of Taurus had Ousir, just as the age of Aries took the Sun to disassociate itself from the Creator's Creation... The era of Pisces will end in Chaos unless there is an awakening of the human soul, with a new Son who will be a new Saviour...

— Several prophets have already announced this, and the books I'm going to publish won't change a thing.

— Don't be too modest! The reaction to your works can become very greedy, but also suddenly so greedy that it is capable of rejecting false prophets who have predicted catastrophes that have not come to pass! This has been the case on several occasions since man has existed, and you will see for yourself! Even after Usir, when the priests of the Sun raised the ram like a god by placing the globe on its skull, the idols were brought down by people wilder than themselves.

And since that memorable time, Amon has become the god of water throughout Berberia, because "amon", in Berber, means water, and therefore the hope of life. The hope of eternally conserving water for one's needs, but also the hope in one's heart of never again seeing the symbolism of the ram as an idol in place of God. This was the order of things, a Messiah arrived with the end of the Age of Aries. The same will happen in a few years' time with the disappearance of the Age of Pisces. God will be trampled underfoot, denied, and everyone will be begging him when the time comes to resurrect a new Son!

— When will this happen?

— You'll find out for yourself as go along.

But don't announce the time too quickly!

— Tell me why, you who know everything...

— Lawless beings, whose greed will always push them towards evil, will try to use this Knowledge to distort its Wisdom for their own profit. You must then be very wary.

— You are a true prophet and you speak only the truth. I didn't come here for nothing...

— I don't have long to live; it's not up to me to break the Will of the One who led you here. I will leave you alone in the next room for as long as you think necessary to meditate. You can learn great things there if you deserve to, but suffer on the contrary if you are unworthy! Would you like to go?

— What is this room?

— A bare room, where you'll have to stay on the ground. But it was in this very place that Usir was resurrected. He speaks to those who are worthy, but punishes the others. Do you have the courage to face the Son?

— Take me...

This is not the place to describe the three very strange and almost supernatural hours I spent there. The novelised narration of *the Origins trilogy* is a reminiscence. It has been criticised by the 'specialists' as being completely invented because it was dialogue-based and no text could provide such a wealth of detail and precision. While it is true that the papyri provide the true and essential framework for the history of the sunken continent and the exodus to the "Second Heart", Egypt, the fact remains that this publication was made possible by the form given to the work. And what made this luxury of detail possible were not the inventions of an unbridled brain, but the result of a concentration between two minds that came together one day, at Ta Mana, at the precise site of the resurrection of Osiris. My intense bibliographical research, which I subsequently pursued in Chantilly, only served to accentuate the heap of details all pointing in the same direction in this monotheism, so that Eternity, which is nothing more than an eternal cyclical recommencement, belongs to God alone.

By way of an accelerated summary, which interested readers will be able to improve on by reading *Les Survivants de l'Atlantide*, let us see what happened to the survivors of the Ahâ-Men-Ptah after the Resurrection of Uzir, once they had docked at Ta Mana, disembarking from their 'mandjit', the unsinkable boats that had carried them to that point...

6

THE SURVIVORS OF THE AHÂ-MEN-PTAH

> *But another perhaps fanciful, but by the same token seductive, supposition associates the Berbers with Atlantis, which would imply a push from West to East, and not the other way round!*
> E.-F. Gautier *(The Past of North Africa)*

> *Who doesn't know that you are the accomplices of those whom God caused to die in the Cataclysm? You are of that race of pharaohs who made the kings of Egypt! You are of the race of Sodom and Gomorrah and of all those who fought against God in unbelief from the beginning!*
> Shenouda the Mystic (5th-century Coptic papyrus)

After the first few weeks of daze, suffering and searching for other family members who had survived like them, the survivors of what had been Ahâ-Men-Ptah began to organise themselves into Ta Mana to survive. This was the first idea to emerge from the cataclysm: to live long enough to warn future generations that a similar misfortune could happen again if they failed to obey the Creator of all things, including the human beings they were!

So the first Councils of Elders, which brought together those who had escaped on their 'mandjit', thanks to God, sought the simplest and most effective ways of learning the lesson of the past in order to prepare for a better future. The pontiff of the College of High Priests had predicted what had happened: it was up to them to learn the hard lessons of their selfishness and impiety.

The divine signs had not been followed, and this was to serve as an experiment, both for the survivors and for their descendants for all eternity. Any divine punishment could be redeemed, but it was still necessary to appease the anger by blind obedience. For the first palpable truth for them, who were in the midst of the "abomination of desolation", was that God had wanted the survivors to understand at last, "afterwards", their disobedience towards this God who was the sole Creator of Creation.

But it was no longer a time for despair, as the Renaissance appeared on the horizon of every dawn, with the Sun appearing *in the East* rather than the West, as eternal reminder of the renewal that had taken place in the same region of the Twelve: in the constellation of Leo.

Usir the Risen had sat for forty-two days, to establish the new multitude in obedience to the commandments of the divine Law, represented by his son Hor, who would thus become the first descendant of the Elder. He would be followed by an unbroken list of Pêr-Ahâ, if they agreed to remain the Sons of God during the long and arduous exodus that was being prepared towards a "Promised Land": Ta Meri. When this place was reached at the end of the eastern horizon that joined that of the Sleeping Ones: Ath-Kâ-Ptah, it would become "the Second Heart of God". He would then unite the Earth of the Younger Ones with the heaven of the Elder Ones, thus rising from the ashes and the dust. But wouldn't the Faith be lost again, destroying all the efforts of those who knew that man was running alone towards his doom? No matter how much the divine force permeated souls, if a few rebelled against it and continued kneel for the Sun, no one could survive the resulting discord!

Before setting off again in search of a new Eden, and in order to avoid a return of the calamities, the Elders decided on the general form to be given to the new religion, which would be that of the exodus. To do this, they and Horus must have flown over the tens of centuries of incessant and exhausting journeys, and foreseen the arrival of the new generations at Ta Meri. What would happen then? Probably total oblivion of the tragic past that so obsessed the Ancients, who were living it in the Present! It was so obvious that the Council almost abandoned its objective. But Horus knew how to lift everyone's spirits, because it was vital that the human race should survive, since the Earth was its possession. From that day on, therefore, every being had to feel that God was watching over their every move, through the thousands of facets of the universe that make up Creation, and which would be typical reflections of each variant of the divine image. So throughout its life, the soul would feel that it was being spied on for each of its acts, whether malevolent or benevolent, and would be judged for it at the end of its earthly life, implacably. If it had failed, it would be irremediably rejected, but if it had returned pure, it would survive eternally.

Gradually, an ethic came to strictly regulate the commandments of the Law so that the people of survivors who multiplied all along the road would maintain their righteousness and their faith in God and in the future. It would be time to review everything once the multitude had reached the Second Heart of God. For, from then on, humanity, becoming sedentary, would have to have other criteria for belief if fear of divine wrath was to remain.

And the great departure took place at the time predicted by the celestial configurations and calculated by the Masters of Measurement and Number, who were among the survivors. On the very first morning, a grand ceremony of thanksgiving took place before eight priests carrying a 'mandjit' on a makeshift stretcher at shoulder height. A shrine was built there, containing a relic of Uzir brought back from Ta Ouz, as well as his clothes. Symbolically, the priests looked towards the west, where the "Sleeping Blessed" of Ahâ-Men-Ptah lay. As for the pontiff facing them, in front of the whole multitude kneeling in thanksgiving, he held in his hands a symbolic pot containing the ashes of a mandjit, whose flame would only be extinguished on arrival in Ath-Kâ-Ptah, the Second Heart-of-God and their future second homeland:

And so it should be, every morning when Ptah would make Ra appear in all his splendour, with the gold of his rays of light in the east, forcing all those who prayed to close their eyes so as not to be blinded. This fervour would be the most salutary for the hard days ahead of this exodus through territories that had also been turned upside down, and which were irreparably drying up.

In the same way, every evening, before the sun disappeared over the sea that had made an enormous liquid shroud of the motherland, the fervent invocation to Ptah should allow Ra, who disappeared over the millions of dead, to warm them, while allowing the living to rest their souls in peace with God.

But, of course, during the evening prayer, the pontiff and his priests would no longer gaze at the ideal point where they would find the Promised Land, but would look at the old continent, preciously presenting it with the ashes of the Ancestors, rekindled by the new flame that would not be extinguished until the new Covenant with Ptah had brought them to the land of the second homeland! In this way, the ever-present memory of the event would keep the fear alive in the very hearts of the survivors, down to the very depths of their souls, as the second drawing opposite shows by the very position of the pontiff staring to the left to present the funerary urn with its reborn flame.

Misfortune, however, lurked around those who rightly considered themselves to be the descendants of Ptah. In this case, it was personified by the rebels descended from Set, who had also partly escaped the Great Cataclysm. They had formed their own clan, further south, and had also prepared to head east in search of a new land that the prophets had promised would be blessed by the Sun and its satellites, just for them. And so the fighting between the two fratricidal tribes resumed.

The traces of these harsh battles can be found all along a route that I have travelled and that I have called: "The Sacred Route of the Rock Engravings". In fact, as at Ta Ouz, there are not just a few drawings carved in stone, but hundreds and thousands all along the imaginary line known today as the "Tropic of Cancer": let's say between the 25th and 35th parallels. And so it was at the edge of a mountainous desert region whose only border crossing with Algeria was the Zenaga Pass. There, the two clans met and fought fiercely, leaving remarkable rock engravings as a reminder of their passage and their battles.

The following map shows the route taken by those of Usir-Ptah and those of Set-Ra.

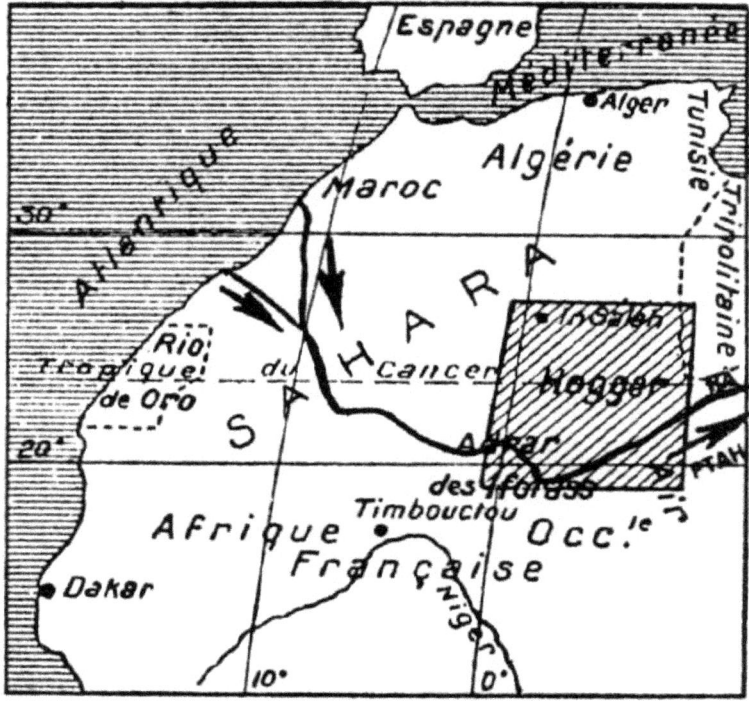

It was therefore easy enough to recount the titanic battles that took place, reborn from the depths of known ages, to attest to this fratricidal duel and the violence of the events that pitted those of Set against those of Usir, the "Manistiou" or the "Blacksmiths of Horus" against the "Ra-Sit-Ou", or the "Rebels of Set". The engravings in the battle zones are significant. In many places they are superimposed on the previous ones, proving that the first inhabitants were dispossessed by invaders who scratched the sandstone, chiselling it with furious flint blows, before these hands engraved their drawings with a different, more rustic conception.

These overproductions are almost life-size, often exceeding one metre in height. All the human bodies have animal heads, either rams or birds.

The Hoggar region is prolific in this respect, which has enabled certain battles and their environment to be accurately reconstructed. The "Rebels" had been firmly established for several decades, a little to the north of where the exodus of Horus' descendants was taking place. In fact, Seth's people, under the reign of a mild-mannered king called An-Sit-Râ, had proliferated in a verdant area that they cultivated peacefully. But his successor, the tyrannical and bloodthirsty Bak-Ra, was only looking for an opportunity to take warlike revenge!

This was given to him by the advance of the enemy "troop" which, he claimed, was going to destroy them. The twofold aim he had in mind was obvious: to revive the struggle, and then to return the promised land "by the Sun", becoming the "Land of Light". He was the first to choose as his emblem the sparrow hawk, whose symbol was plain for all to see: ready to swoop down on his prey, which he had spotted with his piercing eyes, and to close his claws on it like powerful pincers that crushed everything.

The chief's village and the entire tribe were established on the south bank of the Sa-ou-Râ, or "water burnt by the Sun", while those of Ptah advancing on the other bank stopped a few days' walk away, to the north of the river and the rebel camp.

From this point onwards, two types of primitive engraving give a good idea of the events. Those of Horus indicate that in the evening, when the people were full of buffalo meat, the Sun disappeared behind Ta Mana, towards the place where the Blessed were resting, in the Amenta. This prompted the pontiff to tell them that the place they had just arrived would be called Ta Mentit, the "Place-Hopeful-at-Sunset", which combined the place they had come from and the place they were going to, Ta Merit.

Similarly, for future annals, this impetuous, bubbling river would be called Sâ-Ou-Râ, the "Sunburnt Water", which was a linguistic subtlety, as this newfound liquid seemed to be seized by an overflowing fever after the desolate drought of the Sâ-Ahâ-Râ. This water symbolically represented the new Sun becoming the Master of Nature and inundating the new population with its benefits n.[9]

---

[9] These territories, located between 0° and 4° longitude at the height of the parallel of the Tropic of Cancer, all bear Berber names that can easily be written using hieroglyphics, which is always easy to check.

From the very next day, Per-Ahâ displayed a rare organisational genius. The foresight of his pontiff had invigorated him, and he took the useful decisions that were needed. He scattered the great clans of his immense family all along the river, going back up towards the source.

And so it was that the vanguards of some met the rearguards of others! The confrontation took place, but the fight was fairly unequal, with the strength of the weapons going to the 'Manistiou'. But although the rebels' weapons primitive for lack of metal, the flint and quartzite with which they struck their blows killed the biggest beasts. And as they combined strong arms with a certain cunning developed while hunting fast-moving animals such as ostriches and giraffes, they remained formidable adversaries.

The wounded returned to their own camps to tell of the power of their opponents. The Blacksmiths of Horus fortified their camp, and during their counter-attack, much later, the chronology is re-established thanks to these drawings, as men's heads are superimposed in a third engraving on the previous ones, and, by way of signature, this same third hand adds a lion's tail encircling the waist. It is thus easy to re-establish the deeds of ownership of the site: first, there was a "Follower of Hor", then a "Ra-Sit-Ou" worshipper of the Sun, and finally, just to return the favour, once again a "Manistiou".

At Ta Mentit, several statues carved into the basalt rocks of the site have even been found, thanking Ra for the victory of the "Rebels of Sit". A ram's head carved on a cylindrical tenon can be seen in the Algiers museum. To fully understand the hieroglyphic-Berber imbroglio, you need to know that the "sacred" name of Sit, who died at sunset, was Amen (from Ahâ-Men, the "Ancient of the Sunset"), the name given to the ram whose thrashing symbolised the first "Rebel" and his victories over Usir and Hor, as if the living strength of Sit had been reincarnated in all rams.

"Amen" became the hope and faith in the power of the Sun for all the "Ra-Sit-Ou", and over the centuries the name for water was added with the same double syllabic sound. For it was Ra who protected the desert rivers so that everyone could quench their thirst. The whole of Berberia has kept this word, "amen", to designate water, even today. Just like in Kabylia and among the Tuaregs. This winding route has been scrupulously retraced by me thanks to the thousands of drawings that make up the Sacred Path of the Rock Engravings, as shown opposite.

The battles between spear- and axe-bearers and stone-throwers, or the tanks ramming into naked men, are also amply detailed on the rocks of Tassili-n'Ajjer, demonstrating, in the sobriety of the engravings, the revenge that the 'Manistiou' later took on the 'Ra-Sit-Ou'.

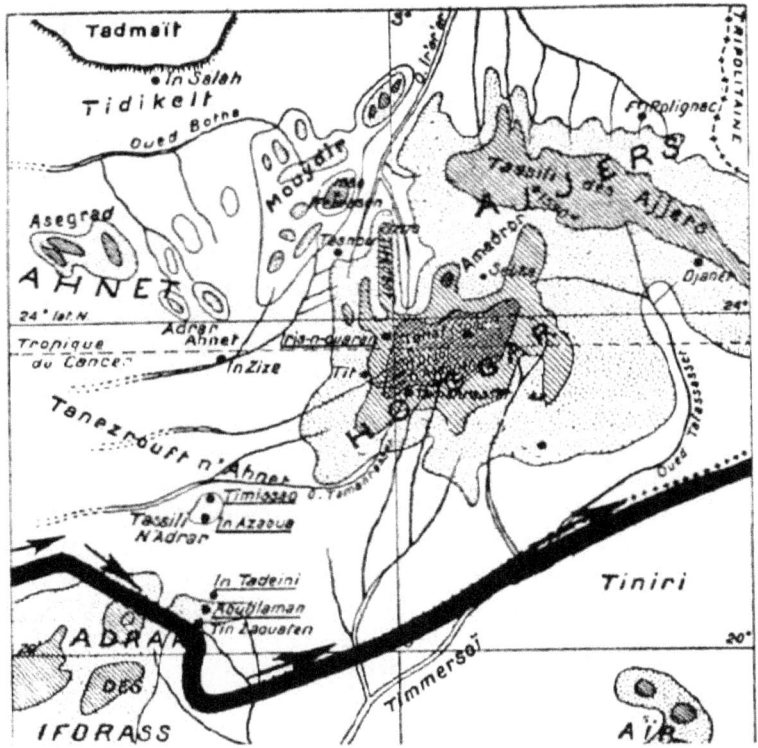

This second battle was very deadly, as both sides found themselves equally armed, the "Rebels" having made a plentiful harvest of picks and axes during the previous invasion. After this bloody clash, the worshippers of Ra were once again driven further east, into another desert. And the advance of the multitude of Ptah also resumed towards the east, where the current settlements of Kabyles and Targuis are the rightful offspring of the Elders, in the same way as the Berbers. This was the origin of the famous "Serk-Kers", the "skull openers". This guild of trephineers settled in the Aurès region, where it is still active today, using the same methods and instruments as ten millennia ago.

In this place, where the entire population born in Uzir stayed longer to regain their strength, the engravings are finer and better incised. The calm no doubt allowed this art to develop, as the "Rebels" had fled to the foothills of Fez to settle down and catch their breath.

There was just one small event, which seemed insignificant at the time, but which later became of paramount importance. The Hor-Vainqueur managed to domesticate a falcon. As a joke, he took the title of Hor-Two-Time-Victor, because his falcon had killed a sparrowhawk. From that day on, the falcon became the emblem of the 'Descendant'. It was in the eternal order of things to ally oneself with celestial harmony.

Taking advantage of this prolonged break, the various oral school groups had gone back to work, repeating over and over again the part of the Knowledge they had conscientiously stored in the back of their minds, without omitting or changing anything, even though they hardly understood all the sentences any more, as they were already losing their original meaning in the thick mist of the new mornings.

The pontiff, to whom was exclusively reserved the class of adult initiates who would train those who would bequeath to later generations the sacred elements destined to re-establish the College for the training of high priests, repeated over and over to his pupils the same phrases accompanied by the same arguments and comments, having himself learned them from his father. He reserved only one final chapter for his eldest son, to the exclusion of all, as had happened to him, and practised for all the Elders of the pontiffs who had preceded him since Ta Mana. The teaching provided was certainly not as good as that of heroic times, but those who wore white robes and shaved their heads were devoted to their thankless task of providing spiritual training for spirits that were unfortunately tired, and far too preoccupied by the hallucinating march of days that seemed interminable, to concern themselves with the future life of the Beyond Life, which was nonetheless more important.

Thus, the only secret element consisted in guiding this immense population along an intangible west-east axis, which they always had to keep on course for, or return to rounding mountain ranges, in order to reach the place promised by God.

It was a simple 'device', rebuilt in Ta Mana as soon as the idea of the exodus had germinated. It was enclosed in a scrupulously guarded cart, which no one but the pontiff could enter. And it consisted of a large bowl, which today we would call a basin, full of water, in which swam an 'object' made of sycamore wood: the *gô-men*.

This little cylinder made it possible to follow a pre-calculated course without any risk of deviation! It therefore held the power to preserve the route to the second homeland and the certainty of reaching it one day or another. The mechanism was disarmingly simple, because the notches made in it were the infallible markers for all the destinations in the world known at the time. A parallel pierced with a small elongated piece of metal was used to fix the point according to the shadow cast every day at noon. Today, this imaginary line is known as the Tropic of Cancer.

Today's southern Algeria saw the establishment of a new medical school, responsible for operating on the countless head injuries sustained during the harsh battles with mace, spear or axe. Anatomy was given pride of place, and we have a treatise of over three hundred leaves, dating from the son of Menes, the second king who reigned four thousand years before our era. Half of the papyrus is in the Berlin Museum and the other half in the British Museum. Operations such as trepanning and caesarean section are described in minute detail. All the precise gestures to be carried out in order to save human lives whose skull has been more or less severely hit, split or broken. Special tools were developed following various tests carried out on "enemy" corpses, as many rebels killed in combat had not been picked up by their own troops. This rapidly became so easy that the skill of the first "surgeons" was passed down from father to son, and is still perpetuated at the beginning of the 20th century, as can be seen from a book by Dr R. Verneau: *La Trépanation dans l'Aurès*, of which the following is an essential extract:

> There is still a small group of trephineers with bizarre medical customs who come from who knows where; who have been performing this singular trephine operation for who knows how long; who learned it from who knows whom; and who, still savage and inaccessible to modern medical ideas, astonish us by their boldness in operating and by the successes they achieve!

Here are the drawings of various instruments found by this doctor, which must not have differed from many of the ten-thousand-year-old originals.

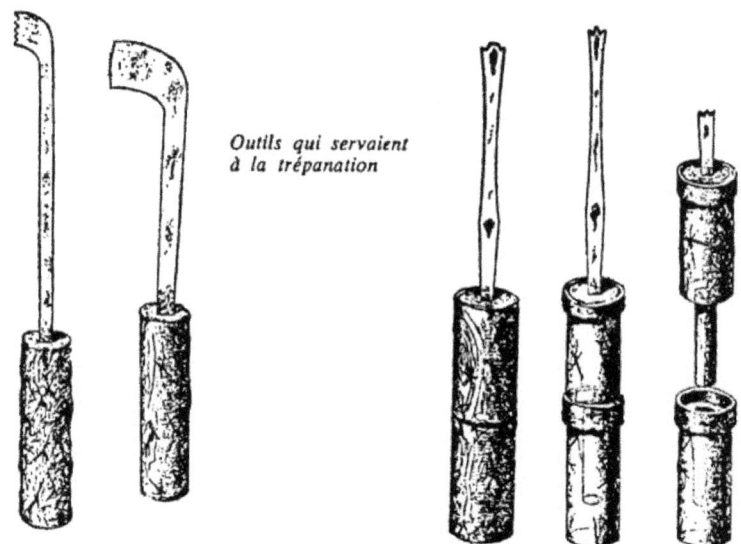

Outils qui servaient à la trépanation

This first school of thought certainly gave rise to the great principle of the equality of all the wounded in the face of suffering. The texts abound in pointing out that we are all alike in the face of death. It is only at this intermediary passage, which precedes the entry into the Beyond of earthly life, that the soul regains its primordial value. All the great themes of monotheism stem from this event. Only those who have lived fully in Justice and Goodness, and in all Purity, will go directly to the Blessed Ones, who alone possess eternal Life.

This specification gave rise to the "opening of the top of the skull", in order to preserve the carnal envelopes endowed with a fragment divine, whether they belong to one clan or the other, because they are likely to continue or begin their good deeds on Earth. Once healed, these heads will be able to bring their souls into line with the Divine Commandments! In this way, only God will be able to judge them.

As the years went by, and then the centuries, the approach of the Promised Land became clearer, after the scattering here and there of families that would become important new tribes. Even today, each tribe retains its own originality within the Arab nation as a whole. But in other places, such as Fezzan, the struggle was so great and the climate so harsh that, apart from the beautiful series of rock engravings, there is nothing left but desert. However, a team of Italian archaeologists are currently unearthing treasures, including real mummies, proving that by reaching the gates of Egypt, the survivors had not only reintroduced trepanning, but also embalming. The remains were already so extensive by the time I was there that it's easy to reconstruct their history.

The fight resumed at the gates of Fezzan, where the rebel families had taken refuge their bitter defeat. These families had grouped together at the bottom of a canyon, leaving a bright spot in a gigantic black stony desert. It was at the end of this dead land that the exiles breathed again, finding there an oasis of freshness, still full of fine white sand. Animals of all species still lived in this area, which covered just a few kilometres, in good harmony. Unfortunately, there were a lot of humans, and they had to eat...

This stage, which was only temporary in the minds of the leaders, lasted longer than expected, and animals of all kinds became scarcer, then disappeared from this oasis, which eventually dried up itself. But before leaving this enchanting place, nostalgia led to the reproduction on the walls of the multitude of animals that had lived there: elephants, rhinoceroses, giraffes, crocodiles, etc., all these engravings measuring around two metres by three s![10]

But now it was time to try and take the 'Second Heart' from those who claimed that this land was promised to them alone. Just then, advanced elements of the Manistiou reached the entrance to Fezzan, looking for an encampment for the next stage. A terrible clash ensued, which dragged on for some fifty kilometres, trapping the two clans in their positions.

The rocky masses that abound in these parts are once again a lasting reminder of this. On the engravings, the figures become "animal", and the two Giants are defined by a hawk and a falcon. The descendants of the first are indisputably "Worshippers of the Sun" and the others "Blacksmiths of Hor". From that onwards, the emblems of the two clans featured this name, which quickly became mythical.

The splendid sculptures engraved on the rocks have the sacred characteristic of being located on the faces that receive the sunset's

---

[10] A 60-kilometre long, winding and almost impassable gorge prevents access to the source of the Wadi Mathendous. It was here that the descendants took the name of Garamantes, dear to Herodotus. The place itself, "Garamara" in the local dialect, has kept its meaning, repeated by my guide: "double sacred place of the Sun"!

crimson rays. This was so clearly intentional that this practice was to be found at all the Pharaonic funerary sites during the four millennia that they were spread out along the western shore of the Nile, where the sun fell asleep on the rocky walls that surrounded them, but where the precession of the equinoxes changed all this.

The reason for this is easy to understand when we admit that the Ancestors, those who rest "Blessed" in the Amenta, on the other side, on the celestial western bank, and who wake up when the daylight disappears in the eyes of those who live in the "Second Heart" of God, see, during the few minutes when the flaming globe illuminates the two hemispheres, the engravings come to life! For they then come to life expressly so that the harmonic link between the two worlds is constant. In this way, life is depicted, work in the fields, fishing, hunting, as well as battles and victories, so that those beyond Life are immediately aware!

Any foreigner in the 20th century who, like me, is lucky enough to have been there and witnessed this extraordinary sunset, in the midst of astonishing solitude, cannot but be overwhelmed. He contemplates the glowing circle, which seems to grow ever larger before sinking behind the rocky escarpments of this desert Fezzan, beyond this high plateau lost in the immensity of , and which before then shoots out its millions of bloody arrows like so many magical strokes striking the engraved silhouettes, suddenly bringing them to life. Our contemporary eyes blink in astonishment several times, as the mobility of the sun's descent causes the shadows to move with disconcerting speed across the sandstone, bringing to life, fighting, and emerging truly victorious, this army thus resurfacing, alive beyond the mists of time!

But these unforgettable moments were all too brief, as night fell swiftly in the Tropic of Cancer. But the impression was no less extraordinary.

What is very difficult to understand in this chronological maze, however, is the fratricidal struggle that pitted the two members of the same family, descended from Geb and Nut, against each other over the millennia preceding their arrival in Egypt, and which continued for just as long before the final destruction of both sides under Cambyses in 525 BC.

The myth of Sit and Hor had become so completely integrated into everyday life that it had already turned into an epic legend which, as soon as it was settled in Ath-Kâ-Ptah, was transformed into a religious symbolism that is inevitably reminiscent of our Christian monotheism, which is on the way to becoming polytheistic. Strangely enough, by not seeking it out, the religion of Ptah, which was re-established at the birth of the first king of the First Dynasty, came closer to the original ancestral truth. But it obsessed the minds of the two rival groups, to such an extent that the universe of each was of an opposite conception to that of the other. And the 800-kilometre distance separating Denderah for those of Ptah and Heliopolis for those of Ra on the banks of the Nile was not enough: for four millennia, the fratricidal struggle continued unabated!

The latent opposition between the North and the South had never ceased to pit the new "Rebels of Sit" against the reigning family of the "Followers of Hor". This hatred was always alive; it haunted and bloodied all the families in the struggle for divine power.

The echoes of these events echoed 2,000 years later, engraved on the walls of the temples of Karnak, Oumbos, Abu-Simbel and Denderah, passions having been unleashed by Ramses I, usurper of the reigning Per-Ahâ, who instituted the 18th dynasty according to Manetho's chronology. His name was Sethi, or descendant of Seth. Ramses II was his son, the first of a long line that included thirteen kings bearing the same surname.

But isn't it astonishing that, in every area, there was such a clear antagonism between the two parties? This was the case from the outset. When Menes united the two lands of Upper and Lower Egypt and settled at the base of the Nile delta, he first built the Ath-Kâ-Ptah, the "Second Heart of God", around which the capital, later called Memphis by the Greeks, was built. But when, in the following dynasty, a 'Sit' took over the sceptre and wanted to keep the same name, the priests of the Sun poisoned him, but he survived and won his case. A few decades later, when a "Hor" returned to power, he renounced this name, even though it belonged to his clan, and introduced Ta-Nou-It, the "Place of the Sycamore Tree of Nut", which became another name for Egypt: "Land of the Sycamores", from the 3rd Dynasty onwards. From this name, the Greeks derived another famous phonetic name: Danaos, which in another way represents the "naos" where the sacred Sycamore tree was planted, which was to enable the coming of Osiris.

As time went on, it was no longer Ptah against Ra, but Amun who was in open conflict with Aten, culminating in the poisoning of

Amenophis IV who, under the name of Akh-en-Aton, wanted to destroy Amun by building another capital and banning the worship of the idolatrous Aries God. This is why the history of the Pharaohs was one of constant to-ing and fro-ing, in which a spirit of revenge was constantly expressed beyond the grandiose, from the 18th Dynasty onwards, ending only with the invasion of conquerors of all kinds and the destruction not only of the civilisation that existed at that time, but also that of times gone by! There was nothing solid left that the sand didn't invade in its turn and make disappear from sight!

But long before this final test, the long march, which had lasted fifteen centuries punctuated by fratricidal struggles, had allowed this slow development of customs. It was almost on the outskirts of Ath-Kâ-Ptah that the last great battle took place, with both sides exhausted.

The "Manistiou" and the "Ra-Sit-Ou" found themselves practically face to face along the present-day border between Egypt and Libya, in front of the foothills that gave access to the last oasis in the far south-east of Libya, which for each clan was like a blessing from heaven, the exclusive ownership of which naturally had to be secured, and which each tried to appropriate.

It was the "Forgerons d'Hor", better equipped with weapons, who won the supremacy in a hard-fought battle. They drove the exhausted Ra-Sit-Ou northwards, a high desert range literally closing off the road to the east, with the now-occupied oasis closing off the strategic opening to the east from the south.

While the Rebels fled back towards the sea, where they regrouped and made their way to the Nile delta in short stages, the descendant who was the last to camp abroad was a woman! As the Per-Ahâ had only daughters, the eldest, Mout-Pet-Ahâ or the "Daughter of the Ancient Scorpion", was called to reign. She ordered a well-deserved break in this soothing place, in a vast palm grove where water flowed in abundance.

When the long-awaited moment finally arrived, the huge crowd swarmed behind the lead carriage, which remained the centre of attraction from every point of view, since it was from its covered and strictly hidden interior that the road signs came. It contained the latest *gô-men*, certainly more sophisticated than the old one and which had been taking them all to their destination for centuries and centuries.

It would seem, however, that the pontiff, a shrewd politician who foresaw the future, dispatched several couriers ahead to explore the best routes, and that he waited for them to return before relying on the solar shadow of his aircraft to embark on this final itinerary.

Nevertheless, as the destination was on the same parallel, the long caravan took the narrow narrows slightly to the south of the oasis, recognised in advance as opening the door to the desert valley, which fortunately only took four lunar months to cross.

One evening, at nightfall, the leading group found itself cornered by an impassable cliff edge, but pleasantly dotted with palm trees and various trees as well as a spring. It was only at the last moment, when the men reached the void, that they let out a howl of joy. In the distance, illuminated by the setting sun, a very wide serpentine stretched from the northern horizon, crossing the entire panorama perpendicularly as far as the south: God's gift, the Nile, had been reached!

In the space of a few centuries, civilisation spread along the thousand kilometres of the "Celestial River", but was clearly separated by sceptres. The main provinces almost all emerged together during this period. These were the "nomes", due to a very specific Hellenic phonetisation.

This weather caused a regularly retrograde sun to pass over the zenith of the twin "Fixes". Their distinctly different brightness seemed to set them against each other on clear nights, like a dark omen. And indeed, they fanned the flames of hatred and discord that formed the core of the drama of these two enemy descendants: the Hawks and the Falcons, for several centuries to come.

For the "Northern Kingdom", that of Lower Egypt, the Nile delta was enslaved by the "Sit Rebels". The first town to be named in the first unified dynasty was Pa-Ouet, located on the Mediterranean coast but well away from the marshy area. It thus became the residence of the first "Reed" kings, later taking the Greek name of Bouto.

The second was Pa-Asit, whose name was changed to Pa-Ousir after unification, and where the Temple of the Sun became that of Ptah. Its current name is Abousir and, in addition to its temple from the first dynasties, it has three pyramids as famous as those at Giza.

Finally, the third important predynastic city was Pa-An-Râ, the sacred locality of the first official priests of the Sun, whose College was modelled on that of the pontiff of the South, quite simply. However, this capital took on added interest when the 32nd "King of the North" decided to settle there himself.

The town then became Kemti, which the Greeks took to Sais. Bouto's disaffection stemmed from the stench of the marshes, the source of various infectious diseases and even the plague. But it is also certain that the predominance of the priests throughout this more fertile region encouraged the king to come and live there himself. The last of submitted to the "Manistiou" of Per-Ahâ Shesou-Hor.

This peace treaty, the most important of all time, preceded by 217 years the entry of the Sun into Taurus, 'the era of the Resurrection of Usir'. This period was devoted by the King of the Two Lands, North and South, of Amenta in the West and Ath-Kâ-Ptah in the East, in other words the Master of the Four Times of the Earth and the Universe, to making colossal achievements in honour of the One Almighty God who had made this possible, which, in thanking the Eternal for his benefits, would unite heaven and earth, in other words humanity and the Divinity, in an Alliance that should be indestructible.

The history of this chosen people therefore really begins at this unified time, around two centuries before Menes ushered in the dynastic era in 4241 BC.

But these most diverse mixtures would not form a single nation behind the One God until the day when the bearer of a single sceptre imposed his hereditary power, derived from Usir. This theocratic monarchy therefore waited in expectation for the imperative affirmation of a "Descendant", a Per-Ahâ from the South to unify the "Second Heart", a kingdom privileged if ever there was one, by the promise kept from the moment of arrival on the banks of the Nile.

The pontiff and the priests, at the sight of the enormous loop in the course of this river made by the Most High, as if with a precise intention, recognised this as the thrice-sacred place where the Golden Circle was being rebuilt, which had been swallowed up long before by the Ahâ-Men-Ptah. Its survivors were hard at work, and all their children would set to work immediately to rebuild the Divine Mathematical Combinations in the gigantic golden structure.

7

THE RESURRECTION OF PTAH AT DENDERAH

No one claims that a statue or a painting cannot be created without a sculptor or a painter; and this creation would have no Creator? Take care, my son, not to deprive the work of its creator. Instead, give God the name that best suits him; call him the Father of all things!
Hermes Trismegistus (Book I, chap. V)

Of all the ruins, the most marvellous is Tentyris. It has 180 windows, and every morning the Sun enters through a different one until it reaches the last one, after which it returns in the opposite direction to make the same journey.
El-Makrisi (*Description of Egypt*, 1468)

Thousands of men, women and children in compact generations had spent hundreds and hundreds of years crossing the gigantic sandy expanse. They had just arrived, after the Libyan desert, on the plateau that dominated the immense loop of the river in the distance, within which grew such a verdant oasis. This miracle became the sign of the Alliance with Ptah: it would be Denderah!

For the high priests, there was no doubt as to the significance of this event: it was here that the Double House of Life, which would be the repository of all the sacred texts, should be established first and foremost. These had become too difficult to preserve orally in their entirety and integrity. This was due to the sudden deaths of those who had learnt one or two chapters as children, but who had not been able to withstand the enormous effort of endurance required to reach the Promised Land alive. So, long before they could enjoy the fertile land and peaceful environment, another prodigious effort was required of the people. In this place, unquestionably blessed by God, they would have to erect what would once again become the glory of the new country after having been the glory of the sunken continent: the great complex that would once again enable the calculation of Divine-

Mathematical-Combinations. The Golden Circle would be rebuilt on this ideal site, scrupulously, methodically, according to plans recalculated on the basis of planetary positions beginning at the next Sun-Sirius conjunction. In this way, it would replace the one that existed millennia ago near the observatory in the capital of Ahâ-Men-Ptah.

The first day of work was devoted to the ceremony of consecration of the holy place, which took the name of Ta Nout-Râ-Ptah in order to place it under the protection of God and of the woman who had given birth to his "Elder". Thus this divine dwelling would be the Double Dwelling of Heaven, where the Divine-Mathematical Combinations would delimit the nocturnal calculations from those relating to the day.

The site soon became a hive of activity unimaginable in our time. Papyrus, which grew in abundance in the river, was used to weave thick ropes. These were used to precisely define the perimeter of the outer wall. Thousands of arms then set to work levelling the area, while another active multitude was already extracting blocks of sandstone, granite and a wide variety of stones. A third group, and not the least, transported the loads, pulling them on sledges powered by logs. The huge excavation to build the underground foundations of the Golden Circle could now begin!

Several dozen architects shared the construction of the shell, supervised by the pontiff himself, whose primary concern was to include countless unforeseen links in the chain of the shell that would serve as impenetrable locks for those who tried to disobey the planned path for the teaching of future initiates. Everything was already compartmentalised and structured on the plans; all that was to assemble each of the apparently disordered parts to the next, so that the Golden Circle could be reborn.

The enormous granite blocks were probably already carved, a few days' sail upstream on the river. It would no longer be the same religious leader who would be at the head of the College of High Priests when these masses of stone reached Ta Nut-Ra-Ptah, but the pontiff knew that from now on the progress of the work would follow its course, whatever happened. As he closed his eyes, he could already see the sturdy sledges with their large runners, pulled by ever-changing teams, shuttling back and forth between the riverbank and this blessed place, thanks to a smooth road to be built, and which would be made slippery with oily river silt spread on the ground, which would stick to the sand as it dried.

The Golden Circle would be an immense two-storey round block with a radius of 7,200 cubits,[11] as in Ahâ-Men-Ptah, since the loop of the river made this possible. It would contain the entire structure of the celestial vault, with all its cogs and mechanisms, its variable geometry and its extremely precise combinatorial calculations.

In the observatory that was being built on the terrace of the great temple, a similar vault, but miniaturised, was used to warn future generations of the Great Cataclysm that had forced a whole host of survivors of divine wrath to flee to this 'Second Heart'. It was a planisphere in all its astronomical development. But when it arrived in Paris, the scientists who studied it described it as a worthless "Zodiac". The underlying reason was that in 1820 the Holy Church was all-powerful and, according to its dogmas, Adam had been born 5,000 years before Christ and the Earth had not existed a millennium before. How could a map of the heavens proving mathematically that a cataclysm had taken place in 9792 BC be accepted at that time?

It is therefore worth describing here this remarkable engraving, which provides a better understanding of the complex whole of the Golden Circle, of which the figurative symbolism of the Lion is the basis and centre of the interpretation that will provide the key.

The catastrophe occurred while the Sun was in front of the constellation Leo. The cataclysm was so violent that the earth pivoted on its axis and the solar globe, which was advancing in the sky, no longer did so, but retrograded, i.e. it appeared to be moving backwards, whereas, being fixed, it was simply the earth that had changed its rotation in space.

But the phenomenon that the survivors of this divine anger remembered was that the sun no longer rose in the west but in the east, and that it set over their country, which had been swallowed up since that day.

So there was a phenomenon of the end of a world followed by a new beginning: a new creation in a space-time in perpetual regeneration. The celestial circle will therefore not be a perfect circle,

---

[11] 7,200 x 0.524 = 3,772.80 m, i.e. a diameter of 7,545.60 m!

but a spiral. This is the first feature of the[12] planisphere from Denderah, on display in the Louvre.

The first engraving is of a lion on a 'mandjit' (lifeboat), and the twelfth is of Cancer, slightly above the royal feline's mane.

To help you understand the description of the twelve constellations included on this planisphere, here is the complete engraving.

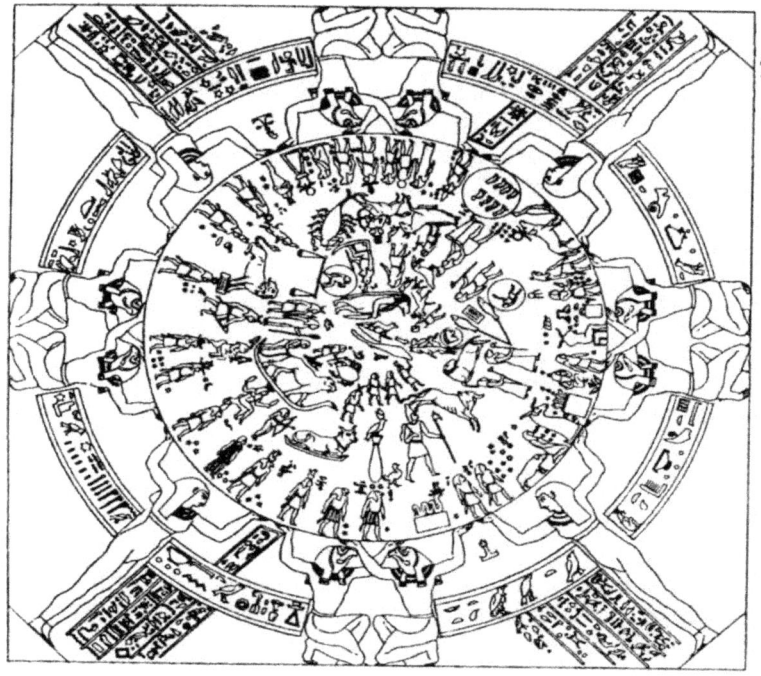

The first figure is therefore the Lion, standing firmly on a "mandjit" symbolised by the serpent of the ancient godless multitude and bearing on its curved tail, clinging to its hair, the image of a small woman representing the cadets from the survivors of the cataclysm. This is, of course, Iset, mother of Horus, the Eldest offspring of all the future survivors of the Second Heart.

---

[12] See drawing on page 161 in *Le Livre de l'Au-delà de la vie*, ed. René Beaudouin, 1979.

Next comes Nut, the Virgin Queen who gave birth to Uzir and thus justified her enthronement under the patronymic of the constellation Virgo. She holds an ear of wheat in her hands, symbolising the divine seed that she carries within her, and which is already following her like a shadow, in human form with the head of a bull. The crescent of the setting sun, that of the Sleeping Blessed, is on his head, and in his left hand he holds the jackal-faced staff, symbolising Set the assassin who is ultimately subservient to his Elder.

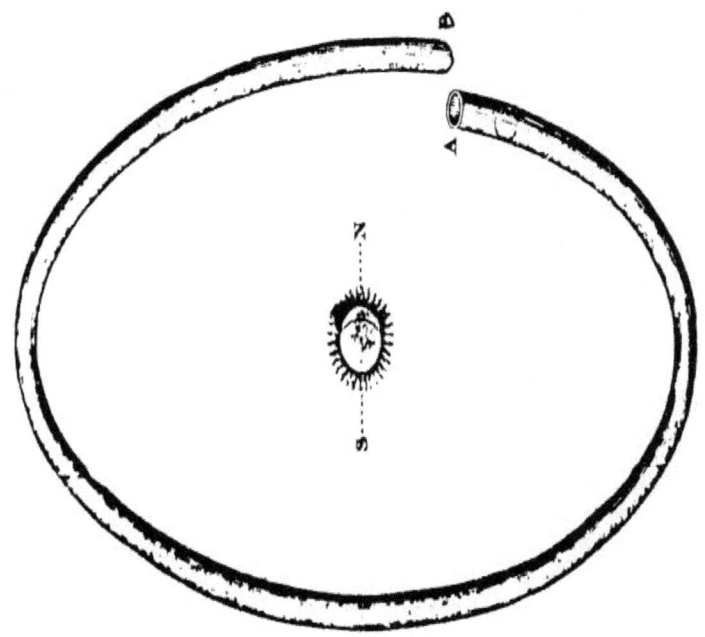

Ce dessin permet de mieux s'imaginer ce qu'est le Cercle d'Or emprisonnant notre système solaire. Vu l'échelle, il est impossible de reproduire ni la Terre ni aucune des planètes près du Soleil.

The third drawing represents the Scales of Divine Justice. This is the only scale that can weigh the actions of each person fairly. It was thanks to the scales that for more than two millennia after this first engraving, there was virtually no war, every conflict being settled during the month dedicated to the scales, in front of a stone dedicated to this purpose and bearing a golden balance, around which sat twenty-two judges.

Scorpio, which follows it in the sequence of the Twelve, owes its name to the last Nar-Mer king, who unified the two fratricidal clans. Its time is one of the shortest in the Great Year, so there's not much more to say about this constellation. The same cannot be said for the next constellation.

Sagittarius, a monster half animal, half man, ready to shoot an arrow from his bow, symbolises for all eternity the divine warning against the actions of the worshippers of the Sun, the descendants of Sec the assassin, without any faith, and their disobedience to the Law of the Almighty Lord of Eternity.

Capricorn follows, lying down, but about to stand up again, as can be seen from the carriage of his head and the tension in one of the supporting legs. On his back is Horus, shown with his hawk's head presenting the staff he is holding as a victor, the insignia of his victory over his uncle Set.

The man walking behind is holding a vase in both hands, with water flowing out in a sawtooth pattern. This is the water-verse, or the constellation Aquarius. The Masters of Measure and Number symbolise this presentation with the image of the Creator opening the floodgates of heaven, either to drown his Creation under a second cataclysm, or to flood away the sins of the world to bring about a golden age accessible to all survivors.

Which will it be? The descendants of Usir or those of Set? The two perfectly identical fish on the planisphere, linked together by a cord but separated from each other by a hieroglyphic ideogram representing three broken lines, in other words the emblem of the flood, give an important revelation: that it will be those who finally respect the Knowledge of the Law who will have their lives saved, whether they are descendants of Usir or simply followers of Set.

Aries, which is precisely the sign of the sun-worshipping usurpers, the symbol of the abhorred Amun, whose capital Thebes was for almost two millennia, is shown looking backwards, lying in the opposite direction to his historical progress, i.e. looking towards the east and not towards Ahâ-Men-Ptah and the Elders, and two figures immediately below his body will not be able to help him overcome the countless remaining difficulties.

The Bull, caracoling in his wake, clearly turns his head towards the east, thus presenting the concavity of his horns towards the setting sun where the Elders of Ahâ-Men-Ptah rest. This celestial bull is most animated, seeming to dart northwards and out of the spiral circle of the Twelve as if it were part of all the living worlds and beyond.

For Gemini, the Masters in charge of symbolism have presented a picture of four figures, the two main ones holding hands: Usir and his wife Iset. The twins, on the other hand, are relegated to the bottom of the engraving of Aries, as explained on the previous page. This substitution must be seen as an unshakeable desire to recall the shame of fratricide that lasted for nearly five millennia before reaching the land of the second homeland.

Finally, Cancer appears just above Leo, as mentioned at the beginning. It's also worth noting that the first representation of this constellation was a scarab, which later became a crab. It was only in Greco-Roman times that it took the name Cancer.

The space inscribed by the Twelve contains a large number of figures. The most important is the central figure, a very large animal that is part crocodile, part hippopotamus, an animal that Egyptologists have described as "typhonian" because it symbolises the most peaceful, but also the most dangerous of the gods: God himself. Ptah the One. He is depicted holding a large cutlass, the same one used by Set, but this is merely a vengeful representation of the engravers, who are human par excellence! For in his beneficent harmony, Ptah had in mind only total earthly equilibrium for his creatures. And that's what the central figure makes clear.

Two other circular series of hieroglyphic figures complete the description of the Twelve to give it a precise date, with Sep'ti, our Sirius, the equivalent of Orion in the Big Dipper, and their respective positions calculated with the help of one of the thirty-six decans broken down at the bottom of the third series.

The large outer circle is supported by four groups of hawk-headed men, symbolising the descendants of the four sons of Horus. Isis stands in the middle of each gap between the groups, supporting the medallion. The explanation in the sacred language can be read along her legs, in several vertical lines. It interesting to note that, to avoid having to carry a lot of extra weight when transporting the medallion to France, Mr Lelorrain simply cut out the planisphere, leaving the giant figure of Nut in place, giving the astronomical direction of the monument with her outstretched hands. Mr Lelorrain also sawed through the zigzags in the drawing below, which, as he explained on his return to Paris, were of no importance! The original therefore had the shape described in the previous engraving.

This makes it easier to understand the meaning of the 'zigzag' line. In fact, the broken line hieroglyphically signifies a movement of water. When there are three of them, it indicates a flood similar to that of the Nile, with very high waters. Five broken lines indicate a flood of water. It is clear that eight or nine of these 'zigzag' lines describe a great catastrophe involving water: the Great Cataclysm that buried the Elder Heart, Ahâ-Men-Ptah, as described in the Denderah sky chart.

If we accept that this representation, intended as a warning to future generations, is indeed the sixth reproduction of an original, it is indisputable that the astronomical science of the promoters was equal to the elaboration of the Golden Circle and its hermetic complex.

The entire loop of the Nile, running north-south, served as a preparatory base for the gigantic construction. Seventy-two years, or two generations of priests, architects and workers, united in a single cause, had completely changed the appearance of this sacred area.

The west-east axis linking the two holiest horizons, the one that linked the Past of the West to the Eternity of the East, stretched its thousand cubits[13] of divine path amidst the apparent superstructures. These were already taking shape, giving a foretaste of what would be the giant complex of this "House of the Universe", still very heterogeneous with the surprising diversity of the hundreds of low walls that appeared here and there, of varying heights. The whole thing appeared to have been built by chance, but every last mathematical and geometrical detail had been carefully studied by a whole section of Masters of Measurement and Number.

The lower half of this structure took shape and before being completed and covered with the ceiling slab, which would form the floor of the upper half, thanks to the contribution of huge cut stones, pulled by "exceptional convoys". Each convoy consisted of five groups of sixteen men toiling on hand-high ropes slung over their shoulders .[14] A foreman chanted the cadence, modulating two notes while tapping on a hollow wooden sounding board. Two other men ran ahead of the extraordinary convoy to pour out their jugs full of water. These were constantly replenished by other carriers of this precious liquid, making the shuttle to the river.

This practice had the dual advantage of ensuring better grip with the ground under the skids, and therefore easier gliding, while at the same time avoiding the risk of sparks from the skids, which were overheated by the weight of several hundred tonnes of cargo.

Thanks to these slabs, the chambers of the "Nocturnal Mathematical Combinations" would disappear into the night, supervised by the Moon. Each of the astral aspects would occupy a different room beneath the ground, linked to the next by a corridor that would change and move with the hours and the days. Numerous underground passages, already covered in black granite blocks, were

---

[13] $48,000 \times 0.524 = 25.152$ kilometres. This is nothing out of the ordinary, because even today, some sixty kilometres from Denderah, is the triumphal way of Aries-Amon, the solar god, which links Karnak to Luxor and measures roughly the same distance.

[14] These ropes, several of which have been found, are actually larger than the wrist. They are made of tightly woven papyrus fibres. They have been dated to over 7,000 years ago by the Egyptian Institute in Cairo, and confirmed by the Chicago Institute to within 240 years.

traps and traps for those who did not observe the strict mathematical laws. So whatever was said on the subject would certainly prevent the 'curious' from getting too close. To the very north of the complex, the perimeter of the Sacred Lake was already visible. It would form the perspective that would block the western horizon. It was almost as large as the Golden Circle currently under construction. It formed an immense basin, the lower level of which had been reached. Its definitive foundation was being consolidated at the points planned for the two foundations of the "Loved Ones-who-descend-the-Light e"[15] with their square bases. Here too, myriads of workers, like conscientious ants, were busy with the sole aim of carrying out the tasks for which they had been trained. This inland sea would complete the true panorama of this holy place, giving it back an ancient aspect of earlier civilisation, while at the same time making it possible to harness the waters of the great river and irrigate the land in times of drought. All this work had been made possible by the revival of sacred writing.

Recreated according to the original tradition, she reappeared in her imaginary form, closer to her Creator. It would not be long before it was officially reintroduced when the Sun entered Taurus, shortly after the Sun-Sirius conjunction. The Son having become the celestial Taurus, it was only natural that the use of hieroglyphics should begin at this precise moment, with the engraving of vital texts. The builders and workers responsible for this holy work would thus be the first to be imbued with the Knowledge of this Law sanctioned by the decrees of God, which can easily be translated beyond all ideograms into a contemporary narrative:

The Elders and their godless people were all drowned, swallowed up beneath the surface of the waters, by this almighty Creator who was moved by a righteous and fierce anger against the hearts of his earthly creatures, which now beat only to do evil. Ptah attacked the carnal envelopes, but not the Divine Parcels. The Souls went to the Kingdom of the Blessed, for they had not been conceived for such misfortune. But hearts are only organs of flesh, like the ears, eyes or feet that carry us. They should be made to beat in unison with each other, not to tear each other apart. For a man's heart is like that of a ram, a gazelle or a

---

[15] This is the actual translation of the hieroglyphic that has been given the name "pyramid", a word that is all the more abstract for the fact that it means nothing in Greek, Hebrew or any other language.

bull. They all have just one identical function, and in the same irreversible sense: to give rhythm to the march of Creation, following the flow of time for the duration of life on Earth. If they beat faster one day or another, it's under the effect of sudden joy, or under the impulse of terror. So how do humans differ from animals? In the vitalisation of hearts by spirits. And, here too, there will have to be a rebirth of Souls, to remind them of their duties.

Human beings possess thought, and therefore a soul, which alone is capable of celestial survival. This is the only difference, albeit an enormous one, between us bipedal humans and our four-legged brothers. When a carnal envelope comes to an end and the heart stops beating the rhythm of life, only that which possesses a Divine Particle, a soul, can allow it to make its way towards the Kingdom of the Redeemed; and even then, following very precise rites, and more rigorous conditions of passage! Living according to the commandments of the Law of the Creator means that it is possible to cross the boundary of the Beyond of earthly life without damage. It's not for nothing that the Elders bequeathed Knowledge! And through this immeasurable Knowledge, they are in contact with present-day Souls. There is a real, tangible link that has been created across the two lands: the Englished and this one, which will soon be Ath-Kâ-Ptah: the Second Heart! It's for this reason that we must follow the teachings of our ancestors, the Elders, for the wise words they have passed on are the fruits of the most beautiful experience lived before this appalling catastrophe, by the Divine Parcels themselves! That's why all the precepts of this teaching must be applied with the utmost rigour, without changing any of the holy words.

The Golden Circle will be the eternal guarantor of this because it is imperishable. It will thus become a magnet for future generations in their quest for Knowledge. Even those who retain only a snippet of truth will hesitate to put into practice everything else that is a lie. Only evil minds will be able to confuse even weaker souls.

The study hall itself, where all the primordial texts were taught during the period of titanic work that lasted almost two centuries, until the day the Sun entered the constellation of Taurus, was enlarged over the decades to accommodate all the religious destined to become Masters of Measurement and Number.

A single door made of thick sycamore wood closed off this room, making it completely soundproof. It was framed by a rectangular lintel on which were carved the three primordial scenes of the rebirth of the survivors of the "First Heart of God", with the mandjit, the sacred boats, in the foreground.

The Divine Triad was thus honoured for all the self-sacrifice it had shown to enable the rebirth of the multitude. This would be consecrated by the inauguration of the Golden Circle.

The last phase of the work had reached its final stage. The "Circle", entirely covered in gold, already surrounded the bodies of the main buildings, imprisoning them as it did the celestial belt of the twelve constellations, thus concentrating even more the radiant influences of the twelve "Hearts", those "fixed" stars which reigned by creating thousands and thousands of Divine-Mathematical-Combinations, thus uniting heaven and earth. And over and over again, the texts repeat the same warnings in a thousand different forms: "Only this Covenant with the Eternal One, sealed by unification, will ensure a universally good and peaceful life. For the happiness and perfection of the creatures of this world are necessary to the Creator to ensure, at the end of the carnal envelope in its place of earthly life, the passage of its divine part beyond the invisible but real frontier, towards the Kingdom of the Blessed redeemed of the Amenta. The man of millions of future generations will continue to doubt his own origin, if he does not already take all the indispensable precautions to remain firmly within the intangible reality of the dogmas and commandments required to preserve the harmony willed by the Law of Creation created by the Eternal One. The unique bond that keeps humanity so fragilely alive on this Earth will only survive on this single but vital celestial condition:

For God nourishes Heaven with his radiance
For Heaven in turn feeds the Twelve;
For the Twelve feed the Divine Parcels;
For the Souls of the West were those granted to Humanity .[16]

In those distant days, the primitive temple was linked directly to the Golden Circle by corridors. It was far more sumptuous than the sixth reconstruction that visitors can contemplate today. Nothing now

---

[16] Inscription located at the entrance to the current north-east crypt, which, due to the equinoctial phenomenon, was in the first construction in the west crypt: that of the "Couchés". At the rate of one degree retrograde every 72 years, this explains the enormous pivot produced over several millennia.

links it to the original monument more than the myth now known as "The Great Labyrinth", which will be discussed in greater detail in the next chapter. But the beauty of the primitive temple can easily be imagined from the one visible today. The edifice consecrated to the Good Mother of God appeared then in all its sacred fullness. Just by looking at it, any human being would realise that they had reached the original Holy of Holies, the primordiality of Ptah, the Lord Almighty. The six pillars of the main entrance, circular but three times the diameter of a human being, were surmounted by a figure of the Virgin Queen, who had become the protector of this high place for observing the sky and the combinations that abounded there.

The imposing mass barely let in the sunlight through several carefully calculated openings, so that its rays highlighted the dazzling whiteness of the priests' tunics as they marched towards the Holy of Holies. These reflections illuminated the walls of the dark corridors leading to the entrance of the Sunset Staircase. This made it easy to reach the high terrace that served as an observatory, and near which was engraved the terrible warning: that of the day of the Annihilation of Ahâ-Men-Ptah.

Their constant foresight into future events was proof of these Masters' formidable ability to calculate the different geometric aspects of the Law. For these were by no means 'visions' of internal clairvoyance, nor 'prophecies' with symbolic phrases whose hermeticism would allow any interpretation, but simple calculations using the celestial configurations in their relationship to one another, which hieroglyphics so aptly call Divine-Mathematical-Combinations.

The Soul of each being had to be accustomed to governing itself, alone with the Knowledge of the future, in order to manage itself within the limits of Good. All the ethics advocated by the Elders were contained within this precise limit, which was willed by Ptah. In this way, the Divine Parcel, strengthened against the evil side of foreseeable events, was able ensure that all events would evolve in the right direction. For the decrees of destiny are not immutable when they tend towards the necessity of Good and not Evil; for the Law that created the Covenant between the Creator and his creatures makes this possible. Hence the axiom: "Destiny directs but does not oblige", taken up in various forms by the Chaldean and Babylonian "magi", who saw in astronomy, according to the Egyptians, a lucrative business for them; and so astrology was born! But astrology no longer had anything to do with the real Divine-Mathematical Combinations.

In the Golden Circle, no obstacle, not even the greatest, could be opposed as an imposition of absolute necessity to the free choice of the divine Parcels to return, in all humility, to the perhaps narrow but necessary path that they had left for a time to stray onto a road that was too adventurous. And while it remains constant that man's inferior actions change the pre-established order through disorder of some kind, even though they take the primary causes of their changes from heaven itself, the freedom acquired in earthly life makes it possible to re-establish total harmony, before the imbalance has upset any attempt to re-establish order.

Moreover, the very fact of this earthly freedom means that many unforeseen phenomena occur because of man's general bodily constitution, with all its complications and interweavings, and not because of his natural acts alone. But here too, fatal necessity cannot be called into question. The temperament of every being must evolve in the right direction, since it is obviously recognised from birth by characteristic data. The same applies to everything that is the object of the Almighty's celestial attentions, whose natural causes and principles receive the influences of the Twelve: minerals, plants, animals and all living things in general. From all their illnesses, all their discomforts, to which they are subjected by a certain necessity, the remedies of our doctors must cure them. Everything is in the One that is Ptah.

The part of the whole that concerns the carnal envelopes is obviously the Belt of the Twelve, i.e. the central celestial zone that imprisons our Sun, the Seven Wanderers and our Earth with twelve stellar groups practically linked to each other in a wide belt, hence the name imagined by our ancestors, and fully justified. It is these Twelve that God uses to send to Earth the infinite number of Parcels that populate, second after second, all the new carnal envelopes. In order to facilitate the study of the Divine-Mathematical Combinations, to make them comprehensible and to be able to retain easily all the terms of this celestial mechanism in perpetual motion, the first Masters of Measurement and Number, those who had in their minds alone all the data of the Universe, writing having not yet been re-established in their time, had to find names and images that were easily identifiable.

And so, on the first day of their arrival on this earth, when they named it Ta Merit, they saw the sign of God's promise to them in the fact that the Great River, at night, was illuminated by the milky whiteness of the heavenly River that dominated it, and which appeared just as long and just as wide. Hence the name Hapy, a contraction of

Ahâ and Ptah, made concrete by the phonetisation of the last letter. Hapy was therefore the patronymic used to thank the Elder Son, Usir, for his double benefit: the celestial sign and the earthly water. Since the first Masters had quite rightly decided to locate the site of the Golden Circle here, as well as the Temple of the Lady of Heaven, it was obvious that the generic name of this celestial river, which had drawn all the Twelve to its banks, had to be that of Uzir's protector, the one who had given birth to him: the Virgin Queen Nut, blessed be she. And the son having become the Celestial Bull, his mother became the Celestial Cow, Master of the Twelve.

Ceci est la représentation à peine symbolique de la Vache céleste nourrissant de ses influx le Cœur des Douze.

The exemplary account of the lives of Geb and Nut, as well as the births of Osiris, Set, Isis and Nek-Beth, are all marvels that can be explained very well if we accept the omnipotence of God. The relationship the Lord and his people in Ahâ-Men-Ptah was a rare privilege. It was justified by the Creator's love for his creatures, linked to him by the Divine Parcels. Evil, having triumphed in the necessity that it instituted in spite of itself, then allowed the regeneration of humanity through the redemption of the human race with Osiris, All our ancient Masters, the preservers of the Word, those who transmitted it to us, did not know our hesitations, our prevarications, our disputes, because they had lived what they were recounting. They were stating facts without trying to convince anyone of their reality!

Autre représentation de la Vache céleste naviguant selon la nouvelle orbe commencée par le soleil en constellation du Lion et qui achèvera l'histoire de l'Égypte avec la fin de l'ère du Bélier.

To seek and find myths in the Sacred Books is as unfounded an undertaking as trying to prove that Ra is the only food for our intelligence! And if the Elders lost the Eden that was theirs in Ahâ-Men-Ptah, this must be seen as nothing more than a momentary triumph of Evil, in order to fight it more effectively afterwards. Unfortunately, it is trying to reappear in its many hypocritical forms, and must be fought in every way possible. It is indisputable that the existence of moral Evil is one of the scourges of the Earth! All the ancient Masters tried to explain this painful phenomenon and reconcile it with the Good. If everything is God, everything should be good, that's a fact, but one of man's creatures has been solicited by Evil: Set! Jealousy and envy prevailed over the need for divine law. Man was created to live happily, innocently and freely in Ahâ-Men-Ptah. Set seriously abused this freedom by making an attempt on the lives of Osiris and his son Horus. As punishment for this sin, he lost everything, but was given a second and final chance to redeem himself.

The help given by Nut, who became the Lady of Heaven, in order to complete and consolidate the redemption, no more injures the resurrection of her son Usir than the death her other son, Set, injures her divinity. On the contrary, by glorifying his wisdom, she stirred up Ptah's mercy. The two brothers of the same mother acted only as instruments of the Creator's eternal power on Earth. If this sign was denied in spite of its obviousness before the Great Cataclysm, it is so clear today that one would have to be blind not to admit it.

This is why the Word can be twofold, whereas the Law is unique in its sacred transcription. That's why only a special elite can have access to it, after going through many equally delicate initiations! And unfortunately, this number will hardly increase over the years, because Knowledge is like a very strong drink taken too quickly: it intoxicates and clouds the mind. The adept then believes himself to be the equal of a false god, and becomes capable of the worst extravagances. Intelligence is such that few creatures can resist the vertigo produced by immense Knowledge. This is why our great Sages from the ancient times of the Divine Triad, and then their Successor Servants, deliberately adopted this form to transmit the Law: through symbols, numbers and parables, so that ordinary mortals could not have access to it.

The purpose of this construction of a Golden Circle on an inhuman scale thus becomes clearer: to make tangible the Law that fundamentally regulates all astral revolutions in a gigantic combinatorial movement that can be calculated and predicted, and whose centre, the geometric point O, is none other than the Creator.

When this cleared Golden Circle appears in all its splendour, each cog in this immense mechanism will come together with its successor and everything will once again become perfectly clear, for the greater good of humanity. Perhaps this is just wishful thinking, because Evil makes the blind, and the Dark will always continue to darken souls. In any case, the 'Great Labyrinth' will once again become the 'Golden Circle', towards which I am slowly but surely making progress. Let's set off to discover it...

8

DISCOVERING THE GREAT LABYRINTH...

The labyrinth is made up of twelve courtyards surrounded by walls, and a walled enclosure encloses them. Their flats are twofold; there are fifteen hundred underground and fifteen hundred above. I have visited the rooms above and can speak with certainty as a witness.

Herodotus (History of Egypt)

Herodotus, in Book II, describes 12 halls and 3,000 chambers, half underground and half above ground. And if it is a forgivable blunder for ancient authors, such as Pliny and Mela, who never set foot in Egypt, what are we to think of Herodotus and Strabo, who supposed that there being 4 labyrinths, only one was in this Kingdom? In this case, the largest labyrinth is independent of the other two. And if it is natural to oppose the authority of one historian to the torrent of others, my reasoning is without reply because I myself saw the three labyrinths, of which I visited the largest: it was on 20 July.

Father CL. Sicard, s.j.
(Unpublished manuscript on the History of Egypt, 1718)

It's hard to imagine the gigantic scale of the construction of the Golden Circle until it's unearthed, but it's highly likely that the monument, known as the Great Pyramid, is about the same size as a doll's house compared to a hundred-storey skyscraper!

Only excavation work will be able to give an accurate account of its grandeur and splendour. And this can only be done under certain conditions, which are still far from being met today, since Egyptologists are not interested in astronomical questions. They only use the funds at their disposal to ensure the consolidation of the current temple, which, it is true, is in great need of them . However, according to the latest news s,[17] excavations have been carried out a few metres outside the outer wall, near which a few slabs have been lifted to demonstrate the existence of the temple dating back to Pharaoh Cheops. But enough controversy, because there are many fascinating documents on the Golden Circle, as well as on the religious buildings that predate the one that stands today in this loop of the Nile.

Any researcher going to the site could have arrived at the same results after reading Herodotus, then compiling all the works on the subject of the Egyptian labyrinth. Of course, there is also the original manuscript written by the Jesuit Father Claude Sicard in 1718, which is in Chantilly and which I have looked through, but the good Fathers have told me that it has been requested several times, the latest being the late Serge Sauneron, Director of the French Institute of Oriental Archaeology in Cairo, shortly before the car accident that cost him his life.

For the reader to come to an understanding of the reality of the Golden Circle, he or she must undertake the same journey, to follow it step by step, as if he or she were taking part in it, to arrive at the discovery of what has become the Great Labyrinth. I'll start with Herodotus' famous passage about the Great Labyrinth, followed by the comments and thoughts that this text inspired in me:

"They decided to leave a common monument in memory of their reign and built a labyrinth a little beyond Lake Mœris, near the town of the Crocodiles. I've seen this labyrinth: it really defies description. Even if you added up all the walls and structures that the Greeks were able to build, you wouldn't come up with a quarter of the expense and work that went into this labyrinth. The temple at Ephesus and the time at Samos are already worthy of praise. The pyramids compare favourably with the most beautiful Greek monuments. But the labyrinth surpasses them all. It comprises twelve covered and contiguous courtyards, with doors facing each other, six by six, all surrounded by a single wall. The interior contains three thousand rooms, half of them on the first floor. Incidentally, I speak from experience. I was unable to see the underground chambers, which are off-limits to visitors because of

---

[17] I was writing this manuscript in May 1981, and excavations in the garden were due to begin the following month, in order to gain access to the earlier temple via a more practicable route than the one uncovered in the current hypostyle hall.

the tombs of the kings and the sacred crocodiles that are found there, so I can only speak of them by hearsay. But the upper rooms, which I saw with my own eyes, really discourage praise. All those doors, all those exits, the countless number of corridors, all those comings and goings filled me with wonder. I went from a courtyard to a hall, from a hall to a portico, I left a portico to fall into a new hall, then into a new courtyard... The entire building has a stone roof. The walls are covered in bas-reliefs, and each courtyard is lined with impeccably crafted white stone colonnades. A pyramid of forty orgyes stands at the end of the labyrinth. Access to it is via an underground passage.

A number of nonsensical passages in Herodotus' account show that this great traveller did not actually visit the labyrinth, and that he speaks only of hearsay. Two in particular: the city of the crocodiles is the ruins of which today bear the name Kom Oumbos, south of Dendera, and where crocodile mummies can still be "admired". The second "rumour" concerns Lake Mœris, named after this Pharaoh. But no one has yet pinpointed the exact location of this lake, let alone the chronological place of this ruler whose name is nowhere to be found!

Now, several important works present the various philological aspects of the name of the first king of the First Dynasty: Mena-Ahâ, which became Mena, or Menes in Greek, in the table of Manetho. Other names include Menkhes, Mendes, Ismendes and Osymandias, each of whom built a formidable structure near Thebes, which is also south of Dendera.

Further details are given by Pomponius Mêla, by Diodorus of Sicily (Book I, chap. LXI), by Strabo in his Book XVII, and by Pliny in his Book XXXVI: "Mendes or Imandes had the great labyrinth built to be buried there. This king was also called Memnon. As such, he had the Memnonia palaces built at Thebes and Abydos before the great labyrinth where he was buried was completed."

Thus begins to emerge the real schema of the only king who was the promoter of this "labyrinth" and of its location. The two palaces of Memnon were built to the north and south of Dendera. If we accept that we are still talking about the same Men-Ahâ, i.e. the Elder of the Sunset, it is easy to make the appropriate comparison, since the writing error stems from Greek phonetics. Mena was the unifier of the Two Lands as a descendant of Usir, or Osiris. As Hellenic phonetics had totally distorted Pharaonic pronunciation (as Khéops for Khoufou, since Khéops should have been pronounced Kéophs, the "p" being pronounced "f"), Menes became Mendes, descendant of Ousir, i.e. Ousir-Mendes, hence Osymandias. This is perfectly logical, as are those of Memnon and Marrhus, which we will see later with Diodorus of Sicily.

The priests of Ptah and the architects of Ména-Ahâ were behind the re-establishment of the Divine-Mathematical Combinations, as well as the design of an immense artificial lake adjoining the Golden Circle, with a pyramid at its centre containing the relics and vestments of Usir. This was the imagined way for the Elder to find his ancestors, who had themselves been swallowed up in Ahâ-Men-Ptah, while the same time watching over and bringing the beneficial rays of the Twelve to this thrice-blessed place through his presence.

On my first visit to Denderah, in the company of my surgeon friend, our guide, with a knowing smile, told us that this place was still called in Arabic: *Ahanas-el Berba*, which means "Mother of Ruins". I've always been struck by the highly imaginative way in which hieroglyphics designate the things and functions of the universe, such as the Divine-Mathematical Combinations, the Twelve, the Belt, etc. And this term 'Mother of Ruins' is one of the most eloquent. And the term 'Mother of Ruins' had been anchored in my memory by the image depicted. And the more I researched the Golden Circle and its complex of religious buildings, the more I realised the most ancient reality: it really was the first-born of all constructions, and therefore the mother of all ruins. And I much prefer the Arabic etymology to the Greek, at least as far as the very essence of the oral tradition is concerned, in the absence of an approximate phonetisation.

Diodorus of Sicily, on the subject of this lost "labyrinth", provides me with further proof when I set out to study it. This passage, admittedly secondary to the one that will be the subject of the next chapter, is found in Book 1, LXI :

> "On the death of Actisanes, the Egyptians regained sovereignty and elected a native, Mendes, whom some call Marrhus, as king. This king did not perform any feats of war, but he did build himself a tomb, called a labyrinth, less astonishing for its size than for the inimitable art of its construction, for those who have entered it cannot find their way out unless they are led by an experienced guide. Some claim that Daedalus, having admired this monument on his

journey to Egypt, built the labyrinth of Minos, King of Crete, on the same model, where the Minotaur is said to have dwelt. But the labyrinth of Crete has disappeared entirely, either through the ravages of time or because a king had it demolished, whereas the labyrinth of Egypt has survived intact to the present day. After the death of Mendes, there was an interregnum of five generations. Then came Ketes, followed by his son Rhemphis. Then came seven generations of idle kings, and finally the eighth, Chembes of Memphis, who reigned for fifty years and built the largest of the three pyramids, which is counted among the seven wonders of the world.

Here, without any possible dispute, we see that this Mendes is indeed the Mêna or Men-Ahâ, unifier of Ath-Kâ-Ptah, since, whatever the names given by Diodorus of Sicily to the pharaohs, the builder of "the greatest of the three pyramids, numbered among the seven wonders of the world" intervenes chronologically in his exact historical place after Ménès. This king therefore has absolutely nothing to do with the one whom later Greek historians called Memnon to personify Amenophis II, the eighth pharaoh of the 18th dynasty, the author of the two famous "Colossi" protecting a fabulous temple built behind them, at the entrance to the Valley of the Kings of Thebes, which has now been completely destroyed and disappeared.

Strabo, the great ancient geographer who, like Herodotus, claims to have visited the labyrinth, speaks of it in a different way in Book XVII, paragraph 37

> "In addition to these works, there is the labyrinth, a monument which, because of its proportions and strange layout, almost equals the pyramids, and right next to the labyrinth is the tomb of the king who built it. After passing the first entrance to the canal on the river by about 30 or 40 stadia, you will see a flat area of land in the shape of a table, on which a village and a vast palace, or rather a collection of palaces, have been built: As many nomes as there were in ancient Egypt, so many palaces, these aulae, to put it better, surrounded by columns, and placed one after the other all in a single line and along the same side of the enclosure, so that they could be taken as the pillars or buttresses of a long wall. Their respective entrances face this wall, but are preceded or concealed by mysterious constructions called crypts, a maze

of long, innumerable galleries linked together tortuous corridors, a maze so inextricable that it would be impossible for a stranger to pass from one aula to another and back again without a guide. The most curious thing is that, just like the chambers, the *aulae*, each of which has a monolithic ceiling, the crypts are covered, but in the direction of their width, with slabs or stones in a single piece of extraordinary dimensions, without any mixture of beams or other materials of any kind, so that when you climb to the roof, which is not very high, given that the building has only one storey, you discover a veritable plain paved with these enormous stones. And now, as you turn round to look at the *aulae*, you a whole string of palaces flanked twenty-seven monolithic columns, even though the stones used to build the walls are already enormous. At the far end of this edifice, which covers more than a stadium of land, is the tomb in question: it is in the shape of a quadrangular pyramid, up to 4 metres square and as high. Imandes is the name of the king buried there. The number of *aulae* in the labyrinth is explained by saying that it was customary in ancient times for delegations from each nome, preceded by their priests and priestesses, to gather in this place to sacrifice together and solemnly judge the most important cases. Each deputation was led to the *aula* that had been specially assigned to the nome it represented.

This paragraph, copied *in extenso*, shows quite clearly that this description only follows on from accounts heard here and there, and there is no need to dwell on it. What is interesting to note, however, is that this passage has given rise to many other interpretations accompanied by highly original drawings, such as the one opposite, dating from the 18th century, which distorted the research of the first Egyptologists who looked for the square building... in Thebes!

Apart from this pleasant improvisation, which confused many researchers in their assessments, the description of the view above the ground in the most ancient period is worth : "As the building has only one floor, you can see a veritable plain paved with these enormous stones".

If there was only a small labyrinth, it could not be a real plain. Secondly and most importantly, the periodic strong winds that blew in the desert sand made an 80 to 100 metre thick shroud over what became the lost labyrinth.

A   nord   B

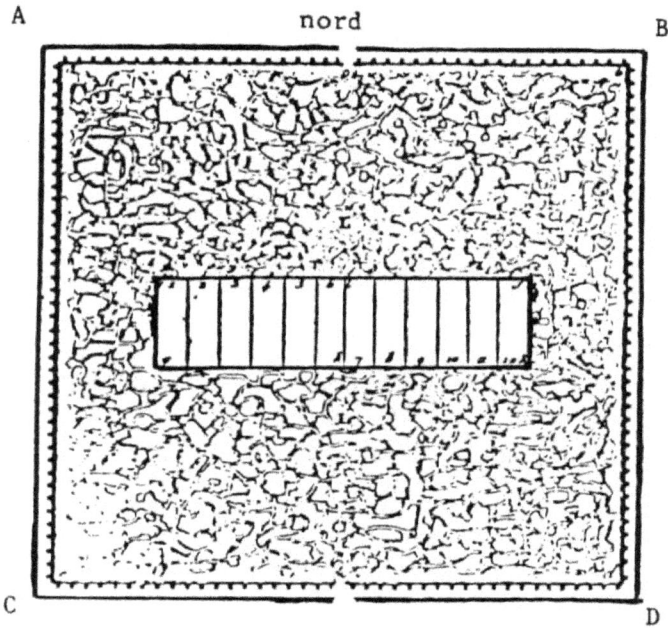

C   D

At this point in my perplexity, which I have to admit was considerable, I heard about Father Claude Sicard at the Collège de la Sainte-Famille in Cairo, which had been run by the Jesuit fathers for a good century. It was Christmas morning 1976, and I don't think I've ever laughed so much in my life!

Two coaches pulled up in the large courtyard of the famous school and flocks of tourists descended to wander in all directions. At Christmas, it's very chilly in Cairo, and that morning in particular it was only 5°C! The Father Superior arrived in a panic, and learned from the group's guide that the group wanted to make a pious pilgrimage to the room that Father Teilhard de Chardin had occupied there during his time as a teacher.

The father panicked, because no-one had come up with the idea before, so no-one could say where the room was! I'll skip over the anger of the American tourists. But after high mass, they visited the premises and the library where, incidentally, the father librarian showed them the map of Egypt drawn by Father Claude Sicard in 1717, which General Bonaparte had used almost a century later to prepare his Egyptian campaign. This good father had travelled the length and breadth of Egypt before coming to die in the hospital in Cairo, relieving the plague victims who were dying day after day during the terrible epidemic of 1721.

These words stayed with me during the night, as I was staying in one of the faculty rooms at the Collège de la Sainte-Famille - perhaps it was Father Teilhard's room? In any case, in the morning I asked about Father Sicard's work and his writings. I learnt that few of his works had survived, that some were perhaps preserved in the new Pare-Dieu library in Lyon, but that there was no certainty. On the other hand, one manuscript was listed in a particular Jesuit 'collection' outside the library in Chantilly. That was how I first heard about it. On my next visit to this 'den of learning' in the Oise region, I had no difficulty whatsoever in compiling it. It's always exciting to have such a work in your hands! For what it contains, of course, but also and above all for what it suggests. On the one hand, there was the text of a clumsy student of Latin, full of mistakes corrected by a stern teacher, probably Father Sicard himself, and on the other, the fine, tight handwriting of the narrator writing the most interesting text I have ever read.

It is not for me to reveal its contents, the only thing that can be published here being what concerns the labyrinth. The extract printed as a preface to this chapter says it all. The father saw the labyrinth, and according to what his eyes perceived, Herodotus and Strabo are wrong! By studying the dates and places, his discovery lies between Abydos and Thebes, precisely where Tentyris, the Greek name for Denderah, is located.

Here is an extract from the manuscript concerning the approach to Denderah, starting from Abydos, which proves the seriousness of the good father, his concern for the truth, and the meticulousness that governed all his research. The length of the lines and the style of writing have been retained in their entirety in the presentation below:

> *Araba village to the west and 2 and a half leagues from the Nile, at*
> *4 leagues from Girgé, and eight or 9 from* Menehiet el nédér *to the south,*
> at
> *8 or 9 leagues from* Hou, *and 17 or 18 from* Dendera *to the north, on the ruins of Abydus. I can prove it: Ptolemy in L. 4, ch. 5 met.*
> *Abydus to the west of the river, then* Diospolis
> *parva, that's all, and* Tentyra *is*
> *Pliny L. 3, Cap. 9 put this town at 7,500 paces from the*

river towards Libya or the sunset, between Tentyris *and Dendera, and Ptolemais,* nenekiet el nédé.
Strabo and Antoninus place it between Diospolis parva *and* Ptolemais.
Araba lies at the foot of a sandy mountain that the Copts called Afud *or* Afodos. *The changed "F in "B" is Abydos in their martyrology on 26 August speaking of St Moyse, a hermit who did penance in the desert near* Abydus.

Abydus olim civitas maxima vidatur fuisse 2a post Thebas, *says Strabo L. 17. Ruins are still there more than half a league long from north to south and a quarter of a league wide from east to west. Here are the remains of Abydus that I visited on 8 May 1715;*
1° *an old monastery of Abbot Moyse, from the village at the foot of Mount Abydos;*
2° *to the south of the monastery is a salt pond. All there's water all year round. Perhaps that's the essence* of the quem patem fornices descenditur in Forcipem Flenos *according to Strabo ;*
3° *to the south of the pond are the ruins of the Temple of Osiris,* in quo, *as Strabo says*, non nec comtori, nec Tibicine, nec est havoudo, facum Sicom aud picavi quem ad modum mos est abis deis. *Elian L. 10, c. 28, states that the sound of was unbearable for the Abydeans. These ruins are an enclosure about a hundred paces long and 50 wide. Everything is granite stone. There are only twenty or so left. still intact. These include a large quarry with very beautiful jeroglifes. The oracle of the god Beka, whose Ammianus Marcellinus speaks of, and the Sepulchres of the great lords who liked to be buried at the the hill. of Osiris, as reported by Plutarch, L. "de Isid et Osyrid", were not the least ornament of the temple. Perhaps that the oracle of Beza was in a separate temple.*
At Abidus, the oracle of the god Beza foretold the future, and some of the consultations held at this sanctuary led to the death of the god. of the black suspicions Constantine conceived. And of a horrible followed at Sezthopolis in Palestine Ammianus L. 19 Cap. 71 ;
4° *to the south of the temple, 2 crossbow strokes away, the palace of Memnon, son of Dawn, apparently the same as* whic

went to the aid of beleaguered Troy in qua a Mnemosis
mividice lapide *Strabo L. 17* Abydus
Regia et Osyris templo inclytum *Pline L. 5 ch. 9 Et Selin C. 35.*
The Memnonium is around 200 paces long and 100 paces wide.
The first thing you see is a fortified building about 75 paces long.
long and almost 35 wide. The floor is made of stone
squares 6 or 7 pitches long by three or four feet
wide and thick. It is supported by 50 to 60 columns

or

Piles welded in several pieces of 6 palms in diameter,
most of which are embedded in the sand, all of which are
covered with very deep jeroglyphs as well as the
floor and the walls. The columns are 10 long and 5,
or 6 or 7 wide, 5 paces apart.
And in 13 wide steps. The sand has robbed us of the door
and the width of the building.

However, this passage, which may seem rather long-winded, is full of lessons. Not only did Bonaparte make use of his work, but so did a number of scholars who aroused the interest of the impetuous Corsican general, who was impatient to leave for Egypt. In fact, a memoir read at the Institut de France on 28 Floréal, Year 5, on the subject of the Great Labyrinth, by one of its distinguished members: the "citizen" David Le Roy, paid a vibrant tribute to the Jesuit father. And when you consider that in those years all the priests' heads were falling off, the churches were burning and there were only 'citizens' left, it took a certain amount of courage, and even a certain amount of courage, to read such a laudatory memoir, of which the following is an extract concerning the Great Labyrinth and the congratulations to Father Le Roy:

"This monument was well worth arousing the curiosity of our modern travellers. Two great scholars have tried to find its location. They are d'Anville and Gibert. They took advantage of the precious map that we owe to Father Claude Sicard. I have also benefited from their writings; perhaps other researchers will benefit from my research.

Before completing this journey of discovery of the 'labyrinth', it remains, first and , to talk about the writings of Diodorus of Sicily, who was the first to awaken in me, in black and white, the echo of the Golden Circle.

This well-known author of Antiquity talks about it at length, especially in his first book describing Egypt. But I had read so much of it that I was a bit disillusioned and had always avoided reading it. But in connection with the tomb of Osymandias and the labyrinth that had to be traversed to reach it, I read a memoir on Osymandias by the honourable Hellenist A.-J. Letronne, read at the Académie des Inscriptions et Belles-Lettres. The full text is far too long for me to reproduce, but it does mention the writings in the first book of Diodorus Siculus from cover to cover! Here are some extracts, the first of which is the very beginning the scholarly paper read at the session of 11 July 1842:

"The description of the monument of Osymandias, which Diodorus included in his work, is one of the most valuable pieces of information we have about ancient Egypt. The colossal proportions of the building, the richness of its decoration, its extraordinary layout - everything in this curious description seems to come together to arouse admiration and give the highest idea of the resources of Egypt at the very remote period when this prodigious monument was built.

"The first modern travellers to the ruins of Thebes were quick to look for the ruins of the monument of Osymandias. But it was not easy to recognise them, even supposing they still existed; for to form an accurate idea of the plan and layout of buildings such as those at Thebes requires a knowledge of architecture that most travellers lack.

The second excerpt that almost made my eyes pop out of my head spoke of the Golden Circle, and it was the first time I had seen this term in French outside my hieroglyphic translation of the inscriptions on the temple at Denderah, particularly in the "Treasure Room". Here is the second passage that almost concludes Mr Letronne's long paper, in which it is clear that he too allowed himself to be influenced by similarities relating to constructions separated by several millennia, and by confusions of apparently identical but usurped place names. I am referring to An-du-Sud, which was originally the name of Denderah, and was taken up again in Dynasty 18 by the priests of Amun-Ra to justify the Theban complex.

If it is true that this famous edifice was destroyed long before the reign of Ptolemy son of Lagus, one cannot help but have some doubts, not about the existence of any tomb of Osymandias, but about that of a monument conforming to the description. In truth, it could be said that this building may have been destroyed in ancient times, like those old monuments whose debris went into the construction of some parts of the buildings at Karnak. But a circumstance in the description itself argues against this. When the Theban priests told Greek travellers that the famous Golden Circle had been pillaged *by Cambyses, they were claiming that the tomb was still intact at the time of the Persian expedition. However, it is hard to understand how such a prodigious monument could have completely disappeared in the space of two centuries; And if one were to say that Cambyses, to whom the Egyptians attributed many ravages that he was unable to carry out, directed all his fury at the tomb of Osymandias, and had it demolished by piece, which is incredible, at least the site of an edifice equal in surface to the main monuments of Thebes combined would have offered an enormous heap of ruins and rubble which, depositing the grandeur and magnificence of the destroyed monument, would have been proudly displayed by the priests; It is hard to imagine then that Diodorus did not see it on his trip to Thebes, and it is even harder to imagine the silence of the whole of Antiquity on this extraordinary monument.*

Who could fail to see in such accounts the intention to exaggerate the power and wealth of ancient Egypt? Ramesses was a great prince, as the Egyptian annals attest, and the Ramesseum *was living proof. But eight or ten centuries earlier, Osymandias was much more powerful and richer still; his tomb alone had to surpass all the buildings Ramesses had built.*

Without mentioning the room of proceedings and other details of a more or less fantastic nature, let's finish with the famous golden circle placed on the roof of the building. It was three hundred and sixty-five cubits *(or about two hundred metres) in circumference and one cubit thick. At each cubit was marked one of the days of the year, with the indication of the rising and setting of the stars for that day, and the* atmospheric *predictions relating to it,* according to the Egyptian astronomers. *Much has been said about this famous golden circle, with the intention of making it at least plausible; and the trouble has been taken to invent hypotheses, all of which fall before the pure and simple examination of the description.*

The difficulties it presents relate to its size, its material and its use.

As for its size, an attempt has been made to remove the difficulty by conjecturing that the word cubit *designates not an* absolute measure, *but a* relative division, *analogous to our degrees. By this means we could reduce its size indefinitely, and make of it, if we wished, a circle of three feet in circumference. The conjecture is not nearly as happy as it is convenient; for it is destroyed from top to bottom by the fact that the circle was* a cubit thick: *Now, a circle of about six hundred feet in circumference cannot absolutely be placed on the roof of an Egyptian monument, however vast it may be, because we know that the surface of the roof changes plane and sinks at each division, going from the beginning to the end.*

If such a circle is impossible because of its size, it is even more impossible because of its material. To reduce the excess of implausibility, it has been supposed that it was simply gilded and not made of gold. I do not deny that the expression has sometimes been used in this sense; but I would not want this opinion to be reproduced to the point of claiming that this is its true meaning, and that good writers do not use this name when expressing that something is solid gold.

Besides, I am not attached to this equivocal expression. I have said, and I repeat, that all the circumstances of the description prove that what was meant was a golden circle, and not just a gilded one. Was it on a thin sheet of gold that all the figures and signs that adorned the famous circle were engraved in a durable manner? To say that it was three hundred and sixty-five cubits in circumference and one cubit thick was to announce that the material was precious. What was the point of talking about its thickness if it had been made of stone? Finally, the priests did not content themselves with saying that Cambyses had destroyed this circle, they said that he had plundered it as he had plundered the gold and silver of the great temple of Karnak. Such a circumstance excludes the idea of simple gilding. It is hard to believe that Cambyses, having so much wealth at his disposal, would have enjoyed scratching stones! The identity of the expressions for the plundering of the circle and that of the gold and silver clearly shows the idea that was intended, that of an extremely precious object, a circle of gold, in a word. This circle is prodigious, no doubt; but it is no more so than other circumstances in the description. There is even something rather singular here. The volume is three hundred and sixty-one to three hundred and sixty-two cubic cubits in round numbers, about fifty-three cubic metres, weighing four million one hundred and seventy thousand two hundred and eighty marcs of gold; which, given the proportion 13, which is the one mentioned by Herodotus, comes to the fifty-three million marcs of silver that Osymandias obtained from the sole product of the mines of Egypt. The coincidence is quite remarkable.

As for the use of such a circle, we have never been able to say what it might have been used for. What we can be sure of is that it was good for nothing. As far as I'm concerned, it's just a clumsy invention, since it's obvious at first glance. According to the priests, the rising and setting of the stars and the atmospheric phenomena they heralded for each day were marked on this circle: this is precisely the character of the parapegms that have been displayed in Greek cities since the reform of Meton; these were, as we know, tables of the rising and setting of the stars for each day of the enneadecaeterid, accompanied by an indication of the astronomical changes that were thought to be linked to them. But there is one difficulty: the golden circle, with its division into three hundred and sixty-five cubits, could only represent a vague year, whereas the indication of the rising and setting of the stars for each day of the year, and the meteorological prognoses that were drawn from it, marked equally for each day, can only have a constant application *in a fixed solar or lunisolar year, such as that of the Greeks at the time, regulated by Meton.*

The invention of this famous circle, impossible because of the place the priests assigned to it, because of the material they claimed it was made of, and because of its very division, brings together all the features that determine the character of the entire description of the monument. It proves that the intention of the authors of this description was precisely that which the simplest common sense would suffice to attribute to them, i.e. to give the Greeks an extraordinary idea of the works of the most ancient Egyptian kings, and to make them believe that Egypt was no longer, even under Sesostris, as rich and powerful as it had been eight or ten centuries earlier.

A royal name quite similar to that of Osymandias, *which is found written on several monuments, would indicate the existence of an ancient king of that name; and it is perhaps, as several critics have thought, the same as the* Ismandes *to whom, according to Strabo, the great labyrinth was attributed, and who was supposed to have been buried in the pyramid located near this mysterious edifice. This last circumstance, if the identity of the characters is real, would prove how vague and uncertain was the tradition about the place where this Ismandes, i.e. Osymandias, had his tomb, since his mortal remains, according to some, were enclosed in a pyramid, according to others, had been deposited in a magnificent monument that he had built in Thebes on purpose. What further shows the extreme confusion of all these historical memories, which perhaps changed from temple to temple, is that this name referred, according to some, to* Memnon *or* Amenophis II. *There is nothing to be gained from all these contradictions. It is possible that, among the sepulchral buildings whose remains were shown to Diodorus of Sicily on the slope of the Libyan mountain or in the plain, there was once an edifice built by the ancient king Osymandias, perhaps more beautiful or larger than the others, but destroyed long before the arrival of the Greeks, like those old buildings whose debris went into the construction of certain parts of those at Karnak.*

Before commenting on this extract, written in 1842, here are the two short passages from Book I of Diodorus Siculus that are of most interest to readers. The first is the one that has led to this labyrinth of Osymandias being located in Thebes:

"1) The priests therefore said, according to the sacred books, that there were (in Thebes s)[18] *forty-seven royal tombs, but that in the time of Ptolemy, son of*

---

[18] See the notes to this paragraph at the end of this chapter, as it is at these precise points that the texts have been interpreted.

Lagus, only seventeen remained, most of which were in ruins by the time we arrived there (in the CLXXX Olympiad).

"2) This is not only related by the priests, according to the sacred books, but also by many of the Greeks who, having come under Ptolemy, son of Lagus, and having written descriptions of Egypt, agree with what we have just said."

The second extract is about the Golden Circle, written two thousand years ago by Diodorus of Sicily:

"16) That all around this room were a multitude of chambers in which were perfectly painted all the animals consecrated in Egypt.

"17) That from these chambers one ascended to the (roof of u)[19] whole tomb; that, when one had reached it, one saw on the monument a golden circle three hundred and sixty-five cubits in circumference, and one cubit thick; that at each cubit the days of the year had been inscribed and distinguished, marking on them the rising and setting of the stars and the atmospheric phenomena which they announced, according to the Egyptian astronomers: It was said that this circle had been plundered by Cambyses and the Persians, when this prince seized Egypt."

Two important points emerge from this passage, the original Greek text of which is appended to this chapter, so that there can be no obscurity.

Firstly, in paragraph 1, "at Thebes" was added by M. Letronne because he felt it flowed naturally from the text as a whole. However, it is indisputable that if Diodorus went to Thebes, it was the priests and many Greek authors who preceded him there who described the tomb of Osymandias. But none of them ever located it exactly! Among these authors, we should mention the very fine description by Hecataeus of Abdera, but nowhere does he mention exactly where it is. Modern authors have deduced from this that, since he spoke of it in Thebes, it must have been in Thebes. However, for the priests who spoke of it, it was in "An-du-Sud", which referred to "the First of the South", i.e. Dendera and not Thebes, which usurped this name from the 12th dynasty onwards. The second highly contentious point, which distorted the interpretation of the location of the Golden Circle, is found in paragraph 17, where Mr Letronne added the expression "on the roof", which does not appear in the Greek text at all, as can be

---

[19] See previous note.

verified in the original reproduced in the appendix to this chapter. Which totally distorts the meaning given by Diodorus, let's face it!

M. Letronne sensed the truth when he spoke of a similarity of name with that of an ancient king, but obviously he shrank from any further research, as this would have led him into an enormous difficulty which would have inevitably brought him down: namely that he would have had to go back chronologically to a date much earlier than that consecrated by the Holy Church at that time, for the birth of Adam, and perhaps that of the Earth itself, since the claim, in 1840, was that our globe had been placed there by God 6000 years before our era!

However, the chronology perfected by Champollion before the young Egyptologist recanted his faith placed the advent of the first king Menes, or Mendes, precisely in 5785 BC, i.e. well before the birth of the first man: Adam... As for the Golden Circle, the priests spoke of twelve millennia...

In Volume I of my *Origins Trilogy: The Great Cataclysm*, published in 1976, I quote a passage from the annals engraved at Denderah on this subject. It is typical of the confusion of the authors who placed the circle 'on the roof'. Here again, in the complex dealing celestial configurations, there was the real Golden Circle, all gold around its perimeter, to be eternally identical to itself in relation to the rays of the Twelve, diffused by Ra "the gold of heaven", and a much smaller circle, on a terrace, used for initiatory purposes, such as the presentation of a newborn child to the Sun, which was the arm of Ptah.

On page 164 of The *Great Cataclysm*,[20] this description leaves no room for doubt about this second "Golden Circle"

"The Annals describe the ancient tradition of this ceremony in detail. The ritual process was based on the appearance of the first rays of sunlight on the Golden Circle to begin the Office. This was an obvious first sign of good fortune, ensuring a long life of Justice, Peace and Goodness for those who benefited from it. This circumference was inlaid with pure, solid gold, making the white marble covering the esplanade even more immaculate, if that were possible. It was arranged in such a way that, every morning, the first rays of the daytime sun were reflected directly onto just one part of it. Due to the phenomenon of the Earth's rotation, each day they

---

[20] A-1, published by Robert Laffont, 1976.

varied slightly from their positions of the previous day, always within the circle, thus touching, one after the other throughout the year, the twelve monolithic blocks of black granite covered with a very specific crystalline material. Each one symbolised one of the twelve constellations that encircled the celestial equator along the Milky Way, bringing Earth and Heaven into harmony.

This was undoubtedly reproduced on the highest terrace of the temple of Denderah, and it is quite possible that Cambyses plundered it completely, as will be seen when the volume "Et Dieu oublia l'Égypte" appears, and which will be briefly developed in chap. 13 of this book.

As for the real Golden Circle, the one with a radius of 7,000 cubits, or eight kilometres in diameter, I'll leave it to the reader to dream for the time being, both about its 'thickness' and its 'metal' quality!

In the days of Herodotus, Strabo and Diodorus of Sicily, it was relatively easy to reach Thebes, the object of all curiosity, but it was almost impossible to get as far as Denderah, which was completely covered in sand and protected by squalid encampments until Bonaparte's armies arrived eighteen centuries later to discover the temple quite by chance . So what about the Golden Circle, which still lies under 80 metres of sand?...

Let's go into a bit more detail!

NOTE ON THE ORIGINAL BY DIODORUS OF SICILY (WITH ADDITIONS BY A.-J. LETRONNE)

This original text is taken from the first volume of the works of A.-J. Letronne, "put in order" by E. Fagnan and published in Paris in 1881 by Ernest Leroux.

The Greek characters printed on the left retain their exact position in the original manuscript. The French translation on the right is that of M. Letronne himself. The parts of sentences in brackets do not exist in Greek, and are therefore due to the addition of M. Letronne alone. In the first paragraph, the third line reads: (in Thebes) and the last line reads: (in the CLXXX Olympiad). All the comments in the scholar's memoir to contradict Diodorus' writing are based on the absurd claim that this enormous construction is located in Thebes. However, there is no mention of the location of the tomb in Thebes, although the other descriptions are there. This is undoubtedly the humorous nuance added by the Egyptian priests who spoke of the "An-du-Sud", one time referring to Denderah and the other to Thebes. Similarly, in the second paragraph, there is a comment: "among whom is also Hecataeus", which clearly proves that this is another addition by M. Letronne.

TEXTE GREC.

α'. Οἱ μὲν οὖν ἱερεῖς ἐκ τῶν ἀναγραφῶν ἔφασαν εὑρίσκειν ἑπτὰ πρὸς τοῖς τετταράκοντα τάφους βασιλικούς, εἰς δὲ Πτολεμαῖον τὸν Λάγου διαμεῖναι ἑπτακαίδεκα μόνον, ὧν τὰ πολλὰ κατέφθαρτο καθ' οὓς χρόνους παρεβάλομεν ἡμεῖς εἰς ἐκείνους τοὺς τόπους...

β'. Οὐ μόνον δ' οἱ κατ' Αἴγυπτον ἱερεῖς ἐκ τῶν ἀναγραφῶν ἱστοροῦσιν, ἀλλὰ καὶ πολλοὶ τῶν Ἑλλήνων, τῶν παραβαλόντων μὲν εἰς τὰς Θήβας ἐπὶ Πτολεμαίου τοῦ Λάγου, συνταξαμένων δὲ τὰς Αἰγυπτιακὰς ἱστορίας (ὧν ἐστι καὶ Ἑκαταῖος), συμφωνοῦσι τοῖς ὑφ' ἡμῶν εἰρημένοις.

TRADUCTION LITTÉRALE.

I. Les prêtres disaient donc, d'après les livres sacrés, qu'il se trouvait (à Thèbes) quarante-sept tombes royales, mais qu'au temps de Ptolémée fils de Lagus il n'en restait que dix-sept, dont la plus grande partie était ruinée à l'époque où nous arrivâmes en ces lieux [dans la CLXXX° olympiade].

II. Cela n'est pas seulement raconté par les prêtres d'après les livres sacrés, mais encore par beaucoup des Grecs qui, étant venus à Thèbes sous Ptolémée fils de Lagus, et ayant rédigé des descriptions de l'Égypte (au nombre desquels est aussi Hécatée), s'accordent avec ce que nous venons de dire.

In paragraph 17 reproduced below, the whole meaning has been distorted by the abusive addition of (toit du) to the second line. There is no doubt that the tomb of Menés, or Ismendès or Osymandias, which has never been found, lies beneath the Golden Circle. This first king, the true Per-Ahâ, therefore the "Descendant of the Elder", is buried at the very centre of the circumference, as befits the Son of God. And this changes the whole real translation of the text originally recounted by the priests and distorted over the millennia until Diodorus wrote:

ις'. Κύκλῳ δὲ τούτου πλῆθος οἰκη-
μάτων κατεσκευάσθαι, γραφὴν ἐχόν-
των εὐπρεπῆ πάντων τῶν καθιερωμέ-
νων ἐν Αἰγύπτῳ ζώων·

ιζ'. Ἀνάβασίν τε ἀπ' αὐτῶν εἶναι
πρὸς ὅλον τὸν τάφον· ἣν διελθοῦσιν
ὑπάρχειν ἐπὶ τοῦ μνήματος κύκλον
χρυσοῦν, τριακοσίων καὶ ἑξήκοντα καὶ
πέντε πηχῶν τὴν περίμετρον, τὸ δὲ
πάχος πηχυαῖον· ἐπιγεγράφθαι δὲ καὶ
διῃρῆσθαι καθ' ἕκαστον πῆχυν τὰς
ἡμέρας τοῦ ἐνιαυτοῦ, παραγεγραμ-
μένων τῶν κατὰ φύσιν γινομένων τοῖς
ἄστροις ἀνατολῶν τε καὶ δύσεων, καὶ
τῶν διὰ ταύτας ἐπιτελουμένων ἐπι-
σημασιῶν κατὰ τοὺς Αἰγυπτίους ἀσ-
τρολόγους· τοῦτον δὲ τὸν κύκλον ὑπὸ
Καμβύσου καὶ Περσῶν ἔφασαν σεσυ-
λῆσθαι, καθ' οὓς χρόνους ἐκράτησεν
Αἰγύπτου.

xvi. Que tout autour de cette pièce étaient disposées une multitude de chambres où étaient parfaitement peints tous les animaux consacrés en Égypte ;

xvii. Que de ces chambres on montait sur le (toit du) tombeau entier ; que, quand on y était parvenu, l'on voyait sur le monument un cercle d'or de trois cent soixante-cinq coudées de circonférence, et d'une coudée d'épaisseur ; qu'à chaque coudée on avait inscrit et distingué les jours de l'année, en y marquant les levers et les couchers des astres et les phénomènes atmosphériques (12) qu'ils annonçaient, selon les astronomes égyptiens : on disait que ce cercle avait été pillé par Cambyse et les Perses, lorsque ce prince s'empara de l'Égypte.

The justification for the name "An-du-Sud" originally attributed to Denderah, and preserved by the hieroglyphic Tentyrite, is given crypt no. 9 of this temple which, I would remind you, is the sixth reconstruction carried out under the Ptolemies in the 2nd century BC:

"As for the place promised by the first Elders, it is the city of An, the seat of Hathor, the good mother of Hor, who is the mistress of this site. An receives the Sun that has lit it since the first day of the beginning..."

As this very long text will be studied in the next chapter, this justification for Thebes' usurpation of An's name is sufficiently demonstrated for now.

9

THE GOLDEN CIRCLE

It seems as if the sea is rolling along the bottom of the abyss, mixed up with the lightning and the hurricane, looking for bones that are still alive!

And over there, in Ath-Mer, a swirling crimson bath covers in blood the Golden Circle of the Temple-God, which was nothing but idolatry!
         Chibet d'Ahou (Annals of the Ahou Scribe)

The study of the site does not tell us anything about the material purpose of the crypts. Fortunately, the texts shed some light on this interesting question. As soon as you enter the crypts, the first thing that catches your eye are the measurements and references to precious materials that are placed next to most of the images of divinities sculpted on the walls.
         Auguste Mariette (Description of Dendérah, 1875)

Since the question is not whether the Golden Circle exists or not, but when and how to enter it, let's take a look at what proves its reality on the , and how it can be approached.

The first point concerns the original purpose of the Dendera site. Those who won't officially admit it today, however, condescend to admit that it could have had something to do with astronomy. Even leaving aside the planisphere and the sacred name of the site: "Temple of the Sky Goddess" or "House of the Universe", the discovery twelve crypts in precise cardinal locations demonstrated, if proof were needed, the validity of what is more than a mere presumption.

So let's start by talking about these crypts, since they are one of the keys to understanding the purpose of the Golden Circle, and how to get there. But if there are indeed twelve of them, one glaring anomaly is immediately apparent: nine are entirely engraved with hieroglyphs and sculptures, and three are completely bare, looking more like cellars or garbage dumps than anything else. What's more, they are arranged over three floors...

Let's go back to the dictionary, as I did at the time of my comparisons, and it said: "from the Latin *crypta* borrowed from the Greek *kruptos* meaning 'hidden', like the underground part of a church where the dead were buried in the past".

If we look at Auguste Mariette's notes, we can read: "There are twelve crypts at Denderah. Six are underground; the other six run through the walls enclosing the rear part of the temple.

"The crypts discovered in the course of our work are the two crypts in room A, the crypt in room O, crypt no. 4 and crypt no. 7, making a total of five crypts. The others were more or less cluttered, more or less accessible, but they were known.

And also this characteristic passage:

"Not all of the twelve crypts have inscriptions. The two crypts in Room A and the crypt in Room O are devoid of inscriptions, but the other nine crypts display the profusion of paintings and texts that generally distinguish the temple of Denderah. As a result, not all the crypts are of equal interest to us. Henceforth, therefore, we shall leave the first three to deal only with the other nine.

"So as not to omit anything general about the crypts, I would add that, in all probability, the builders of the temple did not give all the crypts equal importance. The crypts on the underground level are the real crypts. They alone have their feast days; they alone were furnished with emblems and statues of all kinds. The crypts on the middle level are still worthy of attention, but the texts there no longer have the same precision and the paintings decorating them can be transported from one crypt to another without losing any of their clarity. As for the crypts on the upper floor, they can be seen as a relief in the masonry. However, there are as many paintings there as anywhere else. But there is nothing local about them, and there is not one of them that would not belong elsewhere, in any part of the temple.

From this reading, and before I seriously studied the famous hieroglyphic texts on site, I got an indefinable feeling of unease. It was as if something had been botched in order to prove that the twelve crypts had been discovered, and that there was nothing left to look for! Yet it appeared, both literally and in the normal sense of the word 'crypt', that only five had been uncovered. The fact that there had been secret hiding places on the upper floors did not make them crypts! So I began by looking at the hieroglyphic texts engraved in the upper levels, which were easy to access despite being called "crypts". Such as the one with number 3, which is located under the top of the grand staircase leading to the high terrace, you can see from this plan by A. Mariette:

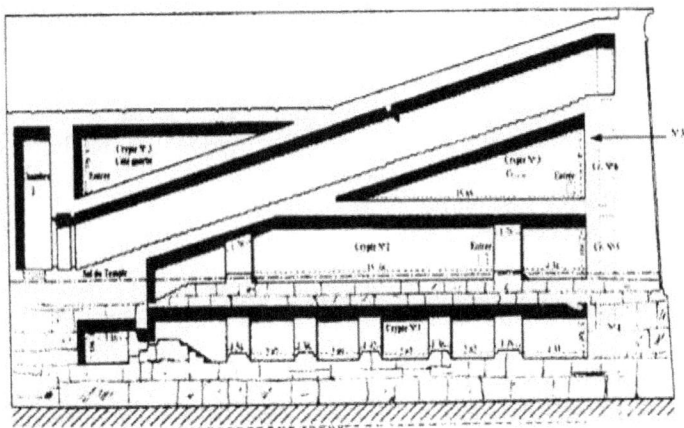

Chamber 3 is entirely covered with engraved texts, the dedication of which is indicative of its purpose, which has nothing to do with a secret hideout or an underground entrance. Here is a *full* reproduction (next illustration).

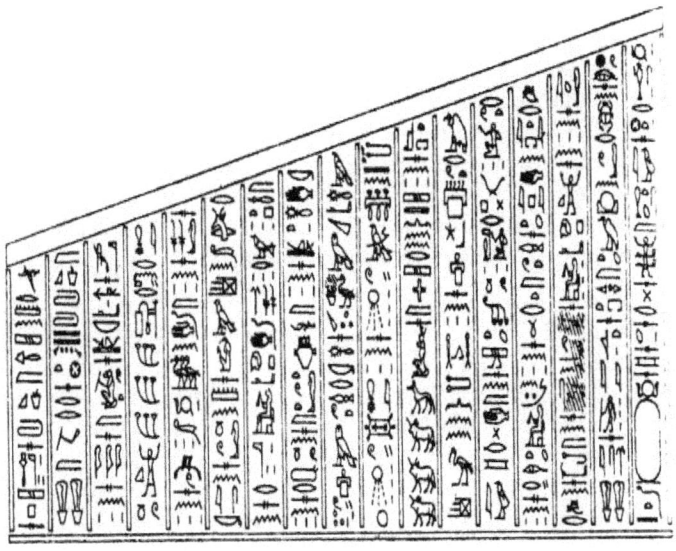

The beginning of the translation gives an idea of the purpose of this room. It is difficult, within the scope of this book, to go any further, as that would require a thousand more pages.

"This room is consecrated by the God of the Universe, the one whose Name is not written, who is the Master of the Divine Parcels as well as the carnal Envelopes, and of all things on earth. All the Judges charged with upholding His Law are represented around the good mother of Hor, son of God's Elder, Usir. Each of them is depicted according to the prescriptions set out in the sacred books. Each drawing corresponds to the words spoken by the descendants of the Elders. The furniture is made of sycamore wood, the sculptures of precious metal...".

This shows that this was indeed a sanctuary dedicated to Isis, hidden of course, with a secret entrance, but nothing like a crypt.

Certain mysteries were not to be revealed. The one concerning the Divine Triad was one of these. Horus, the son of Isis and Osiris, being the direct Elder of God by birth, required additional teaching, accessible only to those who knew the Divine-Mathematical-Combinations and who practised their commandments.

This is even truer one level down, for bedroom number 2... This is a large room, as you can see from the plan on the previous page, located under the staircase leading to the terrace.

The special feature of this room is that it tells almost the entire story of the ancient people whose descendants came to settle in Egypt. This room is the justification for the Past trilogy, as well as for the authority that emerges from Ancient Stellar Knowledge. The excerpt below shows the six main daytime actions combined by Ptah through the 7 Wandering and Fixed Stars of our solar system (Sun, Moon, Mercury, Mars, Venus, Jupiter and Saturn), which reflect the 12 'hearts', emanations of the twelve constellations that form 'the Belt'.

Here, all the sculptures are painted in traditional colours, while the hieroglyphs and engravings remain in their primitive state of relief or hollows in the stone. Unlike the missing parts in the temple chambers, which were usually savagely hammered out when Ra's usurpers intruded, the missing sections of wall were cut out with chisels, either at the end of the 19th century or between 1970 and 1973, by "antique dealers"!

But the engraver's work is remarkable throughout, both in the demonstration of the hypocrisy of Set, the knife-wielding murderer of his brother Usir, whose head has been transformed into a symbolic snake. He is depicted facing left on the north wall, thus looking towards Ahâ-Men-Ptah, the land swallowed up by divine wrath following the assassination. On the north wall, the same scene is depicted looking to the right, towards Egypt, the "Second Heart", where the hieroglyphs reveal that if the antagonism between the Two Brothers continues, it will be the end of the "Second Homeland".

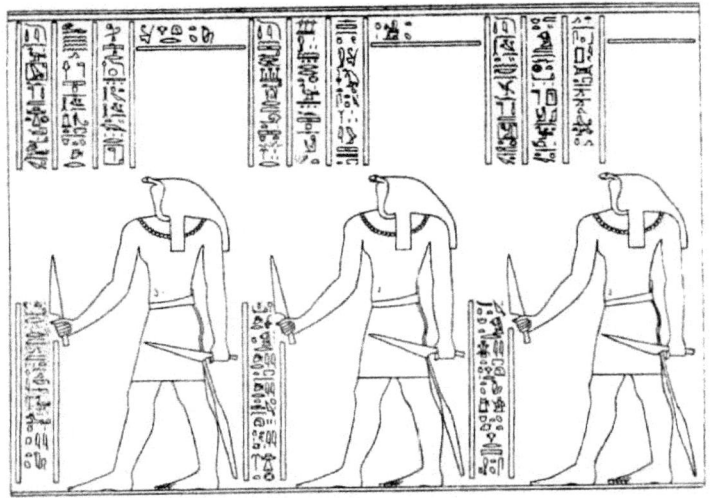

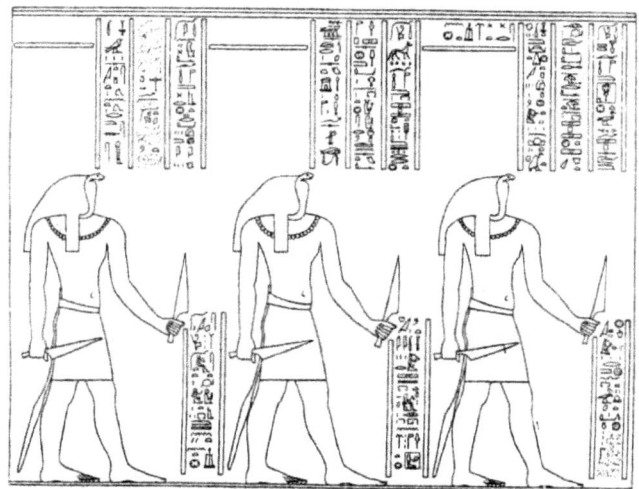

Another remarkable scene is engraved just after the representation of the twelve Divine-Mathematical Combinations, the drawing of which is reproduced here:

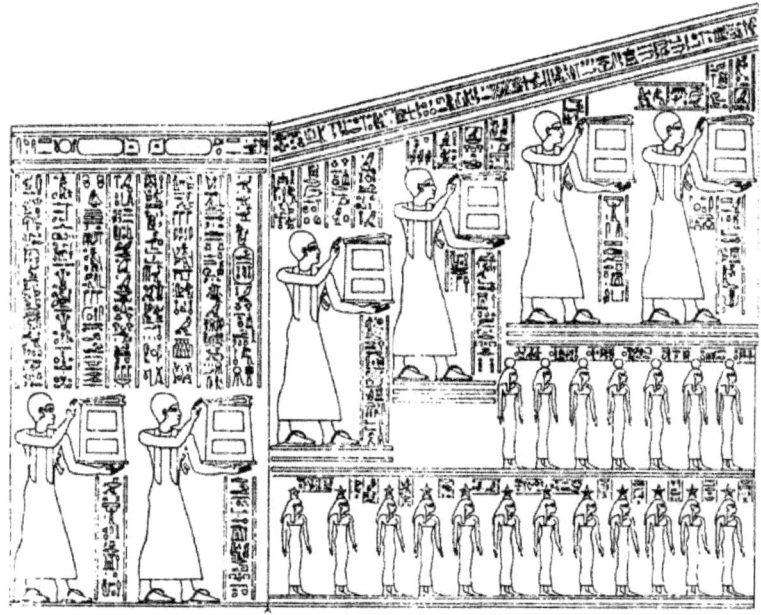

Here we see the six possibilities for divine Justice to be exercised over Souls or to become angry, if strict observance of the Commandments is not carried out: it will be a new flood. In short, the Apocalypse redefined by Saint John or the Golden Age, both symbolised by the urns ready to be tipped over onto the Earth! Here, then, is a figuration so expressive that it hardly needs the preceding comments.

It would certainly be interesting to review in detail the seven chambers described by Egyptologists as "crypts", which are hardly crypts at all, because they justify the theme of my books on monotheism, proving its veracity down to the smallest detail, even when it appears in dialogue form. It is never romanticised. But in this temple I was looking for a certain Golden Circle, or at least its entrance, and it wasn't on the surface or in the upper storeys that I could have found it. So it was in the five real crypts that I discovered that I concentrated my search... before setting off to discover the seven missing crypts, then the entrance to the Golden Circle, and the study of cosmic rays!

For it was indisputable that there were twelve crypts, not only because they represented all the variants of the four cardinal points in relation to the slow equinoctial movement that caused the rays coming from the twelve to vary angularly in obliquity, leaving them always in harmony from one thirty degree to the next. These twelve crypts maintained a permanent link between Heaven and Earth, as well as an eternal accord between the celestial Creator and his earthly creatures. I became absolutely convinced of this when I studied the real crypts!

First of all, here is the basic plan of the temple, showing the location of the underground crypts:

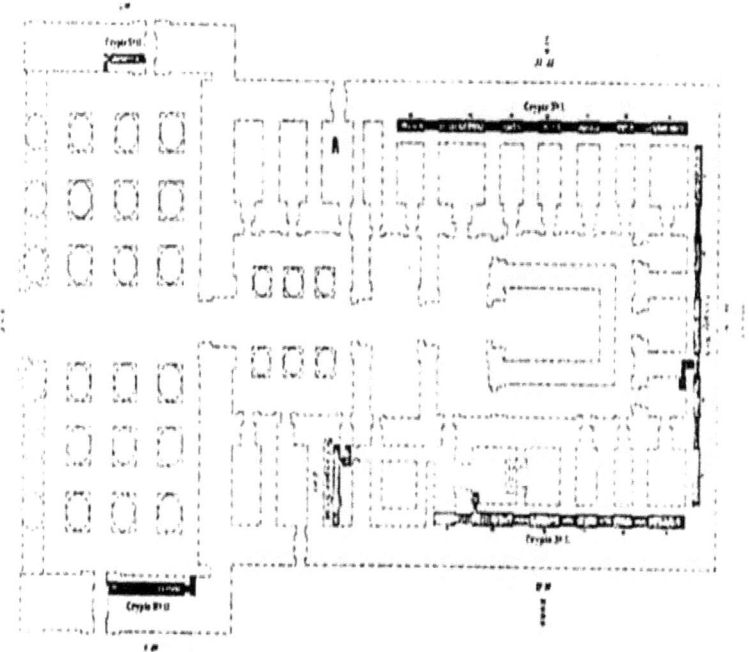

Let's leave aside Crypt 1, which now looks more like a long string of small cellars with almost completely damaged walls and destroyed sculptures, and whose floors have been violently disturbed and excavated, revealing enormous well-shaped holes, but at the bottom of which, obviously, nothing was discovered by the profaners who looked there for "something" at a very distant time. It was nothing more than an exit from a dungeon. The inscriptions still visible, which line the upper part of the carved and destroyed paintings, speak only of incantatory formulae of curses against those who would try to penetrate the secret of the goddess Isis, referred to here as the "White Cow". Indeed, as Osiris was the celestial Bull, his wife, the pure Isis, could only be represented as a white cow.

The crypt shown on the map as number 4, on the other hand, is very pretty and full of surprises! It comprises five rooms linked by corridors. All the engravings have their colours remarkably well preserved. And although the precious furniture disappeared long before it was discovered by Auguste Mariette, a cow mummy in decomposition was still there. And the first thought that strikes any logical mind is to wonder how such a volume could have penetrated this crypt, whose only apparent entrance is a small staircase that the average man has to stoop over to enter this subterranean place? To help you understand, here is a plan of the five chambers, the corridors connecting them and the staircase leading up to them.

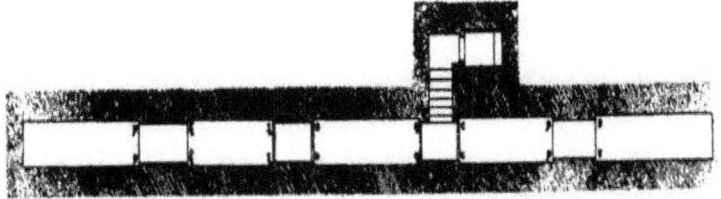

The frieze that dominates the staircase at ceiling level reads:

Entrance to the Abode of the Mother of Mothers, the Pure Celestial Cow, who is the right eye of the sun and the great mistress of heaven. She is the daughter of Geb, the last king of the blessed sleepers of the continent swallowed up by the wrath of the One whose Name is not written, who redeemed the Survivors by giving her his Son to be his husband.

would take far too long to include all the hieroglyphic texts drawn in this book, as the explanation of the crypts alone, even in small print, would run to some five hundred pages! However, the most important text on the frieze in the first corridor, the one that appears once the staircase has been descended, is worth reproducing, as the reader will recognise in it, among other things, the character meaning: "Combinations-Mathematics-Divine, the sky, the earth, and astronomy in general."

You who enter this secret sanctuary of the White Cow purified, to enter the Abode of Hor-le-Pur, his father's avenger, have no fear, for from here on you are under the protection of the Goddess of Heaven and of the Divine-Mathematical Combinations. You will learn to submit to the celestial commandments that have redeemed the souls laid to rest by the sin of Set the fratricide.

Life and Knowledge will be revealed to you, as well as the Past and the Future, thanks to your understanding of the data contained in the Golden Circle. Then you will approach Eternal Life and Blessed Eternity.

As the staircase is deliberately off-centre, since nothing is left to chance in this construction, it was only natural to visit the right-hand side first, since, according to the equinoctial descriptions, this off-centre west wall was originally on this side. In the room we passed through is the most famous engraving, and undoubtedly the most famous: that of Isis breast-feeding her son Hor! Were it not for the hairstyle, this reproduction would inevitably bring to mind "The Virgin and the Child Jesus".

I won't go into the many religious reminiscences here, as they will be detailed in *Jesus the Christ*, which will be published in 1984-1985. But the whole play is full of tableaux retracing Hor's life and initiation, from his birth to his death, in which he appears as judge of the Two Lands: Ahâ-Men-Ptah and Ath-Kâ-Ptah, with a hawk's head and the insignia of his divinity.

Then there is the corridor linking this room to the second, last room on the right-hand side of the underground passage. It is remarkable for several reasons, the main one being that it defines the library of the Golden Circle of Denderah, as well as the five disciplines taught there.

L'enseignement de l'Ahâ fils d'Hor (c'est-à-dire de Têta ou Thoth).

L'enseignement de la Parole dans la Demeure

L'enseignement de la Loi Divine

L'enseignement de la Parcelle Divine dans son corps

L'enseignement issu des Survivants pour assurer le futur des générations de Cadets.

Ten large engravings adorning the corridor hold the key, as they represent, two by two, the protection of each part of the library, some by day, others by night. What is immediately obvious is the first teaching, that disseminated by the books of Teta the thrice-blessed, for it was he who re-established hieroglyphics and therefore God, the calendar and therefore time, medicine and therefore life. Now, this Teta was phonetised in Greek by Theoth, who became Hermes Trismegistus, or the thrice-great!

We know from Clement of Alexandria, in his *Stromates*, book 6, that this Hermes had introduced a total of thirty-six books into Egypt, which contained the whole of Knowledge. Eight dealt with hieroglyphics, four with the Divine-Mathematical Combinations with the phases of the sun and moon, the movement of the five other planets, and the cosmography of the universe; ten with priestly teaching, the Law and its commandments; two books reserved for the cult of Ptah and twelve dealing with anatomy and medicine. At Denderah, then, there was - and there may still be, buried in the Golden Circle - a library whose origins are lost in the mists of time, if we accept that the tomb of Menés or Osymandias lies at its centre. For this Teta, or Theoth, or Hermes, was indeed the son of Menes, the second pharaoh of the First Dynasty.

It's a fantastic leap in time and space, as we find ourselves six millennia in the past, even though the temple is only two thousand years old. It's clear, then, that beneath it lie the remains of another, older temple, which itself communicates, via its astronomical crypts, with the corridors leading to the Golden Circle.

Here are some of the library's protectors, with their significant dedications, who effectively protect the entrance to the Golden Circle, two by two, night and day:

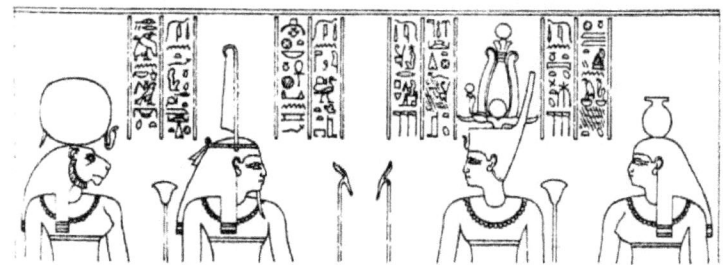

Crypt number 7 was, in a way, the consecration of all the initiatory celebrations taking place in the temple, as it indicated the location of the treasure contained in the Golden Circle.

Consecration is the right word, because every 1,460 years Denderah celebrated the great festival of the New Year, which lasted 365 full days, since a new year of God, personified by Isis, goddess of Heaven, began with a Sun-Sirius conjunction, every 1,461 solar years.

The full calendar of this year-long festival is spelled out in detail in the great hall of the temple. And during the 365 days, believers came from all over Egypt and the surrounding countries, laden with offerings and sumptuous gifts, the list of which is extensively commented on, both on the outside of the temple and in crypt 7.

A whole section of the temple was reserved for the celebration of the great panegyria of the Divine Triad, the sacred barks of Horus and Osiris, coming from Edfu and Esne to join those of Isis. In the centre was the "Chapel of the New Year" and the adjoining room was the "Treasure Room", which was connected by a corridor to Crypt 7 and, from there, led to the centre of the Golden Circle.

In volume 3 of the *Origins Trilogy: And God rose again at Denderah*, I was only able to touch on this festival, because here too several hundred pages would be needed to describe these festivals and the pomp and ceremony that went with them. Perhaps one day all these books will be published. Let's get back to crypt 7, which is apparently in a mediocre state of preservation and has not aroused any particular interest or research! Egyptologists have seen it only as a development of several festivals during the epagomenal days of the vague years and nothing else. Yet the mere sight of the figures of the twelve protectors should have prompted them to meditate, even if the hieroglyphic, as Auguste Mariette writes in his *Denderah* on page 259, "is so crude that we have given up copying it".

Now, in the line traced out for the study of monotheism and the discovery of the Golden Circle that follows from it, the symbolism of the engravings in this crypt is so obvious that there is almost no need for explanation. The twelve are described in detail, giving initiates who have reached that point the code they need to understand the general layout of the various buildings in the complex. Opposite, six of the characteristic figures.

The first of the twelve is obviously Leo, with the Sun on its head, making it the guide for the new celestial 'navigation'. Next in retrograde are Cancer (which was characterised by the Scarab or new life), Gemini, Taurus, Aries and Pisces.

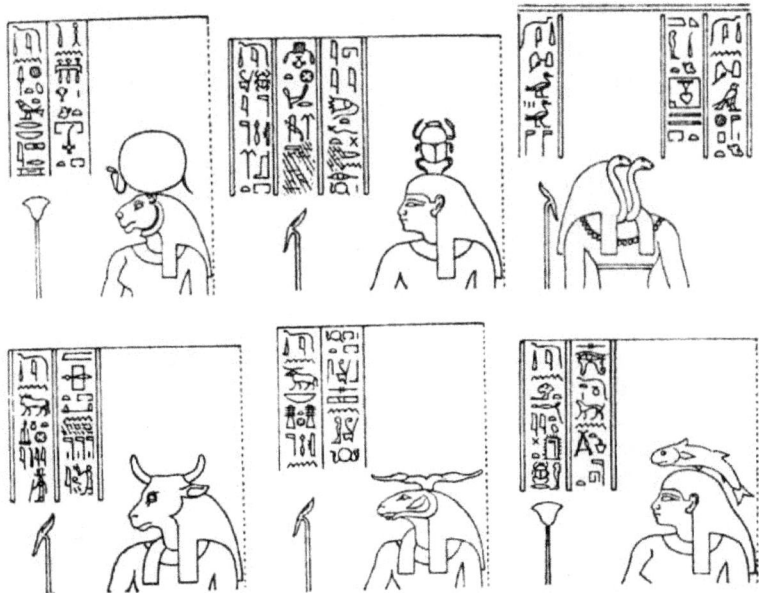

All that remained was to find the locations of the other crypts that would provide the missing links for safe penetration of the corridors giving access to what has become the "Great Labyrinth". The best way to proceed logically was to start in the Chapel of the New Year, in the room describing the calendar of feasts for the Year of God, and end up in crypt 7. I did this meticulously after studying all the inscriptions hieroglyphically. And if I haven't yet mentioned the crypt called number 10, which follows number 7, but perpendicular to the north wall rather than parallel to it (see the basic plan of the temple), it's because logic dictated that there should be "something" opposite. However, the northern wall was cut off a doorway, and all the surveys carried out in the nooks and crannies by successive Egyptologists at Denderah had been negative. However, when we consult the extremely precise plan drawn up by the architects, it is easy to see that the temple of the Lady of Heaven is compartmentalised from top to bottom, from the high terrace to the underground passageways, into an incredible multiplicity of cells that make it look like a beehive or termite mound! New crypts were uncovered in four specific places, and above all, in August 1979, when two slabs weighing several tonnes were lifted and then removed from the site marked A, just at the opening of the south wall, the remains of the temple of Khufu, the famous Khufu of the Greeks, were revealed from the top of the columns, in all their splendour. Just where I had calculated it should be, given the ancient axis of this third construction, which was not at all the , due to the earth's retreat in space as a result of the phenomenon of the attraction of the planets, known as the precession of the equinoxes.

The French Egyptological Mission, headed by François Daumas, was not in Denderah permanently, especially in recent years. So the Egyptians were behind this discovery, which I had already spoken to them about at length, their showing that the site was ideally situated to discover not a crypt, but the upper access to another temple.

As I was on site, I immediately informed Mr Daumas, by letter, of the interest of this discovery, offering to make all my work available to him. There is no modesty on my part in this matter, for it was only incidentally that I became interested in hieroglyphics, and then in Dendera and its Golden Circle.

The handwritten reply I received by return of post, while very kind, was in a way an end of non-receipt. French Egyptologists are not interested in this research, preferring to use the funds at their disposal to consolidate and clean the current temple. Of course, the poor thing needs it, but it seems to me that a compromise could have been found to *also* carry out the research, which is much more important than the rest.

Here is the beginning of Mr Daumas's letter, reproduced *in full*:

Dear Sir,

I'm also sorry we haven't met. Nevertheless, your Tentyrite discovery will be of great interest to me. Far from thinking that Dendara has said its last word, I am sure that there are still some very promising excavations to be made. However, publishing the temple first, which was cleaned by Mariette between 1860 and 1870, seems to me to be the most important thing to do. It is being destroyed a little more every day. That is why I have postponed the excavations indefinitely. My successors will do them.

Given the dynamism of American research in Egypt and the value of the German Egyptologists who are studying my work, my dismay is perfectly understandable! At the same time as I was receiving Mr Daumas's reply, I was receiving a long letter from Washington, from a publishing house that was sending me a contract in two copies, already signed by the chairman and managing director, who was allocating me a deposit of 20,000 dollars (twenty thousand) as soon as I had returned a copy signed by myself, so that I could send him my manuscript including all my research at Denderah...

There was obviously no question of this, and at the time I gave a copy of the contract to Éditions Laffont, having nothing to hide from my publisher. But, on the one hand, Americans are such that it would never have occurred to them that I should refuse such a tempting offer and, on the other hand, a representative from this publishing house had already left for Cairo to await the arrival of a team from ABC television channel who were due to go to Denderah, hard at work, to await my arrival. The contract stipulated that as soon as I received my signed copy I would receive a plane ticket to Egypt.

It was all far too hasty, and smacked of too obvious a desire for publicity, for it not to turn into the simple marketing of a phenomenon that will certainly be far more important and explosive when it comes to light: the Golden Circle! For if the sixth reconstruction of the Temple of Isis at Denderah was decided upon under Ptolemy XI and completed under the Emperor Tiberius, there is absolute certainty that the design of the religious edifice itself, in terms of both its dogmas and its liturgy, dates back to the learned architects of the "Followers of Horus", i.e. the Elders who preceded the founder of Egypt. Before the pyramids were built, before the necropolises of the most ancient tombs were organised, the first Masters of Measurement and Number took possession of the sacred site of Denderah to build an enormous complex to match the workings of the Universe with which they wished to come into harmony. But time and wear have left their mark only in hieroglyphics.

This is why, if French Egyptologists would first condescend to admit that the term goddess Hathor really does mean "Mother of Horus" and not the goddess of orgies like Aphrodite, there would be the beginnings of an understanding that would make it possible to assimilate the major keys! The engravings of Isis suckling Horus, one of which is in the Ptolemaic temple and the other in a new underground crypt separated from the other by six millennia, would provide knowledge of how to access one of the corridors leading to the Golden Circle. I presented these unique and previously unpublished slides on several occasions, and some of the audience members asked the questions they needed to solve the problem!

Similarly, the paintings depicting the death and resurrection of Osiris, with the notable differences they demonstrate over the millennia, and the very place in which they are placed, help us to understand how access to the Golden Circle is gained.

But for this to happen, we must not only admit, but become imbued with the certainty that this temple of Hathor is indeed that of Isis, the Lady of Heaven, the patron saint of Divine-Mathematical Combinations. For this temple would not exist and would never have been conceived in the first place, if Hathor were not the mother of Horus, logically and fundamentally. The essential dogma is personified by the Divine Triad. It only held because all Pharaonic ethics, spirituality and philosophy were based on these precepts.

It was, moreover, because this concept of Ptah was put back into use in Ath-Kâ-Ptah that the antagonism of Set's descendants redeveloped. The opposition of two great principles, set up as notions of Good and Evil, marked the four millennia of fratricidal life, whose incessant struggles over the notions of Amun-Ra and Ptah eventually led to monotheistic Egypt being forgotten and wiped off the map great nations!

The Divine-Mathematical Combinations regulated the entire time sequence of this enormous complex. The year of Sirius, hence of Isis, known in hieroglyphic as the year of God, regulated an immutable mechanism over 1,460 years because it was perfectly run. And during a solar year of 365 days, the temple opened wide to the whole of Egypt for sumptuous celebrations. Because outside this short period - compared to the fifteen centuries or so that existed between two "New Years" - the enclosure surrounding the religious building remained strictly closed to the public. Even the inhabitants of the village of

Denderah could only see the two monumental gates that pierced the high outer wall.

Everything exuded spiritual serenity, punctuated by the slow movement of the Year of God. The interior of the temple was entirely designed for devotion to the Divine Triad and the Good Mother Isis. were altars, offering tables, signs on deposit, chests in which certain sacred images were hidden from view, and other chests in which sacred vestments and the ornaments used to adorn the statues and utensils of worship were kept. Three large sacred boats were kept in one of the rooms of the temple, the Holy of Holies, while other rooms were used to store essences and fragrant oils made on site. The aediculae on the terraces must have had their own sacred furnishings, and it is likely that the thirty-four celestial representations, the statues of the protectors, the small obelisks and the signs used in the ceremonies for the resurrection of Osiris were kept there. As for the crypts, the statues and the emblems kept there were as rich as they were varied and numerous.

The last important thing, decided by Egyptologists to avoid excavation, was that this temple, exceptionally, was built directly on the desert sand under some rather fragile foundations! When you look at the temple as a whole, it's hard to believe how fragile it is, as well as its lack of foundations, especially when you see the hieroglyph for the Golden Circle surmounted by a square representing the domain of Isis:

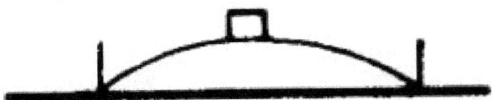

To close this vital chapter, I would like to draw the reader's attention to the engraving below, taken from crypt no. 7, where we can see the resurrection of Osiris by Isis and Nephthys, thanks to the recalling of his Divine Parcel in accordance with the beneficial precepts of the primordial Golden Circle. In fact, *the inverted* hieroglyph of this circle can be seen above the heads of the figures in this scene. And if it's inverted, it's because the Great Cataclysm had passed through there before it was rebuilt in Denderah.

10

DISCOVERING DENDERAH

The time has come not only to study these pieces of information taken at random from a tomb or a temple for their own sake, but to investigate the reason for their presence, the relative place they occupy, the link that binds them together; in a word, to analyse the thought that went into composing the monuments that contain them.
L. De Rochemonteix (Report to the Ministry of Education, May 1878)

Denderah! For anyone who has made the classic pilgrimage to Egypt in a felucca on the Nile, this name evokes the first real vision of the purest and most ancient beauty they have ever had of an Egyptian temple.
G. Maspero (Extract from a letter dated 27 June 1900)

Dendera is the central pivot in the *History of Monotheism*, and the temple that forms its essential element deserves to be considered at length for at least four important reasons:

1. The current temple is the sixth reconstruction of the original building, which dates back to the "Followers of Horus", i.e. to the Predynastic kings.

2. This temple had the only school teaching astronomy that was split into two: one for the day, the other for the night.

3. His Planisphere, or "Zodiac", remains most controversial monument discovered in Egypt, ever since archaeological discoveries were made.

4. The Divine-Mathematical Combinations engraved on the walls of the temple tell the story of an original people led by Osiris, Horus and Isis, the Divine Triad, of which the Zodiac is the very justification, since it represents the map of the sky on the day of

the Great Cataclysm that took place around twelve thousand years ago.

From my first trip to Egypt, when I was preparing a thesis on Pythagoras, all the Copts I spoke to told me a lot about the Temple of Denderah, which was infinitely mysterious, secret and sacred. The Jesuit fathers in Cairo had done the same. It was a place where mathematics and astronomy played a major role. If I wanted to understand Pythagoras' initiation into Knowledge, it was to this privileged place that I had to go first. Here again, by a bizarre combination of circumstances, I was plunged headlong into an impressive 'mystery'.

Denderah is sixty kilometres from Luxor, the great tourist city of today, whose ancient name was phonetised Thebes by the Greeks. This was obviously where I had made my headquarters. Not only for reasons of comfort, but also because at that time President Nasser did not allow those who ventured into the region to move around freely. The headquarters of the Soviet troops was five kilometres from the temple of Denderah! As my health still required intensive care, the presence of the hospital in Luxor, with its doctors and above all a competent chief surgeon who had studied medicine in the United States and Great Britain, was a great reassurance. I mention this doctor because he retired a few months ago and we are still excellent friends. When we first met, he was astonished to see a Frenchman, sick and handicapped to boot, taking an interest in 'stones' that he saw as having only one purpose, to earn foreign currency for Egypt from those who wasted their time coming to see them!

Nevertheless, having never been to visit the ruins, he took me there in his carriage! The first sight I saw was comparable to that of E. de Villiers du Terrage, who wrote as long ago as 1798 in his *Journal de l'Expédition d'Égypte, from 1798 to 1801:*

"The mere sight of the monuments of Denderah is enough to compensate us for the pain and fatigue of the most arduous of journeys, even if we had no hope of visiting all that the rest of the Thebaid contains.

The site is indeed grandiose! Not for its imposing surface area, like that of the Luxor temples, nor for its sumptuousness, like that of the buildings at Karnak. Here, the first thing that emerges is a feeling of respect, followed by a nameless pride in belonging to the human race, which designed the plans and built the walls.

At that time, thanks to the surgeon, our guide gave me a complete course on the Divine Triad... in French. At that time, the Egyptologist in charge of the research was the late M. Chassinat, who had put together a remarkable team, even if his work did not go in the direction foreseen by Viscount Emmanuel de Rougé and Auguste Mariette. As my new friend the surgeon was considered a sorcerer by all the natives, because he operated and stitched up with dexterity all the seriously injured or sick, I benefited from a lesson from which all notion of interest was excluded. I was convinced that our guide didn't expect any 'baksheesh' for what he was teaching me, and he knew that I wouldn't use what he was teaching me for profit.

From that first visit, I understood the undeniable originality of this monument, with all its walls, galleries, columns, ceilings, interior staircases covered with hieroglyphic inscriptions, underground crypts or crypts hidden in the depths of the ground itself, and finally its initiation chambers nestling on the upper terrace, just like the planisphere that has become the Zodiac and is its dominant feature. The temple is entered after crossing a vast esplanade surrounded by a high surrounding wall, pierced at its southernmost point by an impressive portico.

You don't need to be an expert in Egyptology to realise that it is illogical to claim that these splendid buildings, covered in engravings and hieroglyphics, were built solely by workers working under the orders of Ptolemaic architects, when neither of them could translate the sacred language, which has now been lost!

But as a preliminary to studying the four points that put me on the right track, let's look at the major detail that denigrates the anteriority of the construction of the south portico, because here begins the imbroglio over the origin of the builders of the Denderah holy complex. The controversies that animated all the specialists at the beginning of the 19th century bear witness to this! At , the dedicatory inscription on this monumental gate, written in Greek, clearly defines its era:

"For the preservation of the emperor Caesar, son of the god Caesar, Jupiter liberator, Augustus, Publius Octavius being prefect, Marcus Claudius Postumius being epistrate, Triphon being strategist, the inhabitants of the metropolis and the nome have raised this propylon to Isis, goddess most great, and to the gods worshipped in the same temple, in the XXXI year of Caesar in the month of Thoth, the day of Augustus."

Hence the impressive number of "Memoirs" published by scholars between 1810 and 1840 to refute the antiquity of the Temple of Denderah, built during the same period, which, according to its detractors, removed all value from the famous Zodiac, which was transported at great expense to Paris to the Imperial Museum, before becoming the Louvre Museum.

If this portico was Ptolemaic, there was no doubt that the temple's zodiac was too! We now know from papyri that this religious edifice dedicated to Isis was the sixth faithful reconstruction on the site of the original, designed and erected five or six millennia earlier. The foreword by Auguste Mariette at the beginning of this book already hinted at this a century ago.

Thus, Augustus Caesar, having approved the continuation of the sixth reconstruction of the temple, decided to take part in it in his own way in order to win Isis' good graces: he had the south portico built and had his mark placed on it, in order to attract the blessing of his reign. In fact, all the emperors did the same, in a more or less roundabout way, at Denderah. In the Great Hall, the cartouches of Augustus, Tiberius, Caligula, Claudius and Nero perfectly illustrate the emperors' concern to attract the blessings of the Mother Goddess. Even Cleopatra, who had herself represented in the form of Isis, but with her own portrait, in order to receive all the benefits granted to her by Osiris, including four children.

But on that first visit, with the doctor and the guide, I recorded several essential facts:

— Only nine of the twelve crypts discovered were engraved with hieroglyphs, while the other three were more like cellars with bare walls, used to store goods.

— Test pits in the foundations of the temple showed that stones carved or sculpted earlier to build the demolished older temples had been used to ensure the solidity of the foundations. Even inside the current building, as in the ceiling of the south staircase, there are massive sandstone stones from the construction dating back to the 12th dynasty, i.e. two millennia earlier. In other places, figurations show kings of the 6th Dynasty bringing offerings to the good goddess Hathor, gifts that were kept in the crypt specially dedicated to Isis. The same was true of Thutmes III, who brought his tribute of gold to the Divine Triad, which was stored in the Treasury Room before being taken to the subterranean passages leading to the Golden Circle, where it was placed under the protection of Ptah and put to its proper use. I had plenty more to rebel against on this visit!

- As for the orientation of the temple itself. Although this building was consecrated to Isis as the Lady of Heaven, and its "House of Life" taught astronomy and "Divine-Mathematical Combinations", the orientation of the building did not correspond with the data inscribed on the walls! At least, that's what the excavation and topographical survey specialists were saying and writing. In fact, the longitudinal axis of the great temple slopes 16° to the East, from true North, whereas the hieroglyphic texts not agree with this line, since in the chamber it is engraved as being to the North, it is due West. Elsewhere, and in three different places on the walls of another room, it is given as being to the south, whereas today it is to the west.

The second thing I found incomprehensible was, once again, the ignorance of those responsible for deciphering the texts. I've tried to set the record straight, because all they've done is put forward mindless hypotheses to explain the lack of 'intelligence' of the architects and developers of Antiquity. Yet the only logical explanation is perfectly understandable in terms of the phenomenon known as the "precession of the equinoxes", which causes the earth to retrograde on its axis in space. The retreat of Denderah in relation true North was 50 arcseconds per year, or one degree every 72 years, i.e. $16 + 90 = 106°$.

This date is easy to find mathematically: $106° \times 72$ years $= 7,632$ years. If we subtract about 2,100 years from the date of Ptolemy XIII's dedication, this left an anteriority that made the neophyte that I was dizzy, since I obtained $7,632 - 2,100 = 5,532$ years! It was then that the guide told me about some documents in the Cairo museum that referred to King Khufu u[21], who had ordered the third reconstruction of Denderah, providing his royal architect with plans written on gazelle skin and dating back to the "Followers of Horus". This was how I heard for the first time about these predynastic kings, who arrived on the banks of the Nile around the sixth millennium BC and who also

---

[21] This is King Khufu of Dynasty IV, whose full details are given in A-3.

built a Golden Circle, which, if the guide was to be believed during this first visit, has now disappeared.

Needless to say, the doctor began to take a serious interest in Denderah and became as feverish as I was. But I had not yet reached the end of my surprises, and my astonishment was great when I reached the high terrace, where *the copy* of the planisphere taken to Paris more than a century and a half earlier stood. Although it had been darkened, like the rest of the ceiling, by the deposit of candle grease and black smoke, it was nonetheless the great enigma and the Mecca of this temple, still considered to be the most sacred place and the repository of all the secrets of Isis!

That was the day I learned that the original was in the Louvre Museum, where it had been brought by a Frenchman. Since for 150 years it had always been Egyptologists from our country who excavated at Denderah, all the fellahs and assistants working at the temple spoke our language to a greater or lesser extent, which was perfectly the case with our mentor. Although he did not know Mariette-Bey in person, he worked closely with M. Chassinat, whose main preoccupation was to write an enormous multi-volume work on Dendera for the I.F.A.O., which would be the most complete transcription to date .[22] But the origin of the temple, the reasons for those that preceded it, the significance of this "Zodiac" and of the rectangular one painted in the Hypostyle Hall, did not seem to move him. And as the Egyptologist was in France at the time of our visit, I was unable to find out why this lack curiosity. But I did soak up as much as I could of this monument, which seemed to hypnotise me and command me to decipher it by any means necessary.

As I have explained at length in other texts ,[23] let's just say that it unquestionably reproduces the sky chart of a specific day in the past. All twelve constellations are represented, with Leo as the pilot. In fact, it is symbolised by the king of animals, majestically standing on a boat. The woman representing the next constellation, in this case Virgo, holds his tail, and so on down to Cancer, which is set back above Leo,

---

[22] This work, entitled *Dendérah*, now comprises 8 volumes, the last two of which are the work of Mr François Daumas, who continued Mr Chassinat's work after his death.

[23] Particularly in A-l, and especially D-l, which presents the figures of all the tentyrite calendars.

even though it is the last of the twelve. In this way, the image is not a perfect circle, but rather a spiral, so as to speak more clearly to the eye. Leo is therefore the most important constellation in the zodiac, since it marks the beginning of a new time and a new era. Every detail counts here, and you need to be a keen astronomer to decipher each celestial ideogram.

As many works had been written on this subject, I later immersed myself in these readings in order to get a general idea of the subject and to undertake my personal research. Here again, the Jesuit library in Chantilly saved me a lot of time, as all the specialist works were on site, including the astonishing work by Jean-Baptiste Biot, entitled "Recherches sur plusieurs points de l'astronomie égyptienne, appliquées aux monuments astronomiques trouvés en Égypte" (Research into several points of Egyptian astronomy, applied to astronomical monuments found in Egypt). It was published in 1823 and caused a sensation, because its author was no unknown eccentric! His titles included: member of the Académie des Sciences, astronomer at the Bureau des Longitudes, professor of mathematics at the Collège de France, professor of experimental physics at the Faculté des Sciences in Paris, member of the Academies of St Petersburg, London, Stockholm, Berlin, etc. So this was clearly no longer just a bit of fun, or a pastime designed to get people talking unnecessarily about the Denderah "Zodiac".

Although I was still unfamiliar with this fascinating work, it was with our minds in turmoil, and somewhat stunned, that we went back down to the lower rooms, where the beautiful face of Isis, with the graceful, peaceful smile reproduced on the 24 pillars, encouraged me with its thousand facets to regain my composure.

This was how I came to know the first version of the Divine Triad: Osiris, Isis and their son Horus, who was venerated first in this temple in the person of Isis, with two other nearby buildings worshipping Osiris at Esne and Horus at Edfu. The Mother Goddess of a Thousand Names, Isis, received the relics of her husband and son on the occasion of the great religious festivals, making Denderah the most sacred initiatory temple of all, and as our guide showed us in a room the scene dedicated to the resurrection of Osiris reborn to teach future generations, my astonishment was great! After all, even if the was denied to be ancient, it was built at least a century before the birth of Jesus! Now, there was all the symbolism engraved in hieroglyphics of the Holy Trinity and the resurrection of Christ... not to mention the symbol of the cross inherent in the Pharaonic annealed cross, or cross-of-life, which I didn't learn about in detail until later!

This was not the time to dwell on this resemblance, which was striking, to say the least, from the outset. It still took me several more or less hasty trips, depending on the free time I had between my teaching courses, to get a general idea of the conception of this original monotheism in the history of Egypt, which soon became the object of all my preoccupations.

Alas, I kept coming across increasingly absurd hieroglyphic 'translations' on every page of the books I read. Having seen the monuments in situ, it was impossible for me to believe in this idolatrous polytheism, described at length and in grotesque detail, as if to emphasise the savagery of this Pharaonic people, whose greatness was not denied by any of the authors.

From all my reading, two parallel paths took shape. The first concerned texts relating to the adoration and veneration of Ptah by an entire people, of whom Usir (Osiris) was the Son. The other had Ra, or Amon-Ra, as the promoter of nature, as reported by the Scribes of the descendants of Sit (Seth). Usir and Sit were half-brothers from the same mother, Nut, but from two different fathers, Ptah and Geb: Ptah and Geb.

To gain a deeper understanding of the original texts, I had to get hold of the main hieroglyphic dictionaries, as well as Champollion's grammar, which were the most essential works, or so I thought, to enable me to start again a more logical path. But this was very difficult, because all these works were almost impossible to find in the shops. The only place I could have consulted them was the Bibliothèque nationale in Paris, but it wasn't easily accessible.

As if by a miraculous 'chance', while talking to some ecclesiastics about the work to which I now wished to devote myself completely, one of them pointed out to me the 'Les Fontaines' cultural centre in Chantilly, which received researchers and which would welcome me. As soon as I was accepted, I realised how lucky I'd been! But was it just a coincidence? Not only were the books I needed right there within my reach, but there was also a complete copy of the "Description de l'Égypte", a monumental work by Bonaparte's Scientific Commission. There were also many works about Denderah and Champollion, including several books that undoubtedly gave me a better idea of the personality of the 'decipherer' of hieroglyphs, such as 'Les Lettres inédites de Champollion le Jeune à son frère', published by the Marquis de Brière in 1842, which show, among other things, that the great scholar did not become a genius until the age of seventeen, when he became interested in oriental archaeology, which, thanks to his work, later became the foundation of Egyptology.

As "Les Fontaines" was a large hotel complex with 140 rooms a long way from the imposing library in the shape of a blockhouse, the Jesuit fathers agreed to convert my small living quarters into an annex to the study room. They put up shelves and I was able to have at my disposal, without moving from my room, day or night, all the books I needed, which, it has to be said, were in very short supply in a place where spirituality was the focus of most studies.

I was delighted to immerse myself in the study of the 'dictionaries' as a first step. I was very surprised, because none of the five serious works gave the same meaning to the same ideogram. I had Brugsch's *German Dictionary* in particular, in 3 volumes, two English, one French and one German. When I looked up an ideogram indicating the colour black in one, for example, it was red in another, or green in a third! And even in this case, all three spoke of the idea of a colour, which was not the case for other hieroglyphs.

So I had to start again in a different direction. Since Champollion was responsible for the discovery of the alphabet and the 'understanding' of the Sacred Language, I set about trying to pinpoint the reason for such differences, which made any real reading of hieroglyphics impossible. I was astonished to discover that our French scholar had died young, having left his work unfinished; it was published by his brother, who took the name Champollion-Figeac for the purpose. Some archaeologists of the time seized on the 'results' to create an Egyptology for their own use, which would allow them to launch themselves boldly into a science they had no mastery of. I'm not the one to say this, but a number of scholars and luminaries of the time were sounding the alarm. Monseigneur Affre, Archbishop of Paris, wrote a letter to the Académie to draw the attention of its honoured members to the way in which "certain Orientalists were using the work of the late Champollion to create a science that no one would understand, and with the sole aim of obtaining chairs in Egyptology at 5,000 pounds a year"!

In more diplomatic terms, because he was a foreigner and a member of the Moscow Academy of Sciences, Alexis de Goulianof wrote at the same time, in 1839, in his book *Les Éléments de la Langue Sacrée des Égyptiens (Elements of the Sacred Language of the Egyptians):*

"The vagueness with which the French scholar M. Champollion left the elements of his doctrine must, of necessity, have thrown archaeologists into the field of more or less arbitrary hypotheses and, in a way, authorised them to substitute their opinion for the equivocal data of the founder of the theory".

What had actually happened in this conception of hieroglyphics? In any case, no one had understood anything about the original concept of the ideographic writing of this divine language of the Origin. Champollion was close to achieving this when he died prematurely.

Let's take a brief look at the history of Champollion's 'discovery' and the process that led him to create his *Alphabet of Hieroglyphic Phonetic Letters* from scratch.

The "Rosetta Stone", found by Bonaparte's engineers, was written in three languages: Greek, Demotic or the popular ancient Egyptian language, and hieroglyphic, the sacred language of the Pharaonic priests. In the Greek part, the name Ptolemy was repeated three times, and in the hieroglyphic part, three sets of ideographs were enclosed in an oval, which gave Champollion the idea that the contents of these "cartouches" meant "PTOLÉMÉE".

Consulting hundreds of copies of documents depicting cartouches, the scholar came across those of Cleopatra, taken from a bilingual obelisk at Philae. The P, T, O and L of Ptolemy were similar to those contained in the name "CLÉOPÂTRE". Based on this similarity, Champollion composed an alphabet. This is where the mistake lies, because it's just an approximate phonetisation that has nothing to do with the writing itself!

Another 'coincidence': while I was lost in conjecture about the nonsense I intuitively sensed in this abusive alphabetisation, which was not to be found in any dictionary, a distinguished Japanese arrived at the Jesuit Fathers' Centre. It was Mr Takeno, the rector of Sophia University in Tokyo, who had come to complete an important work on Pascal. This Catholic university in the Japanese capital has 40,000 students, so this gentleman occupied a very important position. His erudition was such that one day when we were having lunch at the same table, I spoke to him in detail about this hieroglyphic enigma, thinking that Japanese ideograms could help me. This was indeed the case, much to my delight. The example I used is very simple, but it will be clear to any reader, since it concerns the translation of the New Testament into Japanese.

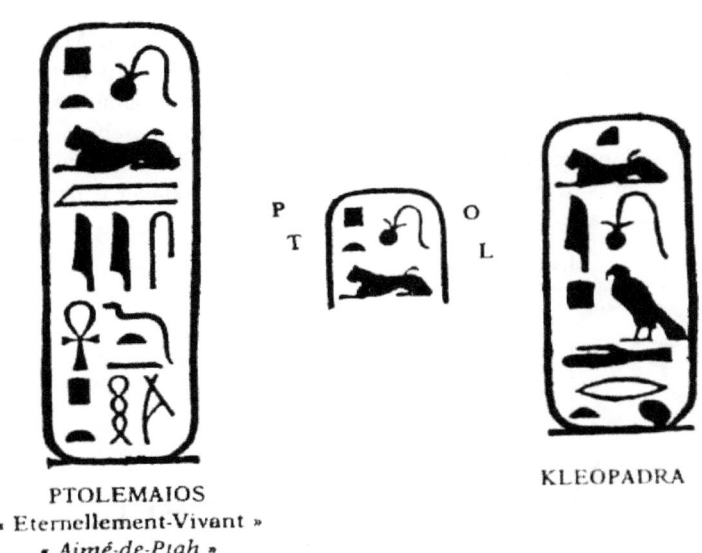

PTOLEMAIOS
« Eternellement-Vivant »
« Aimé-de-Ptah »

KLEOPADRA

Whether it was translated into this language from Greek, Aramaic or even French is of little importance, since Japanese names and surnames have no comparatives in these languages. When it came to translating, for example, the Blessed Virgin's first name: "Marie" or "Maria", not only was there no concordance in Japanese phonetics, but the "r" sound could not be rendered, or written, as its script did not exist! So we had to use a linguistic subterfuge, like hundreds of others in the process of being translated, and put together a hieroglyphic assembly of the most precarious kind, incomprehensible in Japanese, to obtain "Maria"!

Three characters phonetized an almost identical verbal consonance in the same category of sounds: "MA-LI-YA", so Malia is the closest phonetically to Maria, i.e. :

亞 利 瑪

But these three hieroglyphs do not in any way mean Malia in Japanese, because these three signs do not fit together! In fact, this heterogeneous assembly is only to phonetise a foreign name that has to be read out loud or pronounced softly, as if to oneself. And its pronunciation is no more important than its actual meaning. The only laudable aim is to make it sound similar when a foreigner is likely to listen with an attentive ear.

Apart from that, what did these Japanese ideograms mean?...

MA = JASPE

LI = BENEFICE

YA = DEUXIEME

These three characteristic sounds of a foreign first name, phonetising the Virgin of Nazareth, the Mother of Jesus, "Maria", can only strictly imitate, in Japanese, the European sounds to ensure the continuation of the reading of the sacred text! This means nothing other than an otherwise inexpressible whole, and especially not "Mary", since the three hieroglyphs, in Japanese, placed side by side, mean nothing. It is therefore patently impossible for them to become alphabetically: M, L and I.

For the record, I should add that with a mischievous smile the distinguished rector of Sophia University admitted to me that this phonetisation of Maliya had already been used to designate the name of a bloodthirsty tyrant of the 12th century, which made it a most amusing hieroglyphic anaglyph for Buddhist scholars!...

This is why a hieroglyphic translation based solely on the alphabet derived from the principles laid down by Champollion using the replacement sounds used in the royal and imperial Greco-Roman cartouches cannot mean anything sensible, especially as they were designed by priests of Ptah who could not admit these 'barbarian' invaders. Finally, it would be as if, today, we wanted to write in Latin words with meanings unknown two thousand years ago: Chips, electronics or television aerials! Only suggestive imagery would make it possible to retransmit an otherwise untranslatable meaning through any era!

The work Champollion carried out in the frenzy his thirties, just before his premature death, certainly did not have the logical conclusion it should have had. If he had lived just a few more months, the "translation of the cartouches" would really have turned into a solid and lasting work. For he had at his disposal a mass of original documents, alas now lost, which he himself had seen throughout the Ni l![24]

And, once again, I set off in search of a *logical* explanation of the meaning of the engraved texts, because nothing made sense! I had to understand... So I followed a new path: that of the ancient authors who had dealt with hieroglyphics! Sleeping very little, and with the precious books in my room, I absorbed Horapollon, Chérémon, the monk Tzétzés, Aristotle, Father Kircher, Clément d'Alexandrie, and a number of scholars from the first centuries who wrote about this subject with varying degrees of success.

Ceremon, the compiler of *Hieroglyphic Knowledge*, will go down in history as the first person to make public elements of what was called the "Sacred Language of the Egyptians". And this scholar knew what he was talking about, since he was not only one of the most assiduous hierogrammatists at the famous library of Alexandria, long before Julius Caesar, jealous, gave the order to burn it. Ceremon was also the guardian-preserver of the "Original Tradition", the one written on skin manuscripts, which was preciously preserved in the library of the

---

[24] See the important note at the end of this chapter about Champollion's dealings with the Holy Church during his lifetime, which are little known because of his political troubles.

Serapium of Alexandria, not in the Bruchium district, which was totally destroyed by the fire, but in the Rhacotis, where not a single house was affected by the disaster, and where all the documents therefore remained intact.

Unfortunately, only a few scattered snippets of the Greek translation of this work have survived. They were recounted by Latin authors, such as the Byzantine monk Tzétzés, in his book Aegytiaca. This is all the more regrettable given that this work was unique in the annals of history. The work carried out by Horapollon in the fifth century AD should not be counted among the serious works. His treatise entitled "Hieroglyphica" was rejected by all scholars as soon as it appeared, and it is a fact that an unbridled imagination governed its composition. Curiously, it was Champollion who rescued it from oblivion, citing it with great praise in reference to his own work! Our eminent French Egyptologist probably needed a guarantee to ensure that his personal discoveries would not be taken lightly.

In the hieroglyphic language of the Egyptians, the elementary geometric figures were the reduced forms of everything that exists on Earth, or not. They represented the prototypes of things that were significant in their essence. The belief was that these elements formed the basis of the primitive forms of Creation, expressing the Word for all measurable things, just as the Number expressed any quantity. The angle was a bent arm, a figurative expression of the servant; by extension, and in other figurative forms, it became an expression of inferiority or, on the contrary, of Divine Power as an instrument of vengeance.

Many French words have an identical analogy between geometric figures or numbers and ideas of a completely different order, such as circulation, circonvenir, circonspect; and also tort, travers, incliné... These terms are abstract words expressed using hieroglyphics, since they are much better translated by simple drawing.

The same applies to the eye, hand, arm, leg, mouth, head and all human organs. Animals and natural phenomena are also the source of a large number of comprehensible hieroglyphs. They formed the universal principles of things and beings.

The most striking example of this thesis is the "Treatise on Philosophy according to the Egyptians", attributed by specialists to Aristotle. In any case, whoever wrote it had a perfect knowledge of the sacred language of Egypt. We can read in particular:

"I am going to consider the universal or the intellectual, according to the spirit of those who taught, by mysterious figures and notes difficult to express; but to think is to form images. Man's thought is variable, depending on the nature of the spiritual and celestial objects or earthly objects whose forms it takes, becoming almost the same as them. If the forms in our soul were not similar to those of things, we would not know these things in truth, since the truth of a thing is the thing itself. But it is the true, invariable, intellectual forms that man must strive to attain, in order to assimilate to them his thoughts and his soul, raising him by this means alone to his origin."

It was this elevation of the soul, through the study of first causes, that was the goal sought by those who attempted initiation in the "Houses of Life" of Egypt. Although few were chosen, many tried the experiment and gained great wisdom from it. They learned to use geometric images to demonstrate the value of ideas and to formulate the highest thoughts, far better than the words of popular language could.

In the same treatise, Aristotle writes:

"The Egyptians, having known the spiritual forms, explained themselves by an intellectual doctrine superior to human methods. They engraved these sublime concepts in figures on the stone walls of their temples. They used the same method for all the sciences and arts, to indicate that the immaterial spirit had created everything according to the particular models of each being".

These figures explain how man measures the world according to the sacred texts. These are objects that imitate the elementary forms of human thought, forms that have their moulds in things, and that reproduce these moulds. They exist, these elementary forms, and it was in vain to search for a universal language of signs before having grasped these elements; just as it was in vain to search for an alphabet before having analysed the sounds that the characters represent.

From time immemorial, this hieroglyphic art has been the object of respectful consideration, for these images, curious in their strangeness, could only carry a celestial message: that of divine Science. Its symbolic meaning could only be mystical and initiatory, no one doubted it.

This means, firstly, that hieroglyphs have a highly spiritual, ideographic basis, and that for this major reason these signs are not comprehensible to the general public. This means, secondly and logically, that there was another popular script that could be read aloud and was therefore spoken. This is what was later called the demotic language. This suggests that hieroglyphics was simply a written language, designed to preserve the original Tradition.

Clement of Alexandria, who was one of the Fathers of the Church in the 3rd century AD, tried to put this writing back into use, so that the understanding of this religious iconography, engraved on the walls of all the temples of the Pharaohs, would not be lost. He sorted it and classified it, order by order, in his *Stromates*. This was the only valuable contribution since Ceremon that was preserved in the Greek text. As the most important passage has been commented on most of the time in Latin, it is a good idea remind readers of it here, in this excellent French translation by M. Letronne. Here is the gist of chapter four, in book five of Clement of Alexandria's *Stromata*, which Champollion would much later use to convince his detractors and arbitrarily extrapolate from it some parts that suited him, leaving in the shadows those that bothered him:

"Those Egyptians who received instruction first learned a type of Egyptian lettering called epistolographic, then hieratic, which was used by the hierogrammatists, and finally hieroglyphic. Hieroglyphics was of two kinds: one, cyriological, used the first alphabetical letters, the other was merely symbolic.

The symbolic method can be subdivided into several types: one represents all objects in their own right by imitation; the other expresses them tropically, or figuratively; the third expresses them entirely allegorically through certain enigmas.

In this way, if the Egyptians wanted to write the Sun, they would draw a circle; if they wanted to write the Moon, they would draw a crescent. In the tropical method, they changed and diverted the meaning of objects by analogy, expressing them by modifying their image or by subjecting it to various kinds of transformations.

This is how they used anaglyphs when they wanted to convey the praises of kings in the form of religious myths.

Here is an example of the third type of hieroglyphic writing using enigmatic allusions: the Egyptians represented the other stars by snakes, because of the obliquity of their course; but the Sun was represented by a beetle.

We should therefore stop here to explain the method described by Clement of Alexandria, which is beyond doubt, since it is this method that enabled me to direct the complete deciphering at Denderah towards its solution. There is no mistaking M. Letronne's translation, since Clement's intentions proved to be indisputably correct:

"This turn of phrase, using the first letter, was often used by the great Plato, who had brought it back from Egypt. We find it in his *Politics* on page 541, E; in *The Sophist* on page 176, D; and finally on about twenty occasions in *Theaetetus*, where this 'first' articulation was the same: 'primitive sound', 'primary element', 'first letter', etc."

The reality of what Clement said about this first letter is engraved on the walls of the temple of the Lady of Heaven at Denderah, in particular in the text so touching in its fervour, which is called "The Prayer of Isis". What is it about?

This temple at Denderah has preserved all the traditional texts in pure hieroglyphic, throughout the mists of time. It is the only monument built on the successive foundations of the five buildings that preceded it that has not yet been able to be listed in its entirety! The sacred engravings are several kilometres long if you put them end to end! The first of these texts is a fundamental prayer: that of the mistress of the place, Iset, or Isis, who obtained from God her husband's return to life through her intercessory prayer. This prayer is better known by the misleading name given to it by Egyptologists: "the litanies of Hathor". She is the mother of Horus, and therefore Isis, and not any other goddess.

In this engraving, the titles of the Lady of Heaven are arranged in groups, but they have the peculiarity of defining each group title by the same image, and therefore by the same first letter. If this concordance were merely an unimportant trompe-l'œil, it would not be repeated so consistently throughout this maze of rooms dedicated to the Lady of Heaven! There is too much subtlety in all these figuratives for it not to be indisputable that a system of alliteration presides over the understanding of hieroglyphics! He even went so far in his research that almost every word begins with the same first letter to provide the complete alphabet. The usefulness of such an organisation is obvious, especially as it also provides the meaning of certain divine consonances, which explains the term "anaglyph" put forward by Clement of Alexandria, meaning "hieroglyph with a double meaning".

This would undoubtedly be a good subject for a dissertation! But the problem here is different, because the passage from the *Stromata* that immediately follows shows that hieroglyphic writing is one of the processes used to preserve the very spirit of the symbolic form. Here are some typical examples, such as the first, which, one way or the other, indicates how the text should be read:

What we need to understand is that the *Stromata* form a work that deals with the Christian faith, and that just before this chapter on hieroglyphics, this father of the Church spoke of the difference between the order of faith and that which nourished science. Clement endeavoured to show that the former was strict and independent, whereas the latter attached mysteries to the sacred dogmas, which, for the ancient Egyptians, were merely objects of faith and above all a means of expressing thought.

This divine means expressed by the becomes in hieroglyphic: movement, form, geometry, mathematics: THE NUMBER!...

It was therefore appropriate that my research should turn directly to the mathematical papyri, the importance of which I had already glimpsed when preparing my thesis on Pythagoras. Thus, with all my computer logic, I was able to transcribe two-thirds of the ideograms of calculation in their hieroglyphic epistolary context. This will be developed at length in D-2.

With renewed passion, I worked day and night, encouraged by the fathers, despite major differences of opinion on matters faith and dogma. Eleven months later, the manuscript of the first volume of a long series to be called *L'Éternité n'appartient qu'à Dieu* was ready for publication. At the end of 1976, *Le Grand Cataclysme* appeared in all the bookshops, cut down by a good half because it was too voluminous, but perfectly understandable in this form. This gave me a bit of time, not to take a breath, but to plunge with delight into the study of Tentyrite monotheism, its Law of Creation, and the Divine-Mathematical Combinations that govern and regulate it...

NOTE ON THE BURNING OF A BOOK BY CHAMPOLLION

The autodafé of a studious youth includes this sad and little-known page. In 1812, Champollion published a small folio in Grenoble that became all the rarer because its author quickly withdrew it from circulation in order to burn all possible copies! It was entitled *De l'écriture des Anciens Égyptiens*. This little masterpiece disappeared from booksellers' shelves just a few months after it was published, on the pretext that "it might offend the pious"!

This argument stemmed from the fact that Champollion dated the Pharaonic dynasties to the year 5285 BC, i.e. before the presumed birth of Adam. In 1815, the Holy Church dated the birth of Adam to just 5,000 years before Christ and the appearance of the Earth a thousand years before that! So, on pain of being excommunicated and reduced to starvation, he was obliged to burn this writing and make an act of contrition.

It was only by chance, having found a copy at the Jesuit college in Cairo, that the essential passage jumped out at me, because it contradicted without reply the essential data defended by the Church at the time.

As soon as there was no longer any apparent trace of this "youthful fault, forgivable all things considered", everything returned to the liturgical bosom of the Holy Church.

This allowed Abbé Ancessy, in the foreword to his book *L'Exode et la traversée de la Mer Rouge (The Exodus and the Crossing of the Red Sea)*, to quote Champollion's letter in full, in which he burns himself to death in order to survive his text, indicating that the first Pharaonic king dates back to 5285 BC.

Here are *the full text* the memo and letter.

Here is the remarkable letter Champollion wrote in 1827 on the agreement of his discoveries with the Bible; the students he made, and who continue his work, should always have this remarkable statement before their eyes:

> *Paris, 23 May 1827, To Monseigneur Testa, at the palace of Monte Cavallo.*
>
> *My Lord,*
>
> *It was only a few days ago that I received the kind letter you wrote me at the beginning of this year: like the children of Israel, it wandered from office to office for more than four months, and finally arrived, to my great satisfaction. I*

am very grateful to you for preserving for me the feelings of affection which you were pleased to me during my stay in Rome. And I value it all the more because you will always find in me the most respectful and devoted attachment. Thank you for your interest in my studies: they are progressing and consolidating. In a few days' time I shall have the honour of sending you a brochure containing a summary of my historical and chronological discoveries. It is a summary of the dates on which all the existing monuments in Egypt are dated and on which the true Egyptian chronology must henceforth be based.

Messrs de San Quintino and Lanci will find therein a peremptory reply to their calumnies, since I demonstrate that no Egyptian monument really predates the year 2200 BC. This is certainly a very high antiquity, but it offers nothing contrary to the sacred traditions, *and I would even dare to say that it confirms them on every point; it is, in fact, by adopting the chronology and the succession kings given by the Egyptian monuments that Egyptian history agrees admirably with the Holy Books, Thus, for example: Abraham arrived in Egypt around 1900, that is to say under the* Shepherd Kings. *It is also under a shepherd king that Joseph is minister in Egypt and establishes his brothers there, which could not have taken place under kings of Egyptian race, The head of the dynasty of Diospolitains, known as XVIIIe, it is* Rex no vus *which ignored* Joseph *of the Holy Scripture, which being of Egyptian race was not to know Joseph, minister of the usurping kings; he is the one who reduced the Hebrews to slavery. The captivity lasted as long as the eighteenth dynasty, and it was under Ramses V or Amenophis, at the beginning of the fifteenth century, that Moyse delivered the Hebrews. This happened in the adolescence of Sesostris, who immediately succeeded his father and made his conquests in Asia while Moyse and Israel wandered for forty years in the desert.* This is why the Holy Books should not speak of this great conqueror. *All the other kings of Egypt named in the Bible are to be found in Egyptian monuments, in the same order of succession and at the precise times when the Holy Books place them. I would even add that the Bible writes their real names better than Greek historians did. I would be curious to know what those who have maliciously argued that Egyptian studies tend to alter the belief in the historical documents provided by the Books of Moyse will have to reply. On the contrary, the application of my discovery invincibly supports them. Please accept, Your Excellency, the renewed assurance of my tender and respectful attachment.*

J.-F. Champollion.

No one can say what he would do in such an alternative: have to burn a work that is known to be accurate; or lose his job and any possibility of continuing his research in Egypt and his fascinating work as the pioneer of a new science! Galileo had tried his hand at this many decades before, when discussing the rotundity of the Earth revolving around the Sun...

May the Church understand in time that it is useless to pretend not to believe in the Law of Creation as the Divine-Mathematical Combinations demonstrate it to exist tangibly.

11

THE AGE OF TAURUS IN ATH-KÂ-PTAH

His mother Nut stretches out her hands to greet him, saying:
- The Imperishables adore you and invoke you: Hail to you, O Celestial Bull!
You rise from the ocean of sky to come to the rescue of your cadets.
A. Scharff (Aegy ptische Sonnenlieder)

If some day, a man of talent combines astronomical knowledge with the erudition of antiquity, this man will teach his century many things that the vanity of ours does suspect.
François de Volney (*Journey to Egypt*, 1787)

From the mass of documents compiled, both in Egypt and in several French and foreign libraries, there was another question that required a precise answer: the date of the beginning of the 1st pharaonic dynasty. There is such a divergence of views on this vital question among all eminent Egyptologists that, as in the case of hieroglyphics, I had to carry out my own research, based solely on an astronomical calendar, since Têta, the famous Thoth, or Athothis, claimed in the annals of his time to have re-established the calendrical era by starting on the day of the conjunction of Sirius and the Sun. Here, as in all the above, fortunate 'coincidences' meant that my mathematical training was able to solve this tricky problem. The last known and recorded celestial configuration of this importance occurred on 21 July 139 AD .[25]

From this precise date, going back in time, there were four mathematically and astronomically valid possibilities before Jesus Christ: 1322 -2783 -4244 and 5705. It seems that only the sight of ruined buildings, and the chronology established by the Holy Church, inspired the researchers, as no account was taken of the above-

---

[25] This precise date is explained in note 1 at the end of this book.

mentioned dates. Despite certain attempts to get out of the rut, astronomy was left to one side, with ancient and modern Egyptologists stating presumed dates that had nothing to do with the motivation announced by the Sacred Texts, namely the advent of the Celestial Bull and the Sothian Year, i.e. :

Champollion	5867	avant J.-C.
Lesieur	5773	– –
Bœckh	5702	– –
Africanus	5619	– –
Pochant	5558	– –
Sir Flinders Petrie	5546	– –
Hensy	5303	– –
Lenormant	5124	– –
Mariette et Maspero (selon Manéthon)	5004	– –
de Saulcy	4717	– –
Brugsch	4455	– –
Meyer	4244	– –
Borchardt	4186	– –
Lepsius	3892	– –
de Bunsen	3623	– –
Weigall	3407	– –
Moret	3315	– –
Junker	3300	– –
Leclant	3000	environ avant J.-C.

As is easy to see, the window of opportunity is enormous, since the difference between the longest chronology and the shortest is almost 3,000 years! This is obviously just a small sample of the many scholars who have worked on the Egyptian annals to compile their chronology. Today, there are still two chronological schools of thought among Egyptologists, of which the official one is shorter. It is this school that is represented by J. Leclant, the famous translator of the "Texts of the Pyramids", the last in the above list.

The tragedy for all these scholars, whose erudition I am in no way questioning, but whose patent illogic I am, is that once and for all, for them, everything prior to 3000 BC is prehistory and not history. Now, while this concept is accurate for the country that was Gaul later on, it is absolutely not so for the banks of the Nile! A typical example can be found in the introduction to the otherwise remarkable book by Drioton and Vandier, *L'Égypte* :

"For a long time, following Ed. Meyer, Egyptologists had accepted that the Egyptian calendar had been instituted *at the height of the Enaeolithic period*, between 4245 and 4242. It had been assumed that this institution could only have been created at the beginning of a sothic period and, as the calendar certainly existed in 2785-2782, it had been concluded that its creation had to be dated back to the preceding sothic period, *i.e. in the middle of prehistory*. Neugebauer (Acta orientalia) was the first to argue against this view, demonstrating that the scientific knowledge of the Egyptians *of the Enéolithic period* was certainly too rudimentary for them, at such an early stage of civilisation, to have created a year of three hundred and sixty-five days based exclusively on the observation of the Sothian revolution.

I have italicised the three passages to emphasise the comments made by the two authors, which are intended to distort the reality of a specific fact. For if it was the *Enéolithic period* in France, it had not been for two millennia in Egypt! Similarly, for "and therefore in the middle of prehistory", we should have added "on the banks of the Seine, but not those of the Nile".

But here again we come up against the fact that M. Drioton was a canon and that a certain conception of antiquity prevailed.

As has already been said, since the biblical texts announce the birth of Adam five millennia before our era, it was difficult to start the chronology of the Pharaonic kings before the birth of the first man! However, certain prelates of the Catholic Church in the 19th century had their doubts, such as Monsignor Meigrant, Bishop of Chalons, who wrote in a work that was revolutionary for its time, *Le monde et l'homme primitif* (*The World and Primitive Man*), published in 1869:

We must admit, however, that the conclusions reached by the Egyptologists who enjoy great authority in France and Germany - Lepsius, Bunsen, Brugsch, Boeckh - are not entirely in line with the figures for the years recorded in the Bible from Adam to Abraham.

Even those cited by the venerable bishop were, apart from Boeckh, in the middle range! But Maspero and Mariette, who followed Manetho's chronology, are not even worthy of the slightest interest. Yet Auguste Mariette, who at the same time was continuing his research at Dendera, had just published an "Abrégé de l'histoire ancienne de l'Égypte" in 1867, in which he shared his thoughts on the subject, simply by looking at the buildings.

"There is no one who is not struck by the enormous total years to which the addition of the dynasties brings us with Manetho. Through the list of the Egyptian priest, we go back to times that are considered mythical among all other peoples, but which here are certainly already history.

Once again, I had to untangle the particularly tangled skein of the chronology on my own, in order to get off on a solid footing! So the easiest thing to do was to start by delimiting each of the astronomical , then calculate their components and their relationship with the year of Sirius, without worrying about what had been said or written previously. Only then would I attempt to place mathematically the beginning of the Era of the Bull, the cornerstone that would truly enable us to know the date of birth of Ath-Kâ-Ptah, the 'Second Heart-Of-God', protected by Osiris, who became the Bull Celest e.[26]

Once again, good fortune smiled upon me, for among the books I had read a few months earlier about Morocco was M. de Morgan's remarkable study on the origin of peoples. This eminent scholar had just returned from a mission to the Caucasus and left in 1892 as Director of Antiquities in Cairo, although he was by no means an Egyptologist. It was he who, using his own methods, took up the study of Pharaonic prehistory Mariette, in disagreement with the rest of his colleagues, had left off. This book fascinated me, because it called into question the chronological canon of the Bible, from which the main extract below is significant:

> "*I gathered together all the scattered documents, searched in a large number of localities, and bought almost all the flint implements that were to be found in the shops. Thus, little by little, I have come to believe that, while it is possible to admit that some carved flints belong to the historical period, we must attribute to most of them a much more remote antiquity and that the evidence of the true Neolithic age is more abundant in the Nile Valley than is generally thought.*

Jacques de Morgan's precise research culminated in the fabulous discovery of pre-dynastic tombs at Nebadah, *just outside Dendera*, to such an extent that the scholar thought he had arrived at the necropolis of Menes, the first king of the First Dynasty. In fact, the tombs were much earlier than this, which put the antiquity of Egypt back at least

---

[26] To fully understand the exceptional phenomenon of Osiris's resurrection thanks to the Bull's skin in which he was imprisoned and left for dead, it is worth reading or re-reading *The Great Cataclysm*.

another thousand years to the birth of Menes! Near this cemetery, where the mummified bodies had their jewellery and the walls were covered with tricoloured hieroglyphs (white, black and ochre, the only natural colours in those remote times), skeletons were found in the sand, next to which were stone tools. So it had to be admitted that a different indigenous race was living there in those remote times, close by and in good neighbourly relations with a civilisation at the highest stage of Knowledge!

So I had to tackle the era of Taurus and the advent of Menes, before focusing on the Sothian year, that of our own Sirius.

Computer calculations of the different eras give the date of the day of the Great Cataclysm as July 9792 BC. The different stellar positions show that the retrograde left the Sun in Leo for 1,440 years before moving on to Cancer, then Gemini, and finally Taurus.

The size of the constellations was never 30°, as in the astrology of many people after Egyptian astronomy. They were delimited in the sky as follows, just as they are in the Golden Circle:

Vierge et Lion	36°	2 592 années	× 2 =	5 184 années
Cancer et Gémeaux	26°	1 872	× 2 =	3 744
Taureau et Bélier	32°	2 304	× 2 =	4 608
Poissons et Verseau	28°	2 016	× 2 =	4 032
Sagittaire et Capricorne	34°	2 448	× 2 =	4 896
Scorpion et Balance	24°	1 728	× 2 =	2 456
La Grande Année précessionnelle				25 920 années

The rest is simply a matter of elementary arithmetic. From the 9,792, we need to subtract 1,440 years from the retrograde solar passage in front of the constellation Leo, then 1,872 in front of Cancer, then 1,872 in front of Gemini, before entering backwards into "Celestial Taurus", i.e. :

1,440 + 1,872 + 1,872 = 5,188 years.

This left him to enter the constellation of Taurus:

9,792 - 5,188 = 4,604 years.

The Age of the Celestial Bull therefore began in 4604 . It was at this point that the fratricidal battles between the descendants of Set and Horus intensified, with the definitive supremacy of one clan or the other only possible with the arrival of the Lady of Heaven at the celestial reunion with her husband. Now, mathematically, the next start of a Sothian year was 4241, meaning that there remained 4,604 - 4,241 = 263 solar revolutions to achieve unification under one sceptre.

These lengths of time always ruffle the feathers of some readers who pride themselves on logic, because from our revolution in 1789 to the present day, *it's not even two centuries*, and yet, historically speaking, it seems such a long time ago!

And therein lies the good logic, for the science and consciousness of the ancient Egyptians go beyond the stages of understanding of our intelligence, which is limited to a single objective: living well on Earth. In those days, life on earth lasted just 72 years, a mere second of eternity compared to the afterlife! And if we were to approach eternity properly, we needed to know how it worked and every little thing about it, in order to comply with the rigour of its commandments.

So it wasn't simply the flooding of the Nile, as some Egyptologists have claimed, that caused the normal year to begin on the 1st of the month of Thoth, but the annual Sothian sunrise on the horizon.

At dawn on July 20, in the sky above the temple observatory at Denderah, Sirius appeared in the east after a 72-day occultation due to its annual conjunction with the Sun. What we also need to understand is that Sirius, while apparently a fixed star, has a movement of its own. We now know that two stars, A and B, invisible because they are small and in the shadow of Sirius, greatly disrupt its orbit. But the ancients were aware of the specific radiation emanating from , which "coincided", on the one hand, with the annual shift of 6 hours in its first appearance compared with the previous year, and which "coincided", on the other hand, with the beginning of the flooding of the Nile.

And Denderah was particularly well situated for observing the various celestial phenomena. Many non-eyptologists have described them at length. Jean-Baptiste Biot, a member of the Académie des Sciences, professor of mathematical physics at the Collège de France and astronomer at the Bureau des Longitudes, was one of them. Of the two hundred or so papers written on this exceptional monument by various academies around the world, J.-B. Biot's paper, published in 1823, was one of the most listened to and most disputed by Egyptologists and churchmen, of course!

His description of Denderah, in order to make his colleagues at the Academy understand the true antiquity of this moment, deserves to be reported here, because after having seen it many times on the spot, I could not do better:

"It is not, in fact, an arbitrary conjecture that I dare to submit here on the monument of Denderah, nor a new assessment of its antiquity based on the more or less free interpretation of the emblems or mobile astronomical signs that it presents. It is an attempt at a rigorous restitution of meaning, concluded by geometric measurements taken on the monument itself, by virtue of which each star reappears in its place in the emblem that contains it. The star of Leo, the star of Taurus within Taurus, Orion within Orion, Aquarius within Aquarius, and so on with all the others, not only in relative direction, but in absolute position and distance in the fairly numerous cases where positions and distances are specially marked.

Can you imagine anything that looks more like an observatory, with a celestial map carved next to it? And whatever the purpose of the observations, even if they were supposed to have been astrological constructions or determinations of religious epochs, rather than the actual study of astronomy as a science, it was always necessary for the sculpted painting to indicate, with sufficient fidelity, the relationships between the simultaneous positions of the various stars, to which it had been possible to add, either with the help of emblematic figures or by using characters that we no longer know how to read, the explanation of the astrological, civil or religious consequences that had to be inferred from them. These reflections, while confirming in a general way the astronomical nature of the monument, show us that, in order to interpret it in a truly scientific way, we must first discern among the figures that cover it, those, or at least some of those which can probably be considered to be placed in a real situation, and those which are merely emblematic signs of usage, or of phenomena peculiar to certain periods of the annual period, to which, at first glance, the twelve signs of the zodiac appear to relate. "

Thus, a calculation based on a Divine-Mathematical Combination found its very particular use with the "Year of God" comprising 1461 solar years. The shift of one leap day was found at the time of the exact conjunction of the Sun and Sirius, by adding 365 extra days to the 1460 years: those of the "New Year" celebration.

These formal dates are 139 AD, 1322 -2783 -4244 and 5705 BC. Since the Manethonian list has been restored in its entirety with the duration of each reign, as printed at the end of the third volume of the

Trilogy of the Past, the only possible date is the one recommended by E. Meyer a hundred years ago, and which Canon Drioton did not want to hear at all: 4244 BC! What's more, this is the only date that coincides with the entry of the Sun into Taurus. The entire Denderah complex bears witness to this, and not just the Zodiac, as J.-B. Biot suggested. But neither he, nor Drioton, nor Vandier, nor even Mariette had an even more complete view, encompassing the high terrace, the rectangular zodiac, the texts in the caches on level 1 and those in the crypts, where all the hieroglyphics took on their most combinatorial mathematical meaning! To enter the Golden Circle, it was necessary not to begin studying the Divine-Mathematical Combinations, but to possess them in their entirety: to have gone through all the degrees of initiation, as we would say today. And if you haven't studied all this original teaching in the distant past, you need to study again everything about the Sacred Language that has been transcribed into Greek, such as the books of Horapollon, for example, which explain the symbolism of drawings and shapes. This opens up new horizons for understanding the planisphere and its astronomical data, as J.-B. Biot has so clearly seen.

In his first book, *Comment les Égyptiens figurent un cœur*, Horapollon describes the 36th hieroglyph as follows:

"When they want to indicate a heart, they paint an ibis, an animal dedicated to Mercury, the regulator of the heart and reason, because the ibis itself is largely similar to a heart.

There seems to me to be no doubt about the meaning of this interpretation: when the ibis lowers its neck to its chest or hides it under its wings, the tips of the wings protruding from both sides of its ovoid body form a shape absolutely similar to that of a heart.

In the same way, in the beginning, Theta, or Theoth, personified the emblem of Egypt, Ath-Kâ-Ptah, or the "Second Heart of God", with a cup full of smouldering embers surmounted by this heart to symbolise the second heart rising from its own ashes.

It is a similarly hieroglyphised heart that is located at the precise point of the stellar groups visible to the naked eye, which form the "Belt of Twelve". Without a doubt, each of the hearts represents the Sun of each of the constellations, such as Regulus of Leo, Antares of Scorpio or Aldebaran of Taurus, as we call them , within their respective celestial configuration. Each of these positions is meticulously annotated and followed throughout its navigation during a Year of God, in relation to the sothic position. This year was also known as the 'Year of the Dog', or 'Canicular Year' by the Greeks. In fact, this is where the homonymy of the word torrid with canicular comes from, to designate the heat of the month of August that heralded the start of the Sothian year.

Texts do exist that make the link with this antiquity so remote that scholars continue to make it seem mythical. Notably in folio 154 of the original manuscript 2390 in the Bibliothèque nationale, which consists of a mathematical rule copied by Theon of Alexandria, obviously in Greek. It is entitled 'Rule for the Heliacal Rising of the Dog':

"For example, if we want to obtain the time of the rising of the Dog for the hundredth year of Diocletian, we first count the years elapsed from Menophres to the end of Augustus: they add up to 1,605; and adding to them, from the beginning of Diocletian, 100 years, we have a total of 1,705. From this total, we take the quarter, which is 426; to which, adding 5 days, we have 431. From this, we subtract the number of tetraetherides that had elapsed, i.e. 102, leaving 21 (years). The remainder is 329 days. Divide this number, starting from Thoth, taking 30 days for each month, and you find the rising of the Dog on the 29th epiphi of the Diocletian year. Do the same for any other given period.

This very specific example of a calculation using Sirius as the object deserves to be discussed at length, but this will be done in a separate note .[27] The point here was to show, and demonstrate, how easy it is to calculate a date, even if it is two millennia ago, as in this case. But let's return to the Age of Taurus, which reached its apotheosis with the unification of Egypt on the precise date of the Sun-Sirius conjunction. Not only was Usir-Osiris resurrected once again in spirit as Ahâ the Elder, but he was glorified everywhere and in all things, so that no human being would ever again forget either the divine wrath or the redemption of humanity by this Son who had become the Celestial Taurus. Hence the hieroglyphic complexity of this subject, which is only apparent to our pragmatic minds, but which was literally self-evident, even to young children living at the time.

The Bull was called 'Hapy'. When Usir ascended heaven, the Milky Way, the Celestial River, also became Hapy. When the survivors

---

[27] See note 2 at the end of the book.

reached the banks of the Nile, the exact reflection of the Milky Way on Earth, it too became Hapy. Each of them symbolised by a hieroglyphic bull. It was from this Hapy that the Greeks made Apis... the ox! But the phonetisation is good. Hence a triple name with a single script for all three names. For the living, even infants, there was no difficulty in understanding the exact meaning of a sentence in its context. But for foreigners who had no priest to serve as translator, the enigma remained complete!

A typical example today would be a stick with a glowing tip and two red lines across it. In the underground, on the train, or in any other public place, even a child knows from this that smoking is banned! But in two thousand years' time, when has been forgotten, what will this sign with a red-striped smoking cigarette mean? Those who see this "hieroglyph" will no longer understand it; and God alone can say today what interpretation future "francologists" will make of it, if they ever exist!

But the most striking example of this deification of the bull as the earthly representation of Osiris comes from Saqqara, near Cairo. Since the first excavations carried out by A. Mariette and his team, which brought to light the Serapium, or rather the Necropolis of the Bulls, sixty-four grandiose tombs have been unearthed, telling the story of the Pharaohs not over a period of a few decades, but of several centuries.

So it was that whenever a bull died, not only were great festivities organised for its funeral, but thousands of young bulls from all over the country arrived in large formations at Saqqara, as is abundantly explained on several funerary sites. Below, the site of Beni-Hassan, where a scribe scrupulously notes the characteristics of each bull.

If I had one suggestion to make about the Age of the Bull, it's that the age-old tradition of the animal transformed into an idol, a living image of Osiris, goes back well before the time of the present Serapium. It is therefore highly likely that here too, buried in the sand *beneath the present-day necropolis of the bulls*, there is a much more ancient one. Saqqara is entirely covered in desert sand. To find Djoser's tomb, we had to dig down to a depth of 83 metres. It would be necessary to drill some thirty metres beneath the Serapium to find the ancient necropolis referred to in several texts.

But the essence of Usir's message, passed on to the Cadets of the new generations destined to grow and multiply in Ath-Ka-Ptah, during the celestial reign of Taurus, did not go down well, or was at the very least distorted and transformed. From the Second Dynasty onwards, this monotheism, rigorous and intangible in its Great Dogma, became a kind of zoolatry that had hitherto been reserved for those of Set. From the time of King Djoser and the Saqqara period with the 3rd and 4th Dynasties, the Per-Ahâ Followers of Horus felt obliged to introduce the bull as a living idol and object of worship mummifying it dead! And if, at first sight, it was difficult to realise the sacrilege committed against Ptah and his son Usir, what followed would greatly reveal what was in fact nothing more than a polytheism created for the use of Pharaoh alone, who had become a deity!

Here too, it would be easy to draw a corollary with our late Christianity, where the number of holy men, admittedly martyrs, but elevated to the rank of protective gods, make Jesus the basis of a Christianity that has become one thousand percent polytheistic, as will be seen in detail in book C-1, which will deal with its history. But perhaps it is appropriate, here as in ancient times, to have this multiplicity of deities in an attempt to keep the increasingly unbelieving people within the paths originally traced out by the Eternal Almighty. So it was that the Descendants of Thoth, Hermes Trismegistus thrice great, inspired fear of the Celestial Bull as soon as the calendar was reestablished in 4244 BC. Then, as this was no longer enough, it was necessary to create a feeling of insecurity in the soul, with a real fear of exemplary punishment for all disobedience. This is how it was during the two millennia of latent antagonism with the Rebels of Set, so that the One God could reign under the sole name of Ptah.

And so it was with the first temple of Dendera, dedicated in reality to Nut, the last queen of Ahâ-Men-Ptah, who was the mother of Osiris, of course, but also of Set and the twins Isis and Nephthys, so that unification under the sign of the Celestial Bull would not remain an empty word. And the hieroglyph for the sky was symbolised by Nut, bridging the gap between the sunken kingdom and the "Second Heart". Generations passed, as did the pharaohs, and the third reconstruction carried out by Khufu was dedicated to Isis, who unwittingly took the place of his mother from the 4th dynasty onwards. The "Divine Potter" was beginning to lose the clay needed for his modelling, as one of the Pontiffs remarked on the walls of his tomb on the Sacred Hill!

It was therefore on the pretext of making the monotheism of the Ancients more popular that no hesitation was shown in replacing the eternal language of the Word with a certain Word that was more colourful, full of subtle metaphors and double meanings, whose content and form, constantly evolving, became subversive. It was this compromise between Ptah-Un and the solar ram that allowed the great Pharaonic decadence to take hold at the end of this era of Taurus Celestia. It was relegated to the shadows and oblivion of the all-powerful Age of Aries, rising to its apogee with Sety I and the long line of Ramses. Thus was born Moses, whom God invested with the necessary authority to take with him to another Promised Land his oppressed people, made up of Jews and Egyptians combined .[28]

Although monotheism was no longer based on divine grace, it nevertheless had to retain its past integrity. The Golden Circle remains its materiality through the Law of Creation. It was in this Law that the sacred writings were to be safeguarded. The structure of the universe and the mechanism of the cogs that make it up amply demonstrate the indisputable authority of the Creator over all things and all beings.

---

[28] Read or reread B-1: *Moses the Egyptian.*

12

THE AGE OF ARIES: MOSES THE REBEL

For tending the flock is also a preparatory exercise for kingship for those who are to lead the herd of men, the first of all, just as hunting is for those whose natures are destined for war.
Philo of Alexandria (The Life of Moses)

The Egyptian shall not be an abomination to you, for you have been a sojourner in his land. The sons born to him in the third generation will have access to the assembly of Yahweh.
Old Testament (Deuteronomy, XXIII-8/9)

Nowhere in the world has Ath-Ka-Ptah enjoyed such longevity and historical stability in its monotheistic veneration. Century after century, millennium after millennium, dynasty after dynasty, whether Memphite, Theban, Saite Ethiopian, Hicksos or Ptolemaic, only Egypt survived as long as the cult of Ptah symbolised the country at the same time as its creation, which came from the unique Creator of everything it.

This indestructibility lasted for the duration of monotheistic belief. This is clearly demonstrated by the history of Egypt, which proves, if proof were needed, that the most advanced civilisations die of their impiety before any other consideration. This fundamental truth must be understood! And it was blatantly obvious at the time of Moses' birth, which brings us up to the 16th century BC.

The official chronology, known as the short chronology, differs here by only a century, although there is a change of dynasty. It gives the birth of Moses under Ramses II. Nowhere in the Bible is the name mentioned, only "Pharaoh". Secondly, if we accept the theory that this king died in the Red Sea, it cannot be any of the rulers of the 19th dynasty, since everything about their deaths is known. The same cannot be said of Pharaoh Thutmosis II, of the 18th dynasty, whose annals have deliberately disappeared and whose engraved texts have been hammered out.

The work on Moses the Egyptian explained how the reign of Amenophis I began in 1555, that of Thutmosis I in 1532, and that of Thutmosis II extended from 1520 to 1500, only to come to an abrupt end, which remains unexplained because it was erased from the tablets by Queen Hatshepsut, who succeeded her.

For a better understanding, here is this part of the chronology (below).

1500 is therefore the key date in the story of Moses, since it accurately dates the crossing of the Red Sea.

It is easy to date the event, always using astronomical reference points. All the errors made on this subject to this day stem from an attempt to interpret the texts of Manetho. According to this Sybarite priest, it was under a king of the 18th dynasty that the insurrection took place. Not just the Jews, of course, but all the fellahs too, oppressed by the usurpers. Yet it was Amosis who drove the Hyksos out of the country, and it was a Thutmosis who pursued Moses.

But the ancient Greek authors who compiled Manetho made several mistakes in these texts, as in so many other papyri! They transcribed Amenophis instead of Amosis, and, reading from left to right instead of vice versa, they placed Amenophis as the liberator of Moses, and Thutmosis as the pursuer of the Hyksos!

As a result, Theophilus and the African, evaluating a chronology by Manetho based on the enumeration transcribed by Flavius Josephus, embarked on calculations proving that, since this was impossible, it was rather Seti and Ramses of the 19th dynasty! This obviously distorted the biblical data compiled by the Fathers of the Church, who were forced to restrict the antiquity of times even further.

Noms HIÉROGLYPHIQUES	Noms GRECS	Durée Règne	Datation (avant J.-C.)	Fait marquant du REGNE
XVIII° DYNASTIE				
171	AMOSIS	25	1580-1555	Naissance de Moïse
172	AMENOPHIS I	23	1555-1532	Fut co-régent trois ans
173	THOUTMOSIS I	12	1532-1520	
174	THOUTMOSIS II	20	1522-1500	Mort du Pharaon dans la Mer Rouge
175	HATCHEPSOUT	23	1500-1477	C'est l'Amensei de Manéthon et de Champollion
176	THOUTMOSIS III	30	1477-1447	
177	AMENOPHIS II	35	1447-1412	
178	THOUTMOSIS IV	9	1412-1403	
179	AMENOPHIS III	36	1403-1367	
180	AMENOPHIS IV	16	1367-1351	Transforma son nom en Akhenaton

What do we know about the astronomical calendar? Clement of Alexandria, who had all the original elements preserved in the Library of Alexandria of which he was the curator, assured us that the Exodus of the Jews occurred two centuries after the renewal of the canicular year subtracted from 22. This is crystal-clear to anyone who has studied the revolutions of Sirius, the Year of the Dog, whose calculation process we have already explained in detail. It was the Greeks who imagined Anubis, the Guardian of Pure Souls, in this way. So we're talking about the celestial revolution of this star, began in 139 AD and ended in 1322 BC. If we subtract the 178 years elapsed after its renewal, we obtain 1500, to be precise... the year of the death of Thutmosis II, although the Annals do not say how or by whom. Why this obscurity, which seems to have been deliberate?

Let's go back to the reign of Thutmosis I, the father of the man we are interested in. He had three sons and one daughter. As the two eldest sons died young, he focused all his affection on his daughter, the delightful Hatshepsut, seemingly completely ignoring his youngest son. In delicate health, however, Thutmosis I died in the twelfth year of his reign (in 1520) and it was naturally the younger son who was declared king under the name Djhathimes, or Thutmosis II, to follow Manethonian phonetisation.

However, Hatshepsut's mother was only a concubine of Thutmosis I, while Princess Hatshepsut was the daughter of Hemtenphut, daughter of Amosis, and half-sister of the Pharaoh.

Hatshepsut was undoubtedly of much nobler blood... but she was still a delightful young girl of fifteen! And much to her chagrin, although the queen mother wanted to make her the bearer of the Sceptre, the priests forced her to marry her half-brother, Thutmosis II, who was twenty years old, thus becoming, for better or for worse, only the queen consort.

Weak of character in front of his wife, embittered by playing only a secondary role, it is obvious that love did not reign in this couple. Nevertheless, two years later, a daughter, Nefrouret, was born. After that, the couple stopped living together, and each went their separate ways for quite a long time! This Thutmosis was then gradually pushed aside by everyone in favour of his wife: a "strong head", whose constant demands against her husband's weakness bore fruit. And it was not long before she succeeded in her plot in the seventeenth year Thutmes' reign, the date of his jubilee. However, Hatshepsut's husband, who had been alerted to the plot and showed unusual strength, made good her misfortune by reconciling with her husband. This agreement led to the birth of a child, which was unfortunately another daughter! And misunderstandings returned to the household.

At that very moment, a son whom he had had with a concubine at the time of the first separation reached his sixteenth birthday. He was doing his novitiate in the House-of-Life of the priests of Amun when his father appointed him co-regent at his side, a sign of opprobrium against Hatshepsut. Righteous anger shook her, and it was probably this that prompted him, through the Council of Nobles in his pay, to pursue the Jews who were fleeing Egypt, but taking with them all the monotheistic Egyptians of Ptah-Un. They could no longer bear the impious rise of Amun to the azure of this 'heart' given by God to his creatures. It was therefore both an act of lèse-majesté and the queen consorts last hope to wish the pharaoh dead. The death came suddenly during the chase, and no one mentioned how it happened - and with good reason!

Thutmosis III then ascended the throne. The royal architect, in his biographical note, wrote :

"Thutmosis III became the Per-Ahâ on his father's throne. Queen consort Hatshepsut, however, ruled Egypt because of her abilities."

It was therefore she who ordered that no mention should be made of the end of the previous pharaoh. Hatshepsut's abilities were such that in the ninth year of the reign of Thutmosis III, she finally succeeded in having herself proclaimed pharaoh under the name of Maatkara.

It is therefore safe to say that it was in 1500 BC that Moses crossed the Red Sea with his people (Jews and Egyptians together under the halo of the Prince of Egypt). They were pursued by the army of Thutmosis II. It was during this campaign that the pharaoh died suddenly. And Ramses, who was not born until two centuries later, had nothing to do with the story! Only the new "Year of God", beginning in 1322, would make him the pharaoh he would become. Let's return instead to Moses and the Age of Aries, which undoubtedly inspired his rebellion against the cult of Amun-Ra.

His education in the Houses of Life of the Egyptian temples had made him an initiate in his own right: a wise man as well as a high priest. But as Moses was also the crown prince of the throne, he had learned the art of war as well as all the means of keeping God's kingdom intact, and from an early he had become aware the vanity of certain dogmatic principles!

Before he was born and Amosis took the Sceptre to re-unite Ath-Kâ-Ptah, decadence had profoundly upset the country occupied by the Hyksos, the shepherd kings from the east. The oblivion of the prestigious past owed to Ptah had modified the rites, ideas and particular life of each individual, all the more easily because it had been advocated by the three centuries of this foreign occupation. As a Zoolean affinity linked the Sun-worshippers, whose idol was Aries, to the Hyksos, Thebes assumed total predominance over the other capitals and cults on the banks of the Nile.

On the death of Amosis, as a result of a trap set up against the heir, it was Amenhotep I who ascended the throne, and Moses had to flee. It was during this period that the hard labour of the workers was transformed into outright slavery, which included Jews and Egyptians who were not followers of Amon-Ra. From then on, Denderah was forgotten for two centuries, until the great festival of 1322, which opened the "New Year" of Sirius.

In the meantime, Thutmosis I replaced Amenophis, carrying Egypt's reputation far and wide under his banner. But the military campaigns brought to a head the internal slavery of the entire people, i.e. Egyptians and Jews alike.

This Per-Ahâ held the sceptre for only twelve years. His last living son ascended the throne as Thutmosis II, with the difficult task of ensuring the stability of the newly reconstituted empire. He undertook major works that overwhelmed the already miserable population. The Jews were so much a part of daily life that their description of themselves as "nomads" was out of date! They had indeed become fully-fledged natives.

The famous fresco of Thebes, reproduced in black and white in all the textbooks, depicting "Jewish slaves" making bricks under the watchful eye of guards, has, like many other interpretations, helped to spread this baseless legend.

Indeed, it is easy to reread hundreds of comments by learned exegetes on seeing the black and white reproduction of this scene, to understand the origin of this grotesque fabrication. Here, for example, is a text by one of most eminent scholars of the last century, Cardinal Meignan, Archbishop of Châlons, taken from his work on the Old Testament, De l'Eden à Moïse :

> *Paintings in Egyptian tombs and various passages in papyri found in necropolises depict scenes of forced labour. Semitic workers are seen moulding bricks and building walls under the lashes of their overseers!*

Now, all the original reproductions of the paintings in the hypogeums of the Theban region were done in polychrome by M. Cailliaud, according to the exact colours saw in the tombs. And it is the very shades of the men and their hair that give an accurate picture of the situation. Not only are the profiles very clearly differentiated between Semites, Egyptians and captives, but their hair shows the formal proof that all were confused under the same domination. The

Semites had their hair painted yellow, the fellahs black and the prisoners of war white. The Egyptian guards, those with a stick or whip in their hands, have their hair painted black, of course.

This re-established truth, namely that the Mosaic people was composed equally of Jews and Egyptians, would be the cornerstone of the advent of Moses. His flight to eternal glory was only possible because "his" people, the people he led across Sinai, were all oppressed people living on both banks of the Nile. We must not forget that Moses was not only the crown prince of Egypt, but that he had been "brought up in all the wisdom" of that country. "His people were those who believed in the monotheism of the "Elders", whether born of Abraham or Osiris, because they all had the same One God.

Thus, Moses grew up during the troubled period following the invasion of the Hyksos, when the worshippers of the Sun, those of Aries-Amon, were victorious, but the followers of Horus were still the most numerous. As for the Semites, for the first time they felt like strangers in this land that had welcomed them so fraternally for millennia without interruption.

Long before Abraham and his wife arrived on the banks of the Nile, Egypt was well known to the inhabitants of the neighbouring territories. Not only because of its extremely fertile black soil, the silt of which was a divine gift to its faithful people, allowing everyone to eat to their heart's content, but also because constant invasions, in one direction or another, had led to an enormous intermingling of populations.

There is a great deal of evidence for this, such as in the Sinai, where rock engravings tell of the arrival of the troops of Snefru or Cheops, more than five thousand years ago, to drill copper and gold mines with the help of the enslaved populations. This encouraged the conquerors and the native women to mix.

From that time onwards, Semites and Egyptians mixed constantly, as history and chronology show. Whether it was the continual incursions into Palestine, Assyria or the Hittites; whether it was the perpetual famines that drove the nomadic tribes of Chanaan to the welcoming banks of the Nile; whether it was the Semitic occupation of Egypt, which lasted nearly three centuries, with the Hyksos kings.

So, with the departure of the latter, when Amosis, in the name of Amun, took the sceptre, the people venerating Ptah as well as the Jews, who had become their consanguine brothers, suffered the yoke of the "godless" after that of the "cursed"! And this new dynasty, which denied God and worshipped only Aries, was spiritually vulnerable until King Thutmosis II.

The life of Moses, as I have re-established it on the basis of the oldest texts made available to me by the Chantilly library and those compiled in Jerusalem, is also consistent with Manetho's chronology and the historical annals of Egypt. I have kept it all the better because the four pharaohs mentioned by this historian lived during the 18th dynasty, regardless of which Amenhotep or Thutmosis is taken into account. But I repeat, the only one whose annals were suppressed was the second, and from his reign derive those that preceded it.

To better understand life in Egypt at time of Moses, we need to go back a few decades, to the height of the decline of the 17th dynasty, shortly before the beginning of the next one, and with it what all historians have called the "New Kingdom".

This seventeenth dynasty, whose impressive list of kings Manetho enumerates, in fact included those of all the kinglets who held some form of government in one or more nomes, or provinces, under their sole authority, in a torn Egypt. From the time of the departure of the Hyksos invaders, therefore, there were undoubtedly several simultaneous reigns in various parts of what had once been a vast empire.

First there were the 'collaborator' chiefs, who were still very powerful in safeguarding what they considered to be their own heritage; then there were the worshippers of Aries-Amon, those of Set; and finally there were those who, against all odds, continued to venerate Ptah, those of Osiris. The settling of scores that brought the 18th dynasty to an end, in which chaos was only averted at the last second, thus took place in total confusion!

The fight between Apepi, or Apophis, and a "collaborator" of the defeated Hyksos, over a hippopotamus, and the relentless attack by the former's troops on the body of the latter's leader, is the most blatant example of this!

And if, in this fierce and bloody war for power, Apepi did not have the last word, despite the assassination of Sekenen-Ra in an ambush, it was by Kâmenset, or Kamôse, or Kamès, his young son who was initially elected head of the armies, that the Semitic hordes were pursued all the way to their citadel-capital of Avaris. Texts from this period abound in epic accounts of the exploits of certain valiant soldiers close to Kâmenset. The number of hands cut off by the 'Immondes' to count the number of slain was impressive!

But the outcome of this battle not something that this young army leader and king contemplated either, as he too died in an ambush set up on Egypt's new frontier, established in the Fayum desert, more than a hundred kilometres beyond the frontier that marked the Middle Kingdom.

It was only with the succession of the young Nek-Iâmet, the "Descendant of Nek-Bet", the Nephthys of the Greeks, that the situation very quickly evolved in the most favourable way for this Second Heart, which needed it so badly!

This is why Iâmet, phonetised Ahmes by the Greeks and Amosis by Manetho, was considered by Manetho to be the first pharaoh of the 18th dynasty. And the sceptre was given to him exactly on the sixteenth day of the month of Choïak in the year 1580 BC.

The most important thing, which is not written in this Manethonian chronology, is that in the same year a male "carnal envelope" was born, which had no known name to seal the entry of his "divine particle" into this body. However, three months later, the name Moses was given to him by the beautiful young Thermoutis who had found him in the reeds near the beach of the summer palace, where she was bathing in the company of her attendants. For the young and pretty Thermoutis was the eldest daughter of the ancient pharaoh, and the eldest sister, from the same father if not the same mother, of this Iâmet or Amosis. But as she was sterile, she had not been married to him, as she was unable to ensure the pharaonic succession.

Obviously, this event took place to the general indifference of the palace grandees, for two equally important reasons. Firstly, because most of the kingdom's powerful men were on the battlefield in the company of Amosis, and secondly because the divine royal wife, Nefertari, was expecting her first child. The name of this queen should not be confused with that of Nefertiti, as has often been the case, the latter having been the wife of Akhenaten, or Amenophis IV.

Let's leave Moses' life in abeyance for a moment, then, so that we can briefly retrace his future environment. Between his birth and his flight into the Sinai desert, four pharaohs succeeded one another at the head of what became the world's greatest empire: Amosis, who held the sceptre from 1580 to 1555 BC; Amenophis I, who reigned from 1555 to 1532; Thutmosis I, from 1532 to 1520; and Thutmosis II, from 1520 to just 1500.

A few months before the Jewish legislator was born, Amosis became king by marrying Nefertari, the "Beautiful Companion". This very young but fiery 171st pharaoh inspired great hope in all the country's citizens from the moment of his accession. Indeed, his very name, "Born of the Star", was a call for neutrality between those of the Sun and those of Ptah, in order to find common ground to drive the last Hyksos, the godless invaders, out of Egypt.

The ardour of the fighters was further enhanced by the Nubian legions, the black-skinned troops who had been an integral part of the Egyptian army since the southern territories had been annexed to the "Second Heart". And the epilogue to this long conflict took place at Avaris, or Abaris, which was the last fortified retreat of the Hyksos. To the end, they were the invaders, and those who had helped them were the "collaborators".

Everything fits together admirably, so it is wrong to claim, and to write, as many Egyptologists have done, that the Egyptians saw the Hebrews as plague victims and slaves, because they confused these "Ebers" with the "People" that Moses led into exodus almost a century later, the people that included all the oppressed, Jews and Egyptians alike.

Misfortune or good fortune, depending on whether the context is Israelite or Egyptian, meant that Amenophis had no children. It was this primordial fact that unleashed against Moses the almighty power of the priests of Amun, who in no way wanted a pharaoh raised in the veneration of Ptah. So they set up a veritable trap against him in order to shamefully discredit him in the eyes of the large faction of the people who were faithful to their traditional affections for the princess Thermoutis and her adopted son. The plan was almost completely successful, as Moses had to flee. Since he did not die in this odious attack in which he was implicated, he was able, as a result of this Machiavellian act, to take the turn of mind necessary to organise the exodus of his people and become their earthly legislator, as God had willed by impregnating him from birth, through the "Divine-Mathematical-Combinations", with the coordinates of his life. He became the classic rebel by entering into a struggle, initially clandestine, against those of Aries.

Thus, on the death of Amenophis, some time after his shameful flight, the sceptre was given to a distant half-brother of the previous pharaoh, who was entirely under the control of the priests of Amun in Thebes. The name Thutmosis I became his own: "Son of Theta", hence of Theot, which implied that he was destined to return to the ancestral traditions.

But his reign, which lasted twenty-five years, was overshadowed by numerous family deaths that hastened his end. First there was the death of the queen mother, then his wife, and finally his two eldest sons, who were his pride and joy, even though they were from different mothers.

Thutmosis had many other problems to solve, including that of his succession. He had two legitimate children left: a boy and a girl. Strangely enough, it was the latter to whom he turned all his affection. Perhaps because she had been born of the womb of his divine wife, herself the daughter of an illustrious descendant of Set, whereas the younger son had only been born of a concubine without a drop of noble blood. Perhaps it was also because Amenset, who was to become the famous Hatshepsut, already had a strong personality, whereas her younger half-brother was sickly and weak-willed. In any case, the death of Thutmosis I left the dynasty in limbo for a few weeks, with opposing interests. Amenset claimed the throne for her exclusive use, and the priests of Amun preferred his brother to him. In the end, it was he who was declared pharaoh under the name of Thutmosis II, on his sixteenth birthday. Amenset, at the age of eighteen, was forced to marry him in spite of her feelings, so that she would become the "Great Royal Wife".

It was during this troubled period that Moses returned to the land of Egypt. And his talks with the heads of the families of Israel went unnoticed or were deemed unimportant. Pharaoh had other things to worry about, with plague after plague raining down on the land. There was also the education of his son, brought up in the most important House-of-Life of the temples of Amun, in Thebes. And as soon as the young prince was sixteen, he was deemed fit to assist his father as co-regent of the kingdom. A decree formally appointed him to this title in opprobrium against Amenset, still queen-consort.

The violent anger that shook the latter most certainly dictated what happened next, with the crown prince giving up the ghost at that moment. For Moses, preparing for the departure of his people, Jews and Egyptians merged into a single oppressed family, was received in final audience by Thutmosis II, already defeated by fate, and by Amenset.

The Queen kept a close eye on events, intervening through advisors in her pay. When her husband refused to leave, she urged him to get rid of the intruders, whom she accused of setting the country on fire. When the king relented, she inspired him with the idea of hunting them down and exterminating them. It was an easy game for the queen, because in addition to the Jews, a whole section of the population fled in their company: the followers of the monotheism of Ptah. They refused to bend to the will of the Pharaoh and Amun, and were to be judged as impious rebels in the same rebellion! This was truly a crime of lèse-majesté that could not go unpunished. And as this was the last chance for the future Hatshepsut to hold the sceptre of the kingdom, she fomented the death of her husband in this way, helping the fortunes of this holy war to her discretion. It is therefore possible to affirm that it was Thutmosis II who died that year, in 1500, just before our Christian era, crossing the Red Sea.

The first years that followed were very confused. A young prince born of a concubine, supported by the priests and refusing to let himself be dispossessed, made himself king as Thutmosis III. He first ceded power to Amenset, who then became the "pharaoh". He then regained power after a palace revolt and the death of Hatshepsut, which he instigated. Hence also the hammering concerning Hatshepsut's reign of Thutmosis II, in order to erase the traces of his tragic end in the Red Sea!

Thus, the life of Moses is reconstructed with the help of the troubled historical facts of the time and the writings contained in the second book of the Old Testament, designated according to ancient Jewish custom by the word *Chemot*, or "the names", which the Greek translators rendered as Exodos.

But in this second crucial element, the concordance with the first is far from complete. It must be acknowledged that the biblical texts, collected orally, were written down, for the most part, four centuries after the death of Moses by the Levite priests, who were the most faithful to the Mosaic spirit. But the fear of losing some vital snippet of truth led the editors of the definitive text to include some duplicate accounts, or variants that were open to question, especially as this was in the fifth century BC, almost a thousand years after Moses! This is why this spiritual foundation of monotheism, which goes back to the dawn of time, must be read through the thoughts that animated the Jewish priest-writers of the 6th and 5th centuries, corresponding to the deportation to Babylonia, the long years of exile, and the return with the rebuilding of the temple in Jerusalem. It is unthinkable that the long meditations abroad should have influenced the writing of the text of a millennium-old exodus, which was strangely reminiscent of the blindness and decadence of another primitively chosen people of the same God, whose Egyptian origins go back to the earliest times.

The document on the exodus was therefore composed with the sole aim of providing strict teachings, copied from the original commandments, so that Israel would first survive and then live according to rigorous precepts, in accordance with the Tables of the Law and the erection of the monumental temple planned.

It is this Levite distortion that I have deliberately tried to leave out of Book B1, in which the whole life of Moses is amply narrated, so there is no need to go into it in detail here. The wide range of favourable reviews, from Le *Figaro* to Gaston Deferre's *Provençal*, as well as from the Centre de documentation juive to the Office chrétien du livre, whose reading committee includes pastors and priests, went straight to my heart! Indeed, while certain passages, such as Moses' first marriage to a princess of Sheba, or the fact that the Exodus to the Promised Land included as many Jews as Egyptians, should not be too controversial, I thought that the story of Israel's future lawgiver on Mount Sinai would raise a lot of eyebrows. Strangely enough, it didn't!

As far as the substance is concerned, I have provided sufficient evidence in the notes attached to the book that the Ten Commandments already existed centuries and centuries before Moses left the banks of the Nile and that, as High Priest, he knew their content by heart. But for the sake of argument, I need to explain myself at greater length, because it was only after much hesitation, and a stay at Sinai, that I wrote this vital chapter in this way. I spent three days and two nights at the summit, alone, in order to immerse myself, if I could, in the space and time when Moses, the Rebel in love with God, was there. Reading also helped a lot.

Of all the books I have read, Jean Salvador's very learned two-volume *Les Institutions de Moïse*, published in 1881, made a strong impression on me. Not only because of the erudition displayed, but also because of a number of judicious comments, which I have often used to strengthen my view of the process followed by Moses. One of these passages was undoubtedly marked by common sense, and proved that the Commandments had indeed been brought from Egypt:

Moses, brought up among the Egyptian priests, knew all about their science. So while the Hebrews took with them their clothes, gold and silver vessels and tools for pitching their tents, Moses also took with him writing materials and the laws written on papyrus scrolls preserved in the Egyptian sanctuaries.

Moses, prince of Egypt and high priest instructed in all the Knowledge of the Per-Ahâ, had unquestionably learnt the Commandments of the Law by heart. On the way up to the summit of Sinai, they were stored deep in his memory, ready to emerge at the first opportunity. When the patriarch announced to his people his departure for the sacred mountain, he did not yet know what he would come back down from it! But he knew that God would inspire him, even if he did not appear before him, because it could not be otherwise after all the misfortunes he had experienced, and which had led him to this place as Guide of a new people. Unconsciously, when he spoke, he used words and phrases he had learnt in Egypt, which everyone understood because they had come from the country that had been their whole life up to now. The same applied to the name Yahweh, which had existed long before they arrived there. This is what Moses said that morning, in very few words, for in all logic and simple truth, nothing else could be said:

"Tomorrow, I will go to the Mountain to take the orders of Yahweh, so that you may live forever in peace on earth. The Law on which this is based was observed by the first inhabitants, who followed it blindly on pain of seeing no descendants survive them. As long as they obeyed it, they lived happily. When they forgot her, they lost their Paradise, and the survivors of divine wrath had to flee to another homeland, another Heart. So, on pain of losing everything in your turn in the Promised Land we are about to enter, you will have to agree to obey the precepts of the Commandments in order to preserve the advantages you have acquired. Yahweh, the name by which we will honour God, will for the moment have a portable temple and a temporary tabernacle, but our workers will try to weave, carve and shape, with all the love they can muster, the elements that will make it a holy place in the image of our faith and our confidence in the benefits Yahweh will bestow on us. The blacksmiths and goldsmiths are now chiselling the ornaments and jewels that will adorn the sacred place. When we have reached the place where the great city of the Promised Land will stand, we will build a true and great temple, a thousand times more splendid than those you saw in Ath-Kâ-Ptah, which were only dedicated to idols like Aries.

And the thoughts of Moses, of this Rebel of the Ram set up as an idol, and therefore as a false god, as he continued his ascent towards the most holy summit, could only be these: would his many years continue to support him until the end of his task. He reflected on what he should do, wondering whether it would not have been easier to create his Tables of the Divine Law at the foot of the sacred Mountain, in full view of everyone, instead of hiding behind a barrier that was perhaps too holy to be understood by future generations. He had abandoned an earlier faith, that of Ptah, not because Ptah was a false god, but because those who had fought against him to gain and keep power had erected an idol to bring Ptah down. These were false men doomed to destruction. So, together with Yahweh, he allowed all those oppressed by these false men to take their place in a new place.

When he reached the summit of the mountain, staggering and in a state of extreme exhaustion, the patriarch finally had a revelation of what he had to accomplish. Being almost mystical, due to his spiritual training and the countless misfortunes he had endured up to that point, it is indisputable that his mind was capable of perceiving all the celestial waves in response to the mental questions he asked. A veritable dialogue took place during his sleep between his "Divine Parcel" and the One God.

Although I didn't perceive anything similar during my two nights alone at the summit, I readily admit the possibility. I may have been extremely handicapped and exhausted myself, but I didn't feel anything up there, at least in that form. But perhaps it gave me the extra strength I needed to persevere in my task and complete the work begun after my terrible accident. This goal has been achieved, but it has led me to understand that everything is a perpetual motion of recommencement in an eternal world, where the twists and turns only come to demonstrate human vanity in relation to the mechanics inspired by God. I know that the question of the divine authenticity of this Decalogue has been the subject of much ink since the successive compositions of the books that made up the Bible. The point here is not to reopen a controversy that is already endemic, but simply to demonstrate that the Ten Commandments of the Law of the One God already existed long before Moses brought them up to date on Sinai; their authenticity from God himself is beyond doubt.

This unified rule within a rigorous ethic had always been the most authentic form, and the only one, on which the monotheistic edifice, taken up by Moses, rested. If the exit from Egypt was the liberating event for an entire Jewish and Egyptian population, united in a single flight towards freedom, the search for the forgotten God of old was the key event, in order to sign a new covenant with Him. A new covenant, because the first had been made after the resurrection of Osiris, who had come to save the unborn multitude from a new disaster by granting it a "Second Heart": Ath-Kâ-Ptah, or Egypt.

This is why Moses, instructed in all the Egyptian Wisdom, realised, during this slice of life spent at Sinai before continuing on to another Promised Land that he would not reach, that he was reliving a nightmare "already lived" millennia before, after a famous "Divine Wrath"! Now, after having been a fugitive and a rebel, a foreigner without a name and without a homeland, an extraordinary combination of circumstances had forced him to reflect first on what was happening to him, then on what others expected of him, before deciding to attempt to engage in the memorable dialogue at Sinai and the descent of the Ten Commandments that were to change the face of the world once again. Palestine opened its borders wide to allow a human lifeblood to take root in this prosperous land from which milk and honey would flow! Twelve tribes would live in peace with the rest of the world... Yahweh's chosen people would be born while he died on Mount Nebo!

Having also climbed this sacred peak, I contemplated Galilee and the silvery Jordan against a backdrop of fog at sunset. The sad end of the man who died there, alone, remains the symbol of the rebirth of Aries in its non-idolatrous form in Palestine. And the annual sacrifice of the ram will remain its most fervent act until the coming of the Messiah at the beginning of the Age of Pisces.

It was time to pull Moses out of the fantasy in which the first chapters of the Old Testament had placed him, and give him back his true human dimension, on the scale of the brotherhood of blood that closely unites Jews and Egyptians in the same original monotheism, and therefore beyond all fanatical political movements.

13

GOD FORGOT EGYPT:
CAMBYSES THE MADMAN

Cambyses' treatment of the corpse of Amosis was a punishment for the bloody insult he had received from this pharaoh.
A.-J. Letronne (Egyptian Civilisation)

Judging by all his actions, it is clear that Cambyses had completely lost his mind. Otherwise he would not have spent his time making a mockery of the most sacred things.
Herodotus (Book III-38)

It is quite characteristic to note that no sooner had the last quarter of solar navigation along the "Great Celestial River" in Aries begun, than Israel and Egypt lost their identities at the same time! The Hebrews were deported to Babylonia, and the Persians transferred 500,000 Egyptian prisoners to their country, where very few arrived alive. In this way, the main defenders of the Age of Aries were swept from the soil of their two mother countries. Moses and Akhenaten had failed to realise their dream of a monotheism that defended the rights of every human being to live in the peace of God on Earth.

The five centuries remaining until the Sun entered the constellation of Pisces saw an enormous population shift in the Near East, with all the prophecies that were to be fulfilled before the new era. Each country did its utmost to influence events so that they turned out in favour of the strongest or the cleverest. To enumerate the movements between Greece and Egypt, Persia and Egypt, and all the little kingdoms intertwined between these three nations and Israel would require another book.

The third book of Manetho, which contains the names and titles of the last 66 pharaohs, presents a remarkable division of the dynasties for the period we will be looking at throughout this chapter. As for the account of the "great deeds" that marked the reign of Cambyses, we know the broad outlines from Herodotus' account in his *Journey to Egypt*.

Clearly, as impiety took root among the natives and a new idolatry was introduced by the Greeks called in to defend Pharaoh Amosis, the Persians had to act quickly. That's why, as time went on, God forgot Egypt to punish all this wicked world! We must not forget that the Persians, with Zoroaster, their Magi and their Prophets, were well aware of the anxious expectation in which the Egyptians lived. They knew that their end was inevitable! The Divine-Mathematical Combinations had decided it! As in the earliest times of Ahâ-Men-Ptah, the Masters of Measurement and Number had ensured it. The Persians, for their part, formally recognised this. Their priests took advantage of the unhoped-for opportunity presented by Cambyses, who was a weak spirit in a sick body, whose violent ideas prevailed in his desire to submit everything to his will, to influence him towards a holy war. It was certain that the Egyptians would let themselves be killed on the spot rather than defend themselves in the face of fate... And so the army, led by Cambyses, set out to conquer the Zoolaites in a religious war, intended in fact to annihilate the Apis Bull!

For the Persian Magi were certain that while Amun-Ra was coming to the end of his Age of Aries, the same could not be said of those who worshipped the One God in the form of his son, symbolised by a living bull. It was this Osiris that frightened them! They had to destroy this entity at the same time as the idolaters if they wanted to retain their religious power in Persia. The ancient Pharaonic concept of monotheism was not to penetrate Persia under any circumstances! From the outset, therefore, it was a war in which the religious fanaticism of Zoroaster's followers prevailed. The destruction of the thousand-year-old vestiges of another veneration was detrimental to their fetishism. This is more than a personal opinion, for it follows all the texts relating to the history of that period. But none of these "Magi" had foreseen that Cambyses would go completely mad, and ultimately defeat the very purpose for which he had set out to conquer Egypt.

Readers may be surprised to see how well I know this period, but that is because of Pythagoras, whose life I studied in preparation for my thesis. It was 525 BC in Denderah, the year of the Persian invasion. The Great Sage was taken prisoner and brought to Persia in a privileged position because he was Greek, and therefore at peace with the invaders. But it was his status as the Sage in possession of all ancient Knowledge that protected him most effectively. The first volume of *The Extraordinary Life of Pythagoras* was published in 1979. Since then I have received a lot of correspondence asking why the second volume has not been published. It was simply because at that time the Ayatollah Khomeiny returned to Iran and it became impossible for me to travel to Hamadan, Susa and Persepolis as I had wished to do in order to study there in my own way. As everything has to be done at the right time, you have to keep your cool and have the patience to wait. This also enabled me to finish translating the fundamental Pythagorean work: the *Biblion*, which is the book of Moral and Political Laws of his time. It provides a wonderful insight into the lives of the Greeks and their neighbours at a time when the Egyptians were being invaded by the Persians.

Let us therefore return to the banks of the Nile delta, where Amosis lived, shortly before he died and Psammetichus took his place for only six months, killed at that time in a horrible way, at the hands of Cambyses himself. Let us add that we are here under the XXVIth dynasty, known as the "Saite" dynasty, comprising 9 pharaohs who reigned from 702 to 525 , the date when Cambyses behaved like a bloodthirsty madman who tried to destroy everything that Egypt contained in the way of spirituality. The following table illustrates this period.

Noms HIÉROGLYPHIQUES	Noms GRECS	Durée Règne	Datation (avant J.-C.)	Fait marquant du RÈGNE
XXVIe DYNASTIE (suite)				
234	OUAHIBRIPSEM	54	664-610	Rénovateur de l'antique religion de Ptah
235	NÉKAO II	15	609-595	
236	NEFERIBREPSEM	18	594-588	Psammétique II
237	HÁIBRIA	19	588-569	Apriès en Grec
238	KHNOU-IAMET	44	569-525	Amosis en Grec
239	ANKHREPSEM	6 mois	525	Fut étranglé par Cambyse peu après son accession au trône
XXVIIe DYNASTIE (Perse)				
240	CAMBYSE	1 1/2	525-523	Termina fou, perdu dans le désert
241	DARIUS Ier	37	523-486	
242	XERXÈS Ier	20	486-466	
243	ARTAXERXÈS	41	466-425	
244	DARIUS 2^e	19	425-405	

Without going back to the time of the Ramessesids, the annals show that Hellenic settlement in the Nile delta began under Ouahibripsem, or Psammetichus I, who held the Sceptre from 664 to 610 BC, i.e. for more than half a century! This kinglet, head of a province in a branch of the Nile delta, had some serious problems to solve if he was to hold on to his position. One day, just as he was about to be stripped of his prerogatives, he was alerted to the unexpected arrival of a group of Ionians who had come to 'explore' the land - something that had never happened before! They helped Psammetichus not only to establish his authority, but to increase it by fighting alongside him to win the sovereign sceptre, and then to keep it for more than fifty years of a reign in which renewal was the order of the day.

It was during this long period that concessions were granted in gratitude to the Ionians, then to the Carians, Samians and Mimesians, who arrived en masse with their families to defend the pharaoh, and then to trade extensively between Egypt and all the cities of greater Greece. But the most important thing for the Greeks was the discovery of a civilisation that was much older than their own! There they found a legendary world that their genius was able to appropriate. Scholars followed the traders, scattering all over Egypt in search of the sciences and knowledge they did not know. It was at this time that Solon, the Wise Man of Wise Men, entered Upper Egypt, where he lived in an oasis to the west of Thebes, among the Samians. With the help of a priest of Ptah, he spent four years learning hieroglyphics. It is to this scholar that we owe the first study of Ahâ-Men-Ptah, which Plato was to revive a century and a half later under the name of Atlantis!

Psammeticus was not only a fine diplomat and a shrewd trader, but also a renovator of the customs and traditions of the Elders of his time. It is undeniable that the admiration shown him by Greek scholars for the antiquity of Egyptian history had to do with it. The fact remains that there was a tremendous renaissance in the arts and a general return to the spiritual canons of the 3rd and 4th dynasties! The most ancient forms of hieroglyphic writing were revived, giving pride of place to the divine services of Ptah and to liturgies that had clearly fallen into oblivion. But it was above all foreign scholars who benefited.

These Greek colonies of the Pelusian branch of the delta proliferated much and more thereafter, protected as they were by the successors of Psammetichus. Until Ahâ-Iabra, the predecessor of Amosis, who admitted to having an elite corps of Greek soldiers numbering 30,000 men, this was how it was.

This reign is well known, because the Bible describes it as Ophra and the Greeks as Apries. In 586, Zedekiah, king of Judah, asked him to send his army to fight Nebuchadnezzar in Syria. But it was a serious setback, as both sides had Greek mercenaries. So when the army withdrew to its base in Egypt, Jerusalem was taken and sacked. The prophet Jeremiah had left with Apries' troops and stayed in Egypt in the fortress of Tachpanes, where he was given a fraternal welcome. This gives us one of the most beautiful passages in the Bible, in chapter

XLVI, where prophet Jeremiah ridicules Egypt, whose only remaining legacy is the worship of "heifers" by Greek bulls:

"O daughter of Egypt, in vain do you multiply remedies; there is no cure for you! The nations hear of your shame, and your cries fill the earth, for the warriors stumble over one another to fall all together. Pharaoh, king of Egypt, is nothing but a noise that has let the moment pass. Egypt is a beautiful heifer, but destruction is approaching from the north. Her mercenaries are in her midst like fattened calves, and they too turn their backs, they all flee without looking back. For the day of woe is upon them to fulfil the time of punishment!"

And indeed, what was bound to happen one day did happen: the Libyans asked Apries for help against the Dorians of Cyrene, who had dispossessed them of several swathes of territory. The Greek troops who had come to the rescue were ambushed and massacred by their Dorian brothers. The result was a riot among the mercenaries that turned into a terrible military revolution.

To avoid the worst that was about to happen, Apries sent his most trusted general, Amosis, to deal with the rebels. Amosis was notorious for his drunkenness and unpleasant manners, which had enabled him to rise through the ranks on the strength of his wrists, and had made him very popular with all the soldiers. So when the rebels offered to make him pharaoh of Egypt if he rallied the rest of the army to their cause, he simply agreed go over to their side take charge of operations.

Within a few weeks, Amosis deposed Apries and was crowned pharaoh! Two years later, with the help of a few jealous followers of the new monarch, Apries escaped and tried to reclaim his kingdom, but his supporters were crushed and he himself was murdered on the boat in which he was trying to escape. For good measure, the whole thing was sunk to the bottom of the Nile...

Amosis remained the sole master, and he became a real tyrant who made a point of corresponding and maintaining good neighbourly relations with all the minor Greek potentates. Polycrates, the tyrant of Samos, sent him Pythagoras as a friend to initiate him into ancient wisdom. And Thales of Miletus, with whom he had cordial relations. He was also very far-sighted, bringing all the Greeks together in a single city: Nautacris, where they had the right not only to govern themselves, but also to build temples to honour their gods. In fact, his long reign - almost fifty years - was very prosperous for Egypt, which was rediscovering a nationalist spirit. However, religious fervour was deliberately left aside by this pharaoh who loved good wine, good food and his concubines! The priests were not allowed into the Royal Palace of Sais, and Amosis paid no heed to the prophecies about the Age of Aries and the end of Egypt.

They even went so far as to present him with the Stele of Omens, now in the museum in Palermo, Sicily, which must have been found in the ruins Sais later, after the Persians had passed through. In a way, it was an omen heralding the end of the last pharaohs before the last quarter of the Age of Aries (see illustration below).

Yet Amosis should have heeded the prophecies, for a new power was rising east of the Nile. And not only would Egypt resound with lament after Jerusalem, but Greece itself would feel the dread and the passing of Persian swords. For during the reign of Amosis, Cyrus the Great conquered Babylon and the whole of Asia Minor, before thinking of entering Egypt.

In 527, Cyrus sent ambassadors to Sais to propose a "treaty of good neighbourliness". Amosis was furious and had them murdered without even wanting to receive them. So when, two years later, after the deaths of Amosis and Cyrus, each in their own country, their successors came to blows, the most terrible outrages were committed...

Cambyses declared war on Psammetichus in 525, without further delay, as much to take advantage of the element of surprise as to act according to the beneficial celestial configurations predicted by the Magi. A single battle decided the fate of Egypt, as the young pharaoh did not have the military stature of Amosis. A few centuries of mercenaries submitted to Cambyses, while the others fled. And the Persians crossed the delta without a fight to penetrate Memphis and Sais where they were not expected. The troops devastated Memphis, the ancient Ath-Kâ-Ptah of Menes went himself to Sais to ensure a posthumous revenge.

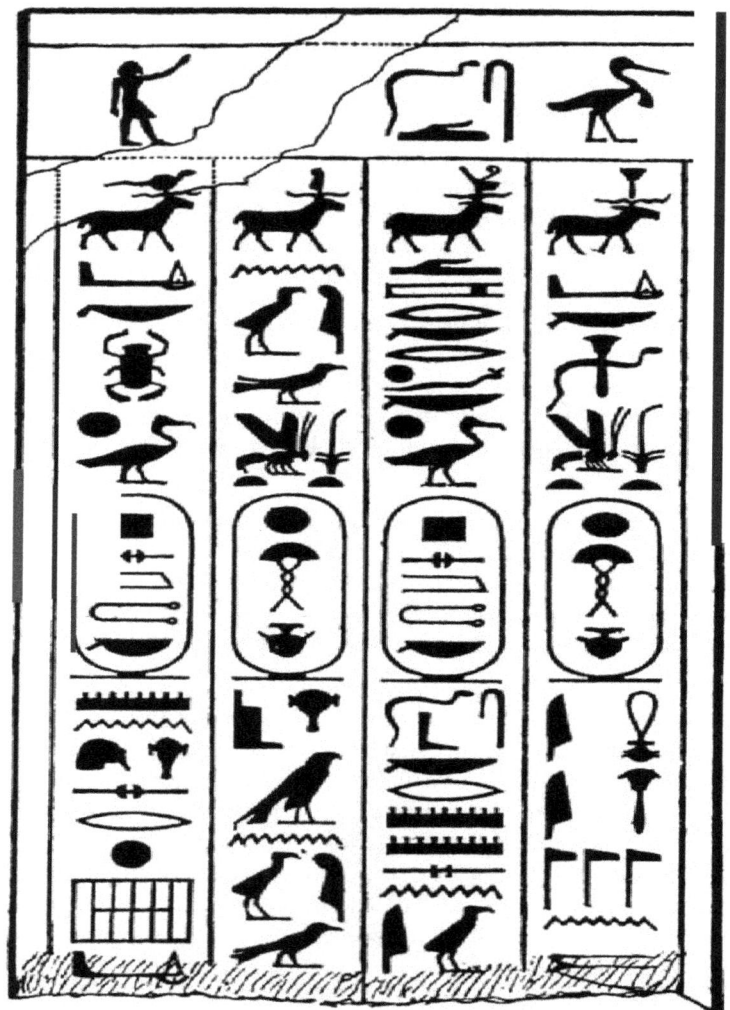

We know a great deal about this period thanks to the writings of the Greeks who were there at the time, including Herodotus, who recounts Cambyses' madness in his own way, which is not far from the truth. In Book II, the Greek historian writes:

"As soon as he arrived at the royal palace, he had the mummy of Amosis removed from its sarcophagus and had it whipped, pierced with goads, had its hair pulled out; in short, he lashed out at it in every possible way. And when his men, exhausted, had to give up (because the embalmed corpse still resisted them), Cambyses had it burnt. This sacrilegious order contravened the traditions of both peoples: firstly, those of the Persians, who regard fire as a god and consider a human corpse to be food unworthy of a god; and secondly, those of the Egyptians, for whom fire is a living creature that devours itself with its own prey. In Egypt, no living creature is ever given a corpse to devour; it is even for this reason that the dead are mummified, so that they are not devoured underground by worms. Cambyses' order thus offended the customs of both peoples. But the Egyptians affirm that the mummy on which the Persian worked was not that of Amosis: "It was that of another man of the same age, they told me, for Amosis had been warned by an oracle of the fate that awaited him after his death. So, to ward off the threat, he had the man who was whipped in his place buried near the entrance, in his own burial chamber. And he instructed his son to take care to place him at very bottom of the sepulchre." For my part, I am convinced that Amosis never took such precautions, and that the whole story is an Egyptian invention designed to save face.

As for what happened in Memphis, the pious citadel of the One God, Herodotus' account not only doesn't fit in with reality, but it lends the king of the Persians ideas of nobility that he had absolutely no idea of, and that his madness would have forbidden him anyway, as the Greek historian assures us in other passages!

The affront committed against the Persian ambassadors two years earlier by Amosis could only be erased blood, and the revenge was going to be terrible! When the Royal Palace was taken over, the entire Pharaonic family was brought to Memphis to await Cambyses' decisions. The princely families and Egyptian nobility were already there. All the women and girls, whatever their age, had been given to the victorious soldiers. As for the two thousand men, they had all been tied together by the neck, barely free to breathe so as not to die of asphyxiation or strangulation. They had waited, harnessed in this way and penned up for four days, for Cambyses to decide to bring them before him.

This took place in the great courtyard of the temple of Ath-Ka-Ptah, rebuilt on the orders of Amosis, still abhorred by Cambyses, even though he had taken his revenge on the mummy at Sais. He had brought out the pontiff's throne, and it was with a sniff of disgust that he came to sit on it the 2,000 men stinking in their own filth were all kneeling awaiting his sentence. At the foot of the throne, spread-eagled, Psammetichus, his wife, his son and his three daughters, all completely naked, waited in anguish and unable to turn round to see what was happening, having been lying in this position for several hours, even before the arrival of the 2,000 men chained together by their necks!

To reach his seat, Cambyses savagely trampled on the bodies of the pharaoh and his progeny, then ordered them to straighten up and kneel down. They did so, except for Ladicea, the wife of Psammetichus, who conveniently fainted when she fell to the ground. The pharaoh and his son, on their knees, naked under the bright sun, had to watch their two thousand most faithful companions go to the sword, one after the other, before their heads were cut off! It took five hours for the butchery to end! Cambyse had followed the abominable carnage with feverish eyes and gasping breath. And Psammetichus' three daughters had long since fallen unconscious beside their mother.

But Cambyses was not satisfied, and signalled to one of the executioners to seize the king's son so that he could suffer the same fate as his companions. And his head was cut off and fell into a veritable sea of blood. Cambyses then got down from his seat, sneering, and lifted Psammetichus by the hair until he was at his full height, before letting go of him with a quick movement and grabbing him by the neck to strangle him with his powerful fingers. It was at this moment that sweet Ladicée chose to regain consciousness. She screamed so loudly at the sight before her that she clearly went mad. Exasperated, Cambyse plunged his dagger into her left breast to stop her hearing. This death was probably better for her, because her daughters were fed to the three leaders of the invading armies, who carried them off on their shoulders, running and laughing at their lucky stars!

From this day, the madnesses of Cambyse went *crescendo*. Herodotus recounts his second exaction, still in Memphis, a few weeks later. The temple courtyard had been cleared and, surprise, surprise, a bull that met the standards of the celestial deity had finally been found to replace the one that had been dead for 26 months, and whose death had been blamed for the atrocities committed, since no longer was Ath-Ka-Ptah's protector watching over his creatures. All the priests fell in adoration before the new Apis, the living resurrection of Osiris, who would save them all from disaster despite the ominous prophecies.

Herodotus recounts this in great detail in his second book:

"When Cambyses returned to Memphis, the god Apis (whom the Greeks call Epaphos) appeared to the Egyptians. The whole country immediately put on their festive clothes and celebrated the event. But Cambyses, convinced that they were in fact rejoicing at his defeats, summoned the city's notables: "Why," he asked them, "did the people make no demonstration when I first passed through, and are they giving vent to their joy just as I am returning after suffering so many losses? - The god Apis has just appeared," they replied, "and as this is a very rare event, everyone is in the habit of celebrating it with festivals. Cambyses did not believe a word of this explanation and condemned the notables to death for lying to him.

Once the notables had been executed, it was the turn of the priests to appear before Cambyses. They told him exactly the same thing, and Cambyses ordered Apis to be fetched. We'll see," he said, "what this god, who supposedly appeared to the Egyptians, is going to do. According to tradition, this Apis (or Epaphos) must be a bull born of a cow that is unable to calve again. The Egyptians say that he is conceived by a bolt of lightning that falls from the sky on this cow and makes it fertile. You can recognise Apis by the following signs: he is black with a white triangle on his forehead, the design of an eagle on his back, a tail with double the number of hairs and, under his tongue, the design of a beetle.

So the priests brought Apis, and Cambyses went berserk, drew his dagger, aimed at the beast's belly and finally hit it in the thigh. And he shouted to the priests, bursting into laughter: "Stubborn people, have you ever seen gods of flesh and blood who bleed when you hit them? That god is worthy of you! In any case, you won't laugh at me!" And he ordered the priests to be whipped until they bled, and any Egyptian caught celebrating the festival to be arrested. The priests were flogged and the festivities came to a screeching halt. Apis, wounded in the thigh, bled to death and completed his death in his sanctuary. The priests buried him without Cambyses' knowledge.

This madness was followed by many others. But in the meantime, a fixed idea was taking shape in the cracked mind of the King of Persia: "If he were to die, what would become of him? He had long ceased to believe in the value of the Persian Magi, or in their gods. On the other hand, he had come to realise the faith of the Egyptian priests, who all allowed themselves to be slaughtered without shouting or defending themselves, simply by praying to their God Osiris to receive them to his side. His disappointment at not knowing the great secret did not last long, because he learned from one of the Greek dissidents under his command that the great temple of this God of Egypt was in the south of the country, not in the north: very close to Thebes.

Cambyses once again led his troops and, despite the total submission of Upper Egypt, he behaved like an omnipotent invader, setting Thebes on fire, destroying, pillaging, stealing and raping everything in sight. He shouted and laughed in incessant delirium:

"Break all these rams! The time of rams is over! The bull Apis is the God! I want to honour Osiris in his kingdom..."

It was while the Persian king was on his way to Denderah that Pythagoras was taken prisoner in front of Thebes. This scene, described in *The Extraordinary Life of Pythagoras*, is entirely accurate in context, as is the dialogue between the Persian surgeon and the Greek sage, which I reproduce below for those who have not yet read the book. Pythagoras, wounded and unconscious, wakes up:

— My weakness should excuse me at this point from a dialogue worthy of an essay, you who must be a learned doctor. May I ask in turn I am and who you are?

— I'm Naboniram, the second physician to our king, Cambyses; I'm the one who cuts off limbs... or patches them up, depending on the case and the rank of the wounded! Anatomy and skeletal bones are my domain. Your slave having shouted enough as soon as you fell to the ground, that you were Greek, to be heard not only by the troop, but by the leaders of our armies, you were brought to my tent with a good escort. Your right leg was broken halfway down your thigh, and the break was very clean. You were unconscious, but your heart was beating normally, which enabled me to use a technique I had learnt in our capital from a doctor who had arrived from Asia.

— What have you done to me? Is my leg cut? I can't feel it.

— You've been very lucky, Pitagoras! You've still got your leg, and you'll soon be walking again.

— How is this possible?

— You're very lucky, I told you. Not having to worry about you stirring and shaking, I cut away the flesh and fitted the two pieces of bone exactly one inside the other. Then, using the method recommended by my yellow friend, I placed and firmly held two strips of fine gold at the break. Then I closed the flesh over the whole thing, placing a mattress of special herbs around it to prevent any inflammation. Finally, two planks hold your leg completely immobile, because a white cloth surrounds the whole thing solidly.

— But how can I walk?

— I'll be removing your bandages in a few months, and little by little your legs will start working again, I can assure you.

— I thank you for this, Naboniram; my life is entirely yours. Especially as it can't have been easy to get you this gold...

The doctor laughed:

— When I said you were very lucky, it was also because of the gold! Because here, in Thebes, there was so much of it and so much of it everywhere, that no one raised the slightest protest when I took these two gold strips from a loincloth of their ram-god, which was at the top of an impressive pile of precious metals and gems!...

Ouaset! Ouaset! What was left of your splendour and culture? The Pontiff was right. But to answer the doctor, my voice lacked the desired warmth:

— Yes! I've been very lucky...

— And as you have the gold of a god in your thigh, you also have the chance to become a god yourself right now!... You are "Pitagoras Golden Thigh! This will be your name in our Persian language during your stay in our country.

— In Persia?

— That's right, Pitagoras Golden Thigh! I've been asked to sew you up so that you can join our scientists, initially in Ecbatane, where there's a sky observatory.

— So I'm a prisoner, despite your friendship for the Greeks?

— Er, no, stranger. You'll be our guest of honour for a while. Not our prisoner! As for the Egyptians, they left on foot, in herds, hundreds of thousands of them, across the burning desert. You will go to Persia with us, sitting on a donkey, or on a cart, when your leg is free of its bandage.

But that doesn't tell the whole story, because doctors already had a different status. The same was not true of soldiers. A few pages later, the young priest who had saved Pythagoras told him what had happened in Thebes:

— I have seen countless groups assembled here in Thebes! All those who weren't killed during the invasion, or who didn't have time to hide, were taken prisoner. But the three days they were gathered here were the most horrible I've ever experienced! I saw the Persian assassins kill all the young children, so that they would not encumber the columns of prisoners and delay their advance. The women were left with the soldiers at night and thrown back to the men in the morning, screaming, desperate and naked. During the three days, only once did I see food being brought in! I don't need to describe to you the awful scenes that took place to get a few crumbs! This morning, all the groups left on foot, escorted by savages armed with a dagger and an axe; girded with a shield and carrying a spear. The men were chained together at the feet, and the women whipped to walk as fast as their companions, to the laughter and jeers of the guards. But here, it was by the hundreds, by the thousands, that the lying bodies, dead or dying, were fed to the roaring beasts so that they could devour them.

As for Cambyses, at the same time, with a small "elite" troop in his devotion, he arrived in front of the entrance pylon of the temple of Isis at Denderah. The college of priests had already assembled in the great courtyard, at the entrance to the hypostyle hall, to receive the King of the Persians, without apparently showing the slightest fear.

Somewhat bewildered by this calm and the prevailing silence, Cambyses trembled with impatience, after staring for a few moments at the smile of Isis, which was reflected from pillar to pillar, seeming to taunt him. He called out to the pontiff Khan-Fé, alone in front of the gathering of high priests, in his long white tunic, in a violent diatribe. An interpreter hastened to repeat the phrases in the popular Egyptian language:

-I am now the king of this country. Everything belongs to me, even the title of Per-Ahâ. That's why I want you to take me to where Osiris, your God, lives. I want to talk to him!

The pontiff suppressed a disdainful smile before replying in Persian:

— You are indeed the master of Ath-Ka-Ptah, Cambyses; but Osiris can only be perceived by those who are pure of heart...

Cambyse stomped his feet.

— Well, what! Don't I have a pure heart?

The pontiff did not reply to this aberrant question, so the King of the Persians approached, raising a hand under Khan-Fé's nose:

- I destroyed the temples of the Sun of Thebes, your enemies. I had their priests killed and I hoarded their gold for myself. But I'm willing to give some of it to your God as a token of good faith.

— There's too much blood on your hands, Cambyse!

— I can add yours to that, and that of all your priests!

Take me to Osiris without further delay!

— You may not come back, because your heart is not pure.

— You admit this place exists, pontiff! Don't try my patience, just hurry up and obey.

After a brief moment of reflection, the pontiff decided:

— I will take you to the resting place of our Elder. But I cannot force Osiris to manifest himself to you if he does not wish to, or to spare you if you want to survive the sin you are committing.

— He'll talk to me, I want him to, come on!

— You can pull down our temples, kill our priests, but you will never force Osiris to speak to you. Or else fear his wrath, for it will be commensurate with your unforgivable sins!

Cambyses raised his fist to the face of the pontiff, who did not move back a millimetre. The Persian king, drooling, stopped himself in time. He stammered:

— Lead me, lead me to your God... quickly, before I crush you!

— So be it, Cambyse, but you're not prepared for this meeting.

The pontiff turned to enter the temple without bothering to see if the King of Persia was following him. The high priests opened a passage for him to pass. Cambyses followed in a hurry, accompanied by about twenty soldiers. But when he reached the small staircase leading down to the crypt of the resurrection of Osiris, the pontiff stopped to signal to the soldiers not to go any further. They stopped, clearly content not to descend towards the unknown that filled them with dread. A priest handed his religious leader a burning torch and the two men descended, while the pontiff's voice echoed strangely:

— You want to see the place where God's Eldest Son lives: we're going there! There are twelve crypts like this one, all around the temple. Each one personifies one of the twelve "Hearts" of heaven, which form the great belt that governs all the Divine Combinations. The abode of Osiris is that of the Soul of the World, because each of the Parcels of this soul is implanted in human bodies at birth.

As they walked along the corridor, the engraved shapes seemed to come to life under the changing reflections of the glow of the flames. Cambyse felt a cold sweat break out on his back, but he wanted to go all the way in order to attain eternal life. He had become Pharaoh, and therefore the equal of Osiris: he shouldn't be afraid! Fear of what?

When they entered the crypt, Cambyse was relieved to see that it was quite large and spacious. One entire wall was occupied by a strange engraving: a man lying on his deathbed, watched over by two kneeling women. The Persian king let out a long laugh, followed by hiccups:

— What's that? Is that your God? But he's dead!...

— He was dead, but he has risen again. His wife and sister called his Divine Parcel back from the centre of the Soul of the World, where it had gone, so that he could be with us to judge the living and the dead!

— I don't believe you, pontiff! This is a story to frighten the people and squeeze them to fatten you all up! I want better proof than this: let him judge me in the flesh, if he has risen from the dead!...

The pontiff held out his torch towards the stage, speaking in a loud voice:

— Look, Cambyses, look with open eyes, if your mind remains closed. You want to speak to Osiris: here he is! Kneel down and ask forgiveness for all the horrors you have committed. If you are not struck by lightning and your soul is not reduced to ashes with no hope of being reborn in the eternity beyond this earthly life, then it is I who will perish, for Osiris cannot tolerate such infamy! Kneel down, Cambyses, and await eternal death!

The king raised both his hands, as if to move the vision away from the wall, and he shouted:

— No! No! Take me back to the sun! The sun, quickly, quickly... I'm burning, I'm burning!...

With a gesture of contempt, the pontiff pushed aside the king who was clutching his arm, setting his tunic on fire without realising it:

— Back off, Cambyse, I warned you! Let's go back into the open air, but it's too late to save your soul!

Cambyses took terrible revenge, killing all the priests and destroying the temple, which was not rebuilt until three centuries later under the Ptolemies. The king of the Persians pursued all the places of worship in Egypt with his madness. It was in front of the Serapium at Saqqara that he went completely mad! The chronicle reports that after ordering the destruction of all the sarcophagi containing the bodies of the mummified bulls, then piling them up and burning them, he suddenly his helmet and shield and ran screaming into the desert, shouting that he was on fire!... That was how the bloodthirsty madman disappeared from history. Although the 64 Apis were saved in this way, not much remained of the spirituality of the ancient Ath-Kâ-Ptah.

However, during the Greco-Roman occupation that followed that of the Persians and before the Sun entered the constellation of Pisces, the great Alexander, who had fallen in love with Egypt, began restoring the places of worship. But it was a last gasp. The true monotheists came together in a different spiritual population, which kept the patronymic of "Heart-of-God": Kâ-Ptah, which became Koptos in Greek and Coptic in French.

Their rallying sign was a fish engraved on a scarab in the eye of Isis, to deceive those who wanted to destroy them by preventing them from reuniting. At the beginning of the Age Pisces, the Messiah appeared. And the fish became the symbol of the first Christians.

14

THE AGE OF PISCES : JESUS THE CHRIST

My brothers, observe the feast days, first of all the feast of the Nativity, which you must celebrate on the twenty-fifth day of the ninth month. After this feast, give the greatest solemnity to the day of the Epiphany, in which the Lord manifested his divinity to us; and this feast must take place on the sixth day of the tenth month.
Apostolic Constitutions (Book V, 13)

Here properly begins the drama of the passion, of which the struggles of the preceding days were only the prologue. The Evangelists recount this heart-rending drama in an impassive tone that disconcerts us.
Ferdinand Prat s.j, (Jesus Christ II, 320)

Inevitably, chronological questions will interfere with any recounting of the life of Jesus, because the key point is obviously the precise date of his birth. It is easy to recalculate it very accurately in the historical context between the years that preceded the Christian era with Herod, and the years that followed with Pontius Pilate. A large calendar is appended to this chapter to make it easier for readers to find their way around. Before getting to the heart of the matter, a specific example will enable us to judge the validity of this chronological return to astronomical time: that which concerns *the very day of Jesus' birth*. The earliest texts can be found in the "Apostolic Constitutions" (Book V, page 13). There is no reason to doubt this authenticity, since it is approved by the learned and masterly demonstration made by Simeon de Magistris, already reproduced in the *Patrologies* of Migne (pages 523 et seq.), which refutes only a few additional alterations by Paul of Samosata, and proves that Saint Clement, pope and disciple of the Apostles, as much as of Saint Hippolytus, preserved the strict truth. In order to understand the passage from these "Constitutions" quoted at the beginning of this chapter, it must be said that all the dates, days and months, are based on *the Hebrew calendar*, which was the only valid calendar at the time of the Apostles, almost all of whom were of Jewish origin and knew nothing else! And the holy year began on the day when spring returned. Consequently, the first Christians called April the first month of the church year. With this axiom established as law, the 25th day of the 9th month was the 25th of December in the Roman and pagan civil years. As for Epiphany, the 6th day of the 10th month was therefore the 6th of January.

You don't need to be a doctor of religion, or a great cleric, to understand this. The rest of the imposing work of the "Constitutions" regulates everything with this calendar, which was only changed during the reign of Charles IX in France. But that is enough to prove here that these two feasts do indeed date back to apostolic times, because it is certain that the composition of the texts is not very far removed from the time when the Apostles lived. The manner and tone totally demonstrate that these dates existed as such, as a reminder of the obligation to celebrate them. And at that time, there would have been an outcry in the Church, as well as among those who persecuted the Christians, or bursts of sarcastic laughter against the announcement of these two dates, if they had been false. At no time did anyone raise their voice or write for or against reality. The older generation were still living through the period. As for the younger generation, their parents had confirmed the assertions, and they remembered them as accurate.

There are also three points of reference, this time in the holy books, which make it possible to pinpoint this date: in Saint Matthew and Saint Luke :

a) Jesus was born before the death of Herod the Great.

b) Three events took place between the birth of Jesus and the death of Herod: the adoration of the Magi, the flight to Egypt and his return after Herod's death.

c) The birth of Jesus coincided with a general census of the inhabitants of the Roman Empire.

Since Herod's death occurred in 4 B.C. and there is historical evidence that Jesus went to Jerusalem to celebrate the Jewish Passover in 7 B.C., when he was twelve years old, it is easy to determine the year of the Messiah's birth.

In our current calendar, therefore, Jesus was born on 25 December 5 BC. The calendar at the end of the chapter explains why this particular year was chosen. Let us add that the Kâ-Ptahs (Copts), following in the footsteps of St Clement of Alexandria who said, at the beginning of the second century, that the baptism of Jesus was already celebrated on the eleventh day of the month of Tybi, the Egyptian month corresponding to 6 January.[29]

This new tangible proof suffices here, so as not to lengthen the unnecessary in this too short chapter, readers being able to refer soon to *Jesus the Christ* for all further details.

We are in the year 751 of Rome, during the reign of Augustus, which corresponds to the year of Jesus' birth. The Roman Empire was all-powerful. It brought together under a single sceptre almost all the peoples of Europe, Asia and Africa, the greatest force of conquest and political organisation the world had ever seen. Greece and Italy, the islands and coasts of the Mediterranean, Asia Minor and inland Asia, Syria and Phoenicia, Egypt and northern Africa, Spain and the Gauls, Germania from the Danube to the Rhine: Rome had conquered and conquered everything. Its legions, generals and governors covered the globe. The strategic routes from the Forum stretched as far north as Scotland, as far west as Lusitania and the Ocean, as far south as the Thebaid and as far east as the Arabian desert.

Everywhere, authority came from the Roman people, along with their law, language and customs. The rest of the world, North Germania, Armenia, the Parthian kingdom, India and China, Arabia and Ethiopia formed the borders of the colossal empire.

Augustus reigned, concentrating all forces and powers in his hands. He was tribune and proconsul, prefect of morals and high priest, "Imperator" at last. He bore a name reserved for the gods. He sent surveyors to measure the world, censors to inventory its wealth and count its subjects. He built roads, aqueducts, temples and cities, and gave his people plenty of bread, games and festivals.

But this satiation of bread and constant feasting were taking place in Rome. When Jesus was born, Herod was the ruler of Judea on behalf of Augustus! He was the son of Antipater, a half-Bedouin nomad from Edom, and he suppressed all those who seemed dangerous to him

---

[29] Clement of Alexandria, *Stromates*, Book 1, 21.

before finally seizing power. It was only later that he sought to win the favour of the Jewish people before that of Augustus, the Caesar of the Roman Empire.

It was in this tumultuous yet propitious atmosphere that the Messiah was born, on 25 December of the year minus five, in Bethlehem, a small town not far Jerusalem, to the south, where Herod's administrative complex was located. All the censuses were taken there. It was therefore an important stopover for all the caravans, who were only passing through after stopping off in this mountainous basin overlooking the plain of Jezrael. Many caves on the hillside provided accommodation for caravanners in need of shelter.

A short time earlier, Zechariah was born in the days when Herod was King of Judea. He belonged to the "class of Abia", that is, the class priests who, by lot, had to perform one week's service a year in the temple in Jerusalem.

The rest of the time, as there were too many priests, he officiated in the mountains of Judah, not far from Ain-Karim, where he lived with his wife Elizabeth, herself of the priestly race of Aaron, i.e. of distant Egyptian origin. This is why this young priest had a singular life that isolated him somewhat from the Jewish communities, even though he was a priest himself. Perhaps it was for this reason that, at first, the instinctive question of believers was: "Who sinned so that the couple had no children: he or she? For time had passed, and although highly respected, the household was kept apart for the disgrace of not having offspring, the idea remaining that God did not want this because there was a secret sin, if not in Zechariah, at least in Elizabeth the Egyptian! But the years passed peacefully for both of them!

Now it happened that on the first day of the Sabbath, a Friday, Zechariah, having placed grains of incense on the embers of the sanctuary, bowed down to worship Yahweh on the right of the altar of incense, close to the seven-branched candelabra. A great fear shook him when he straightened up, for an angel was watching him benevolently. The holy texts tell us:

"Do not be afraid, Zechariah, for your prayer has been answered. Your wife Elizabeth will bear you a son, and you will call his name John. He will be a cause of joy and gladness for you, and many others will rejoice at his birth. For he will be great before God. He will not drink wine or anything that intoxicates, and he will be filled with the Holy Spirit from his mother's womb. He will bring many of the children of Israel back to the Lord their God. He will walk before the Lord in the spirit and power of Elijah, to turn the hearts of the fathers to their children, and to turn the unrighteous to the righteous, so that the Lord will have a well-prepared people.

No one can say whether Zechariah had prayed for this son or whether Elisabeth had remained the pious child of ancient Egypt, but after nine months John was born in the little village of Karem, which became Ain Karim. It was he who later baptised Jesus.

From this precise point, it is appropriate to make a few remarks about what follows. Just as, in Pharaonic times, believers renewed their faith in the birth of Osiris from his mother Nut, fathered by Ptah under the sacred sycamore tree, each time they read this passage from the Sacred Writings, those of Ra shrugged their shoulders and sneered, because for them it was Ra, the Sun, who had given birth to the first human.

This in no way prevented the great Ramses, an idolater of the Sun if ever there was one, and whose name alone is an insult to Ptah, from having his title accepted by Isis in a famous engraving in which the divine goddess of Heaven, placed under the sacred sycamore tree, gives birth to him so that he can be called "Per-Ahâ", or Pharaoh, i.e. "Son of God"! (see illustration below).

Today, atheists shrug their shoulders when they read the texts of the New Testament, while those who believe in the divine birth of Jesus find renewed hope in the thought that God can do anything, provided we live in purity and according to the commandments of the Eternal One. But all it takes is a major drought or an for even unbelievers to turn up in church and beg for mercy! You never know...

So why not accept this fact, without wanting formal proof, of the divine conception of Mary begotten by God?

I shall therefore simply recall what happened to Mary, Elizabeth's cousin, six months after the conception of the man who was to become John the Baptist. The angel came to visit Mary to inform her that she was blessed among women, having found favour with God. "You will conceive and bear a Son whose name will be Jesus. Therefore the Holy One to be born will be called the Son of God.

THE GREAT HYPOTHESIS

As the angel had added, as proof of this unique possibility, that he had visited the elderly Elizabeth six months earlier and that she would bear a son by her husband Zechariah, despite the advanced age of both spouses, Mary visited her cousin Elizabeth. The rest of the story is well known to everyone, and need not be mentioned here, including Mary's splendid canticle and her dialogue with Elizabeth. The same goes for the birth of John the Baptist and the misadventure of Joseph the betrothed. Let's turn instead to the three Magi...

The book of Daniel was full of the succession of empires to calculate the time of the coming of the Messiah. All the prophets and Magi had also made their calculations on this subject, of that there can be no doubt. It was feasible for those who knew the movements of the Divine-Mathematical Combinations, with their various precessional cogs bringing the Sun to the entrance of the constellation of Pisces to give birth to a "Fisher of Men". Three of them set their sights on a specific point: Jerusalem, for which they set off. Their caravans, rich and shiny, aroused curiosity and much envy. They enquired in many parts of the city about the place where the greatest man of the new age was to be born, because, they said, "we have seen his star rise from the east and we have come to worship him".

We're not in France, but in the Middle East, where the sky is similar to that of Egypt. The starry night is almost indescribably beautiful. It's not a kind of opaque veil as it is over Europe: the stars twinkle, vibrate and breathe to their own rhythms, as you can recognise their different pulsations in their sparkling, distinctive colours. Here too, the Milky Way is an enormous celestial river of light, not a pale cloud like in our Western sky. And everyone can follow the appearance, ascent and disappearance of the stellar groups, or constellations, that border this river of diamonds. The same goes for the big stars that surround them, as was the case for the Magi, who were perfectly informed about the one they were supposed to be looking at.

This star was undoubtedly Sirius, or Isis to the ancient Egyptians, whose reflections at certain times are blindingly bright, brighter than those of Venus, for example, which is always visible first. This year, from 18 February to 20 March 1981, Sirius was 17 times brighter than Venus when it appeared! Now, with the annual displacement of the star in relation to the Earth's precessional retreat, Sirius was in its prime position, precisely in December at the beginning of our era.

But let's return to the questions of the three Magi, which reached the ears of Herod, who was moved by the birth of a "future King". Concerned, he immediately summoned the religious leaders and doctors and asked them where Christ was to be born. They all replied: "In Bethlehem of Judah". The Scriptures were clear, tradition unanimous: and a prophet had said unequivocally: "And you, Bethlehem, land of Judah, no, you are not the smallest of the towns of Judah, for from you will come the Ruler who will govern my people Israel."

The wise old tyrant had the Magi called in secret, and asked about the precise time when the star had appeared to them, and what their investigations meant. The answer satisfied him but not reassure him. Herod, after a moment's reflection, said to them:

"Go to Bethlehem, for he is neither in Jerusalem nor in any other village near the city. Look for this child there. And when you have found him, come and report to me, so that I too may go and worship him."

It does not seem that the Magi detected the ruse in the hypocritical words of the bloodthirsty despot who, aware of the prophecies, was working to pass himself off as the Messiah! And to understand the sequence of events that followed, we need to look at the topography of the place. Jerusalem and Bethlehem are only a two-hour walk apart. Once you leave the mountain of the city itself by the Jaffa Gate, and have crossed the deep ravines, the landscape changes and you immediately discover the territory of Bethlehem, even though the town is not very close. Herod's knowledge of this place is explained by the fact that his palace was close to the gate of Jaffa. Every time he went out, he passed through Bethlehem. On the famous night of the murder of the children, no one in Jerusalem was worried about Herod's soldiers leaving the city, as they did not pass through the city but went straight through the famous Jaffa Gate. On several occasions when I was passing through Jerusalem, I passed through this famous gate to remind myself of this atrocious scene. I was accompanied by another Elisabeth, who helped me and made the task much easier, so I didn't forget a thing on those panoramic walks that took us back almost 2,000 years!

Finally, if this bloody night was possible, it was because of the census. Here again, atheists or those who are ignorant of ancient history may think that this is a fabrication, because it is hard to see how, in those days, a whole population could move around like that, just to declare their civil status. But the Roman Empire was all-powerful and tyrannical. Augustus had decided on this general census because he had little confidence in Herod. It was not just a question of declaring one's identity before the scribes of Rome, but also of carrying out a survey of the real resources of Palestine and a general establishment of the land register. Rome was preparing the transformation of the country into one of its provinces, and it had all the officials qualified to do this.

A striking example, which I recovered in Egypt at the same time, when the country was already under the domination of Rome and censuses took place every 14 years, is an "Apograph". This is the document drawn up precisely to enact a similar census, which was carried out even in smallest villages of the Thebaid, and one of which was preserved and found:

> *I, Gaius Vibius Maximus, Governor of Egypt, make known: As the census of families is imminent, it is necessary to order all those who, for whatever reason, are away from their place of birth, to return to their original home to take part in the performance of the customary census.*

The orders must have been much the same in Palestine, even though this was the first census before the country was annexed. As for the Magi, after finding the baby and worshipping him, they went straight home. They were tired, and it would have been a long diversions for them to return to Jerusalem, since that was not their route.

Herod then flew into a rage and ordered the massacre. Given Herod's mentality, this is easily explained, as I have done at length in my *Jesus the Christ*. Let us add here that it was useless, since Joseph, Mary and the new-born baby had already fled to Egypt. It took six days to make this journey by donkey through the desert, where even today anyone can disappear without a trace! This was the time Herod waited before sending his henchmen to Bethlehem, so sure was he of seeing the Magi again. In his fury, he ordered the murder of all boys aged two and under!

During the Holy Family's stay in Egypt, Palestine was practically under siege. All meetings were forbidden throughout the country, and even walking in groups was forbidden, on pain of immediate arrest. And anyone taken to the Hyrcania prison disappeared forever! But Herod was becoming increasingly ill. When the people were certain that he would not recover, he rose up, led by the two rabbis Judas and Matthias, and removed the golden eagle, the insignia of Rome, from the entrance to the temple. However, the dying man still had the strength to have the ringleaders arrested and to watch them burned alive before dying himself! His body was transported with great pomp to the fortress of Herodium, south of Bethlehem, to be buried with unprecedented pomp.

During this time, the Holy Family rested on the banks of the Nile, waiting patiently for the order to return. Near Heliopolis, at Matarieh, we can still see the venerable remains of the sycamore tree known as the "Virgin Tree", under which, according to oral tradition, Mary rested while nursing Jesus. What is certain is that she fled to Egypt and stayed there until the storm calmed down. If Egypt had not welcomed Jesus at his birth, Christ could not have existed afterwards, since the baby would have died in the bloodbath that flooded Bethlehem. Here too, Egypt played a very important role in the origin of Christianity, albeit an episodic one. The Copts are still very much aware of this today.

We need to open another parenthesis here, because the Coptic monasteries of the Fayum desert possess a multitude of completely unpublished manuscripts and papyri, not only copied in Coptic from the 4th to 9th centuries AD, from more ancient papyri, but also from Abyssinian, Syriac, Aramaic manuscripts, etc., which are still in existence today.

Copies of the so-called apocryphal gospels exist, including the *Gospel of Nicodemus*, which Sozomen and many other early-century writers recount in their Ecclesiastical History, in Greek or Latin. In this Gospel, which is known and recognised by the Church, the episode of Matarieh and the sycamore tree is recounted, even adding that where the shade of the holy tree stopped, a spring gushed forth so that Mary could wash the tunic of the little Jesus. Although several 18th-century authors still report the presence of this fountain in the middle of the desert, it has disappeared today.

The Gospel of Nicodemus tells of the Holy Family's stay in Egypt, where they visited eight cities, the first of which was Men-Nefer, or Memphis in Greek. The angel then ordered Joseph to return to Nazareth.

It is nevertheless disturbing to read these texts from the first centuries, written at considerable distances from one another, and which all, more or less, recount the same events. It is to this problem that I draw the reader's attention, because it is impossible for so many scribes to invent *the same story*. It must have happened!

Some readers, perhaps too fervent and unconditional followers of Catholicism at the end of our era, will say that I am too tempted to trace everything about the One God back to Egypt! That's true, of course, but because that's the reality demonstrated by every monotheistic act from Menes to the present day, i.e. for 6,000 years!

When I was at Chantilly three years ago, a Synod of the Fathers of the Holy Spirit brought together some one hundred and twenty prelates of that order from all over the world. One evening, I was asked to speak before them, to explain my attribution of original monotheism to the pharaohs, and to the existing reminiscence between Osiris and Jesus, between the Divine Triad and the Holy Family. The discussion got very heated and lasted until after 2 o'clock in the morning! Exasperated by the procrastination and disputes based on form rather than substance, I retorted and concluded that, if the Holy Family had not taken refuge in Egypt, there would never have been a Christian era, and that they themselves would be elsewhere, woodcutters or farmers, but certainly not distinguished bishops! I was certainly wrong to get carried away, but the original Egypt provides the link between Ahâ, the first Adam, the Elder Son of Ptah, who populated Eden; Ahâ-Men-Ptah, who was swallowed up by divine wrath. The lands that border the Nile are the resurgence of this disappearance. All the monuments and texts provide a glaring explanation.

But let's get back to Joseph and Mary who take Jesus back to Nazareth... After birth, it is death that is important, the rest being barely a second of eternity in the combinatorial paths calculated by God. What comes with death, and afterwards, with the Beyond of earthly life, corresponds to the two millennia of the Piscean cycle, which will usher in the Age of Aquarius.

Jesus, as the Christ, knew not only the hour of his earthly end, but also the way, atrocious for a human, in which it would occur. Ever since his break with the people of Galilee, his life had become a journey without respite or moral rest, far from Capernaum and the lake, passing through towns and villages where he tried to remain unknown. He travelled along the borders of the countries of Tyre and Sidon, as well as the Decapolis, before continuing his journey with his disciples towards Caesarea, in search of an even deeper solitude. Jesus knew that his end was approaching, and he wanted to prepare for it as he had to, so that divine history would continue according to heavenly desires.

It was on that famous evening that he asked his friends the question of confidence: "What do people say that I am?

If he asked this question, it was not interrogatively, but to oblige his disciples to proclaim aloud, in opposition to popular assertions, what they thought of his person. And they replied according to the Sacred Texts: "Some say you are John the Baptist, others Elijah, others again Jeremiah, or some other resurrected prophet of old".

Through Peter and the others, this testimony accurately reflected the opinion of the Jewish people, who no longer saw in Jesus the prophesied Messiah. *In their eyes, he was once again one of the prophets who had foreshadowed the true Messiah!* It was a moment of disaster. Yet that same evening became the evening of the Transfiguration. The Messiah finally appeared before all the disciples, whose splendour each of them would recount without contradicting himself. It was at that moment that, for all the disciples, Jesus definitively became "the Christ", in all the majesty of the Kingdom, which would be the Kingdom beyond earthly life. And so, when the fatal day arrived, Jesus wearied the emissaries of the Sanhedrin, the divine doctors of the Jewish schools, who had come to question him. He knew that they would not forgive him for calling himself "Son of God", but his wisdom, which frightened his judges, earned him the applause of the people, who recognised him as the Messiah. So when Jesus was brought before Pilate, he knew what he was up against. Pontius Pilate was then governor of Syria and Palestine, one of the most important posts in the Roman Empire, because these two countries, situated between the Nile and the Euphrates, were a key military bridge between the ancient centres of Asian civilisation and Roman power.

Pilate, like the leading soldiers of his time, was very ill-disposed towards the Jews. What's more, this was under the ministerial yoke of Sejan, who reigned from 23 to 31, that is, two more years after Jesus' death. And this Sejan was hostile to the Jews, just like the emperor Tiberius himself. So, as soon as Pontius Pilate arrived in 26 AD, he showed everyone that the tide was turning and that there was no longer any question of going easy on the Jews. The uprisings were put down in bloodbaths, which need not be repeated here. But since Pilate's "agnostic" ideas were well known, Jesus met a "modern unbeliever" on his arrival before the governor, whom he confronted calmly.

Objections have been raised against the historical character of this gospel trial, since the coexistence of two courts of law as different as the Jewish court and the Roman court could not interfere as the biblical accounts have transmitted them to us. Here again I take issue, because apart from the texts, there are Egyptian documents from the time of Christ himself which record the same minutes of these two aberrant trials.

Shortly before the interrogation began, Pilate had received news that a prisoner had been brought to him from the Sanhedrin. Since he had heard about this peaceful but proud Jesus, who thought he was the Son of God, he had listened to the report of the centurion who had taken part in the arrest. So he began by asking the rabbis in the most official tone: "What grievance do you have against this man? The answer embarrassed him, for he understood that it was in fact for matters of religious heresy that he was being asked to pass judgment. So he turned the problem around more kindly, saying, "Judge him yourselves according to your laws."

The reply was immediate and unambiguous: "This man deserves to die, and we are not allowed to put anyone to death! Because when he stirred up the people, he forbade them to pay tribute to Caesar.

Pilate was thus obliged to interrogate Jesus himself, on pain of the Sanhedrin sending a denunciation to Rome that would show the lightness with which the government regarded such a serious accusation! At the very least, he would have been disgraced!

Tertullian gives a perfect account of this scene (Apol., XXI):

"The teachers and the foremost of the Jews, rebelling against the teaching of Jesus, which confounded them, and furious to see the people running in droves after him, forced Pilate, commander in Judea for the Romans, to abandon him to them and crucify him. He himself had predicted it. That's not enough: the Prophets had predicted it long before".

These words fit in perfectly with the Gospel account, which shows that there was no judgment given in the Praetorium, but only violence on the part of the Jews, coercion on the part of Pilate and suffering on the part of Jesus. For it is very true that the Jewish doctors forced Pilate to give him up to them, and that they forced the governor to act against his deep conviction concerning Jesus' innocence.

The "Praetorium" in Pontius Pilate's palace, referred to by Tertullian, was decorated with a mosaic pavement, or *Lithostrote*, which symbolised elevation in Hebrew, and which the Jews called *Gabbatha*.

So, once again, this is a real symbol designed by God, so that Jesus would be judged as a criminal in this high place, called the "Praetorium" for the cause.

Similarly, Lactantius, but later (276/311), wrote along the same lines as Tertullian in his *Institutions* (Book IV-18):

"When the Jews had seized Jesus, they brought him to Pontius Pilate, who, as the representative of the empire, was then ruling Syria. They asked him to bind him to the cross, accusing Jesus of nothing other than calling himself the Son of God and King of the Jews. When Pilate heard these accusations and saw Jesus said nothing in his defence, he declared that he could find nothing in him worthy of death. But these unjust accusers, together with the people they had incited, began to shout and stubbornly demand his crucifixion with violent and threatening cries. Pondus was then overcome by these cries and by the urgings of the tetrarch Herod, who feared he would be dethroned. Nevertheless, he did not pass sentence, but handed him over to the Jews to be judged according to their law.

The real tragedy of this "judgement in Pilate's Praetorium" lay in the fact that the Jews, who were the accusers before the Roman governor, did not show themselves to be defenders of the outraged Jewish religion, but rather traitors bent on losing Jesus by any means possible! This is why, ceasing to be Jews, they committed the infamy of defending Rome's interests by accusing Christ of stirring up the people and asking them to stop paying taxes to the oppressor occupying Palestine.

Moreover, there is judicial and legal proof that Jesus was condemned to death for a political crime, not a religious crime of blasphemy or sacrilege, and even less for having preached a new cult in contradiction with the Mosaic law. In fact, this proof is the very record of the sentence pronounced by Pontius Pilate, by virtue of which Jesus was led to his death by the Roman soldiers.

In Rome, there was a practice that has since been borrowed by French jurisprudence, which was to present a sign in front of the condemned with an extract from their sentence so that the public would know for what crime death was required. Pilate had a sign placed at the top of the cross on which were written four words: *Jesus Nazaremus Rex Juderum*, which have since been reproduced everywhere by the abbreviation I.N.R.I.

The cause of this condemnation was thus marked: Jesus had to die because he was the "King of the Jews". And what proves the politicisation of this crucifixion was the conduct of the princes of the priests. Their hatred - is not too strong a word - did not overlook the smallest detail. Fearing that the four words would be taken literally, they asked Pilate not to put the words, but "I.N. was called R.I.": Jesus the Nazarene was called "R.I.". Jesus the Nazarene called himself King of the Jews! And Pontius Pilate, annoyed at the hypocrisy of those who had forced him to this horrible end, replied harshly: *Quod scripsi, scripsi*, in other words: "What is written, is written!

On this subject, an exchange of correspondence between Theodore and Pilate exists, and here are the two extracts relating to this judgment, which confirm it. The first is from Theodore to Pilate:

"Who was the man against whom you were accused and who was crucified by the people of Palestine? If many of them brought this charge justly, why did you not grant them their just request? And if they asked unjustly, why did you transgress the law and order something that was far from just?"

Pilate replied, "I did not want to crucify him because he was showing signs; but I had him crucified because his accusers said, 'He claims to be King!'"

But the most important letter was the one sent by Pontius Pilate to Herod Antipas, in response to a letter he had received from him.

This precious document is one of the official apocrypha, recopied in Syriac from the 2nd century and taken from the Codex Thilo. Here it is transcribed in full in French:

Pilate to Herod the Tetrarch, hello!

"Know and consider that on the day you handed Jesus over to me, I had pity on myself and testified, washing my hands, that I was innocent of the blood of the One who rose from the tomb after three days; but I fulfilled your good pleasure over him, since you wanted me to join you in crucifying him. But now I have heard from his executioners and from the soldiers who watched over his tomb that he has risen from the grave: and above all I have been assured of the truth of what I had been told, that he was seen alive in Galilee with the same form, the same voice, the same doctrines and the same disciples, having changed in nothing, openly preaching his resurrection and the eternal Kingdom. And behold, heaven and earth rejoiced, and behold, my wife Procla believed in Him because of the visions she had seen when you sent me word to deliver Jesus to the people of Israel because of their evil intentions towards her. Then, when my wife Procla heard that Jesus had risen and that he had been seen in Galilee, she took Longinus the centurion and the twelve soldiers who were guarding the tomb with her, and went off as if to a great spectacle to see the arrival of the Messiah. And she saw him followed by his disciples. And as they looked at him in amazement, he stared at them and said, "What is this? Do you believe in me? Know, Procla, that in the testament which God gave to the patriarchs, it is said that all those who had perished would live again through my death which you saw. And now you see that I am alive, whom you crucified; and I endured many things before I was buried. Now listen to me and believe in God my Father, who is with me. For I have broken the bonds of death, and have broken down the gates of Sheol, and it is my coming that will come next." And when my wife Procla and the soldiers heard these things, they came and told them to me, weeping, because they too had been against Him when they plotted the ill-treatment they did to Him, so that I too was afflicted on my bed and put on mourning clothes and took with me fifty soldiers and my wife and went to Galilee. And as I walked along the road, I testified that Herod had done these things with me, that he had arranged them with me and that he had forced me to arm myself against Him and to judge the Judge of all and to scourge the Anointed One, the Lord of the Anointed. And when we came near Him, Herod, there was a great voice from heaven and a terrible thunder, and the earth shook and gave off a sweet fragrance; nothing like it had ever been seen in the temple of Jerusalem. When I stopped on the road, Our Lord saw me; he himself had stopped and was talking to his disciples.

But I prayed in my heart, for I knew that it was he whom you had delivered to me, and that he was the Lord of all created things and the Creator of all. But when we saw him, we all fell at his feet with our faces to the ground. And I said aloud: "I have sinned, Lord, because I presided over the tribunal that judged you, who justly avenge all things. And alas! I know that you are God, the Son of God, and I have seen your Humanity but not your Divinity. Herod and the children of Israel forced me to torture you. So have mercy on me, O God of Israel".

This letter was one of the reasons for Pontius Pilate's arrest in Rome, the other obviously being the earthquake and the darkness that ensued for a moment over the entire surface of the empire. The arrest order signed by Tiberius was therefore issued, decreeing that he be put in chains and taken back to Italy.

It was while sitting in the Pantheon, in plenary session before the assembled Senate, that the emperor had Pilate brought before him. The first questioning of the former governor of Palestine was for "exposing the empire to complete destruction through his negligence and incapacity".

It is beyond the scope of this article to discuss Pilate's trial, which was subsequently continued in the Capitol, and which forced Tiberius to take new, harsher decisions against the Jews of Palestine. But by looking at the minutes of the orders given to Licianus, Pilate's successor in Jerusalem, it is easy to form a fair opinion.

The cries of the huge Jewish crowd in Jerusalem were far removed from Rome and the special atmosphere of that other trial! But Pilate still had to hear the screams in his ears: "Death! Death!" This furious, howling mass continued to shout "Death! Death!" when he had asked a slave to hold the basin in which he had had water poured over his fingers. The Jews had long been familiar with this ceremony performed by the governor. So there was a great hush among the multitude, who knew they had won. Pilate's voice rose to say: "I wash my hands of your decision and I remain innocent of the blood of this victim. You will all answer for it. The crowd unanimously endorsed the accusation: "Yes! Yes! May his blood fall on us and our children!

Although Pontius Pilate was the first to suffer, the Jews have borne a large part of it ever since, without any mention of cause and effect. Whether or not Jesus was the Son of , the origin of evil dates back to the day of the crucifixion! Death on the cross was the most painful of all, and the circumstances that accompanied it made it all the more infamous. With this form of mortal torture, and although no vital organ was affected, the condemned man died very slowly, through the exhaustion of his physical and moral strength, from the terrible suffering he endured from the fastening of the long nails! What's more, this infinite human suffering, in all its horror, was left open to the unhealthy curiosity or hateful vindictiveness of the assembled passers-by. The slightest cry uttered by the victim, the slightest movement unleashed in the body by a more acute pain, was answered by the joyous howls of the delirious crowd! Not to mention the swarms of flies and mosquitoes that swarmed around the bloody hands and feet...

All this was certainly fresh in Pontius Pilate's mind as he himself awaited his death warrant! But while he was perfectly familiar with the process of disintegration of the human body, having often observed in minute detail the ordeal endured by those condemned to death, he was less familiar with the suffering that preceded the journey from the palace to Golgotha, which everyone knows the "Via Dolorosa": the Way of the Cross!

There is no question here of opening the debate as to where Jesus set off from on his way to Calvary: Antonia or Herod's fortress. The distance from Golgotha to the two fortresses is the same, as is the altitude. Golgotha is at 755 metres; Antonia at 750 metres; and Herod's palace at 755 metres. However, the route with the carrying of the cross is much harder from Antonia, with a significant difference in altitude followed by an identical climb. But it was from Herod's palace that the sad procession set off.

The crowd was large and unruly, and the sight of Roman soldiers using whips to clear their way is not at all extraordinary in the context of this day that marked the life of the world for more than two millennia!

Here is the map of Jerusalem on that day. It is easy to recognise Antonia's fortress, at the very top of the second wall, and Herod's Palace just to the west, with Golgotha, outside the walls and between the two, marked with a cross (see next map).

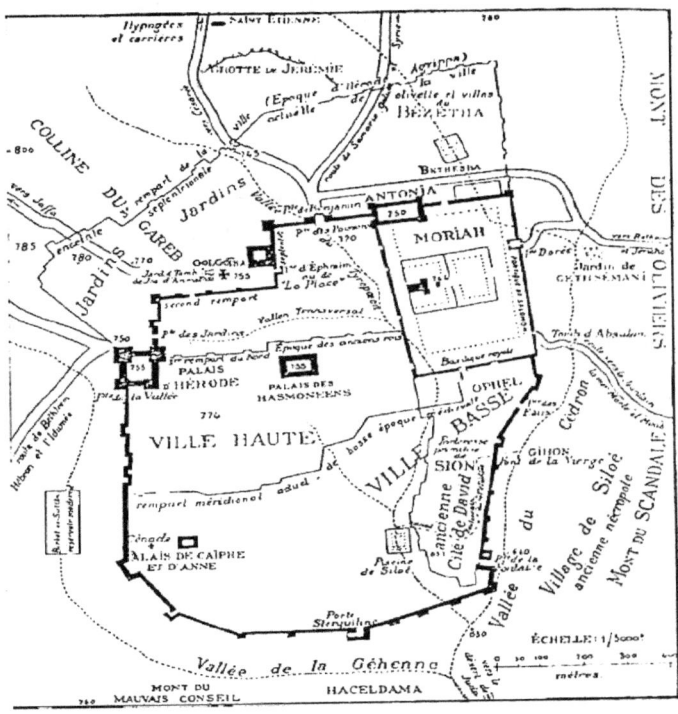

The Western Gate, or Garden Gate, just to the north of Herod's palace, opened not only onto the road to Jaffa, but above all onto the splendid gardens of Mount Gareb; this gate did not become the gateway to Jaffa until eleven centuries later.

So Golgotha, which in Hebrew means "the place of the skull", will remain eternally the place of renunciation to save the soul of the world!

But what a different path this cross has travelled up to the present day! I was in Jerusalem at Easter 1976, "waiting" to enter the Holy Sepulchre. Not to mention the sheer horror of the building known as the "Holy Place", which was locked with a large bolt on the outside to prevent anyone from entering during the 45 minutes allotted to the Congregation who were there to celebrate "their" Mass according to "their" conception of that Easter Day! It was important to avoid any dogmatic incidents.

On the esplanade, I overlooked the crowd from above, between two Israeli soldiers armed with machine guns, stationed there to protect the crowd from any terrorists ready to drop a bomb. And this swarming, gesticulating mass, bearing large crosses similar to that of Jesus Christ, was literally fighting over questions of dogma or precedence. They had come to blows, to the great joy of the soldiers, but to my great shame! How was this still possible after two millennia of Christianity?...

What more unfortunate concrete example could conclude this end of an era in which the fallen Pisces symbolised the beginning?...

RESTITUTION OF THE HEBREW CALENDAR (4726-4744)

ÈRE CHRÉTIENNE	PÉRIODE JULIENNE	Lettre dominicale	NISAN NÉOMÉNIE VRAIE	NISAN NÉOMÉNIE MOYENNE	NISAN 1er ou 2ème	PÂQUE LÉGALE
av. l'ère chr. 7	4707	D	31 mars, 4 h. 15'	31 mars, 0 h. 31'	31 mars	Mardi 11 avril
6	4708	C	20 mars, 5 h. 45'	20 mars, 9 h. 19'	20 mars	Samedi 3 avril
5	4709	BA	7 avril, 1 h. 45'	7 avril, 6 h. 52'	7 avril	Jeudi 23 mars
4	4710	G	27 mars, 11 h.40'	27 mars, 15 h.41'	28 mars	Mercredi 11 avril
3	4711	F	15 avril, 11 h.29'	15 avril, 13 h.13'	15 avril	Dimanche 31 mars
2	4712	E	5 avril, 4 h. 27'	4 avril, 22 h. 2'	5 avril	Jeudi 20 mars
1	4713	DC	24 mars, 19 h.45'	24 mars, 6 h. 51'	24 mars	Mercredi 7 avril
apr. l'ère chr. 1	4714	B	12 avril, 17 h.10'	12 avril, 4 h. 23'	12 avril	Lundi 28 mars
2	4715	A	1 avril, 22 h.52'	1 avril, 13 h.12'	1 avril	Dimanche 16 avril
3	4716	G	21 mars, 23 h.28'	21 mars, 22 h. 1'	22 mars	Jeudi 5 avril
4	4717	FE	8 avril, 16 h. 48'	8 avril, 19 h. 34'	9 avril	Lundi 24 mars
5	4718	D	28 mars, 22 h.20'	29 mars, 4 h. 22'	29 mars	Dimanche 12 avril
6	4719	C	16 avril, 20 h.30'	17 avril, 1 h. 55'	17 avril	Vendredi 2 avril
7	4720	B	6 avril, 11 h.16'	6 avril, 10 h. 44'	6 avril	Mardi 22 mars
8	4721	AG	26 mars, 1 h. 28'	25 mars, 19 h.32'	26 mars	Lundi 9 avril
9	4722	F	14 avril, 4 h. 2'	13 avril, 17 h. 5'	14 avril	Vendredi 29 mars
10	4723	E	3 avril, 14 h.56'	3 avril, 1 h. 54'	3 avril	Jeudi 17 avril
11	4724	D	23 mars, 18 h.37'	23 mars, 10 h. 42'	23 mars	Lundi 6 avril
12	4725	CB	10 avril, 11 h. 0'	10 avril, 8 h. 15'	10 avril	Samedi 26 mars

- 8 (4,706) Census of Roman citizens.
- 6 (4,708) 25 March (25 December): Nativity.
- 5 (4,709) At the beginning of the year: Adoration of the Magi.
- 4 (4,710) Death of Herod.
- 3 (4,711) The Holy Family returns from Egypt.
+ 6 (4,719) Judea becomes a Roman province.
+ 7 (4,720) Jesus, aged twelve, arrives in Jerusalem for the Passover.
+ 29 (4,742) Jesus is baptised by John the Baptist.

15

WHAT I SAW AND UNDERSTOOD

If you want to save yourself, the door is open. It's up to you to know the Son of God, to become perfect to be happy.
Justin (Dialogues, VIII, 1 -42)

My earthly passions have been crucified, the fire of material desires is no longer within me, but living water murmurs within me saying to me in intimacy: "Come to the Father!
Ignatius of Antioch (To the Romans, VII -A.D. 1 02)

According to Descartes, extent is the essence of bodies. I am not a Cartesian, and my sickly body interests me only insofar as it allows my Divine Parcel to act in the direction I wish to go. For my part, I would say that the soul possesses the unfathomable density of space that propelled it into the carnal envelope, remaining its owner during the earthly sojourn.

It is not my intention to philosophise here, but simply to recount what I have seen, and which has therefore enabled me to understand the whole of cosmic reality, if not all its details. No more than to talk endlessly about the near-fatal accidents that developed certain mental and spiritual faculties. But rather to start from that primordial moment, at the end of the last coma, when I discovered the glimmer of light that was missing to bring together all the scattered elements of understanding that I had already accumulated. Up until then it had been a simple understanding. Then came the beginning of Knowledge.

This light came with the confirmation of the exactness of the combinatorial geometry that presides over all natural births, whether of things or beings: namely, of the very real existence of the Law of Creation. The appearance that reality is coarse in its generality, and that only the idea that we form of it allows us to detect the truth, and therefore purity, then takes on all its value. The example given below of generations who do not want to understand the mentality of their

Elders, whatever the cycle, is typical of this fact. The eternal recommencement in another space of time, at the beginning of each era, should permeate all those who seek to understand. What's more, admitting that the eternity of this Space-Time combination is the sole fact of divine will is for those who have finally understood. Such readers will not be surprised by the apparent paradox between those who can understand and those who want to and succeed in doing so. The difference lies solely in the powerful hold of the Parcel, the Soul, over the mind, which is merely reasonable reason. This was my personal proverbial sentence in Volume 2 of the Origins Trilogy: *The Survivors of Atlantis: Human reason possesses no reasonable reasoning in its conception of God.*

It is not a question, for the sake of simple reason, of forcing a protocol convention of adoring God for his creation and the commandments that flow from it. Worshipping something, someone, or God, is within the reach of the simplest human being who is willing to bend the knee to do so. Everyone manages to do it in full view of the world or in a more or less hypocritical disguised way in church. You have to comply with the rules of society, even though this is no longer the case. But the reason I'm talking about is the reason of the soul, the reason that is woven from birth into living in harmony with heavenly decisions. He will do good when he has to, and he will refrain from any personal will when the celestial combinatorial configurations are harmful to him. First of all, it takes a certain amount of trial and error to get used to this cerebral calculation, which does not depend on any contemporary religious formulation, be it Christian, neo-troist, theosophical or spiritualist, if the latter sect has any real spirituality.

Philo of Alexandria said that sleep characterised and symbolised the ignorant, the blind who plunged themselves out of the material world in this way, in order to ignore the truth.

A primordial Coptic document (another one!) from the year 148 AD, found in 1945 near Nag-Hamadi, halfway between Cairo and Denderah, but already in Upper Egypt, has since been authenticated as a fifth Gospel by all the world's scientists and scholars: the *Evangilium Veritatis*, or simply the Gospel of Truth.

Here again, the Coptic copy was made by a scribe from a Greek text of the Alexandrian School, but no one can say in what language or by whom the original was written. If I mention it here, it is only in relation to the truth, as I will go into more detail about this Gospel in the last chapter of this book.

In fact, this precious text from the middle of the second century speaks of the duality strangely felt by those who wish to know the "unthinkable", the "ungraspable" and the "incomprehensible". Leaflet 17 announces that the desire to know is not an intoxication of the senses, but "a search for the One from whom it emerged: that whole which is in itself". It is this lack of knowledge that produces powerlessness, anguish and fear. This has affirmed forgetfulness, then lies, whereas Knowledge engenders Truth, stable, unshakeable, unalterable, perfectly beautiful.

Ignorance, then, does not come from sleep, but on the contrary from the refusal to open our eyes to this very simple yet sufficiently complicated beauty that it is the cause of sleep agitated by the jolts of anguish and terror.

I experienced all this during my prolonged hospital stays. I had the time to open or close my eyes, to reflect, to see the light, or to remain immersed in darkness. I was looking for the Light and it came to me, little by little, by dint of reflection.

In this fascinating Egypt, I had meditated for a long time, but the agglutinating presence of the imposing mass of tourists, even at night, meant that I could not meditate as I wished, except at Denderah. However, I couldn't stay locked up with Isis in the dark, or with just a single candle for lighting. I had to put the results of my reflections down in black and white, and have the hundreds of slides I took developed so that I could study the hieroglyphics carefully. Because it was all there, engraved, drawn and reproduced as a warning to the future. Nothing else was possible!

My overall understanding of the facts had already enabled me to discern the community principle of these ancients, who saw only two classes: that of their people and that of foreigners. They understood, practically without studying, the need to place themselves under God's protection. It was innate in all the natives of this second land. The others, those who lived elsewhere, were indifferent to them, and for that reason they remained in ignorance. They did not seek to spread the good word; those who were interested only had to come and settle on the banks of the Nile. The others thus became infidels of Ptah, but not enemies; they remained foreigners unworthy of instruction.

Their great fear stemmed from the predictable fact that their future generations, those of their younger siblings, would forget the lessons of the past and become strangers on this soil blessed a second time by Ptah: Ath-Kâ-Ptah, the "Second Heart of God". This was the main reason for the indestructible teaching engraved on the stone walls throughout the Temple of Denderah. That was the reason for the huge blocks stacked up to support this sacred writing, destined to defy time, only to be found again later, if Ptah decided to forget Egypt at the appointed time.

The people formed a single, real entity. From the Pharaoh to the most humble of labourers, all were equal before the Ultimate Judge who weighed the souls as they entered the Beyond of earthly life! Equality was not an empty word, since everyone ate their fill and clothed themselves without problems. In short, it was full-blown socialism before its time! The difference, which is still valid today, lay in a parallel conception that originated in certain corners of the so-called popular mind. These souls could not penetrate the cosmic world, because it was beyond their comprehension.

There was therefore no contempt on the part of the priests, nor any specific initiation to attain Knowledge of the Creator and his creation. There was no pretence of trying to hide anything by means of 'Mysteries', in hermetic parables, but the desire to leave hieroglyphics to those capable of understanding it one day, should it no longer be read by those who had the capacity to do so.

All this is very well explained in texts that have been unduly added to the so-called Book of the Dead, from which I have extracted the whole of chapter XVII, which is in fact a large part of Tentyrite theology. Others confirm, by their titles alone, the reality of the foregoing. One chapter, which is still famous because it is apparently obscure, states that this "book will thus be transmitted from generation to generation without accident", although it is very simple to decipher for anyone who accepts the value of this original monotheism in which the Per-Ahâ, or pharaoh, played the just and equitable role of Son of God. In this same chapter CXXV, the prohibition on allowing it to be read by any man "except by his sons" is a clear indication of what he has decreed.

Whoever possesses the papyrus must be worthy of it. For this reason, he must show it only to his Cadets, who will pass it on in the same way.

Even more explicit is this warning in chapter CXLVIII:

Nowhere, never, in all eternity past or to come, does anyone but the pure know this book, which is the truth. You are reading it now, but nowhere, nowhere, will another impure eye interpret it in its own way, so that no unholy ear may hear it. Let it be read only by you, and heard by those to whom you teach it.

This is why, when the Greeks flooded into the Nile delta in the 7th and 6th centuries BC, all the temples wove a kind of veil that decreed obscurantism by systematically introducing mystery. When scholars questioned the priests, they took refuge behind the absolute authority of the sacred texts... only slightly disguised! Thus, the incomprehensible hieroglyphs of the Hellenes became the following sentences: "What this book says, don't tell because the gods would get angry. That is why it must remain the greatest of mysteries". Or again: "Never tell this book, for it would be an abomination to make it known to men". Here, only the word "stranger" has been replaced by "man", and this pious message must have made the priest smile because, for him, a man could not be a stranger, but one of his fellows from the people chosen by Ptah to possess the Knowledge of his Creation. It was probably from this restriction that all the Greek authors' affabulations arose. Herodotus recounts his irritation at being put in his place by a priest of Sais: "If I were to tell you why the sacred animals are mummified in this way, you would penetrate to the divine, about which I can tell you nothing. And if I have ever touched on this subject, I have not so without being compelled to do so by necessity.

Diodorus of Sicily was even more explicit:

"The Egyptians perform many incredible ceremonies in honour of the sacred animals, the explanation and origin of which we are unable to give, because the priests keep these doctrines secret and are forbidden to talk about them."

It was a duty, a true obedience to the precepts of Ptah, not to reveal to outsiders anything of what formed the very 'Heart' of this blessed land. And this concept of duty at every moment increasingly led, as time went by, to a struggle within the souls of the scholars in possession of the keys to the sacred texts. The instinct for self-preservation in the face of the approaching end set in motion prodigious systems for preserving the writings! Fear never drove any of them to betray the mental pact linking their Divine Parcel to the One God. And this was true long before our time!

The myth of Prometheus, for example, which is one of Hesiod's finest jewels, prophesies Christ! I was fascinated by the undeniable reminiscences of the original traditions and the beginnings of Christianity. Here's a brief outline of the story of Prometheus, in which one of the protagonists, Chiron the Centaur, is the hero: Chiron the Centaur, is featured by Nostradamu s![30]

Prometheus was the son of a Titan, Japet, and therefore a Titan himself and father of Deucalion and Hellen. At the time he lived, Jupiter had just dethroned Saturn, who was therefore king of the gods, presiding over Olympus. To take revenge for human disinterest in his new glory, Jupiter hid food from mankind, forcing them to work hard to obtain it and survive. This degenerated into a memorable dispute between the various gods and creatures of the Earth over the share due to Olympus, and the sacrifice this entailed for mortals.

It was at this point that Prometheus intervened. To arbitrate the dispute fairly, he divided an ox into two pieces, placing on one side all the bones covered with the animal's fat, and on the other the flesh under the entire skin of the ox. Jupiter, king of the gods, pretended to be fooled, and deliberately chose the bones covered in fat. And to punish Prometheus for his rebellion, he hid fire from mankind. But the Titan's cleverness enabled him to find it and introduce it to mortals. Jupiter's new revenge: it was Pandora, the first woman made of silt by Vulcan at the behest of the King of the Gods, in order to seduce Epimetheus, Prometheus' Titan brother. It was she whose curiosity punished the whole Earth, for she opened the amphora from which all the evils of mankind flowed! And Prometheus was bound to a column where an eagle arrived every day to devour his immortal liver, indefinitely. It was Hercules, Jupiter and Alcmene's own son, , who freed Prometheus, who thus lost his immortality. It was only later, thanks to Chiron the Centaur, that he regained it. What is important here is the similarity between this myth and the divine wrath against humanity, followed by the redemption of the survivors. Unquestionably, Hesiod, followed by Aeschylus, is narrating a distorted Egyptian oral tradition, which was itself taken up by the Hebrews, before becoming the traditional Christian foundation.

---

[30] See page 63 of the book *Nostradamus trahi* by Élisabeth Bellecour, published by Laffont, 1981.

Since the ancient Egyptians had launched the tradition, it is not surprising that the Greeks should have sought an ideal far superior to the one born of their mythology. But that their disappointment at failing to achieve it should have triggered in them a destructive spirit of what they had given up trying to understand because *they* had not wanted to *integrate* with the Egyptian people was the beginning of their decadence!

For the ideal sought is that of every man with a soul and a heart. But for the ancient descendants of Ahâ-Men-Ptah, the only humanity was that of the people of Ptah. To reach this ideal, they had to accept that they were no longer foreigners, but *residents* of this land: men in their own right!

It was the first glimmer, the spark that eventually gave rise to flame and light. I had seen this little light in hospital, even before I started convalescing, while talking to a priest about Moses and Egypt. It was at this point that the priest took his Bible out of his pocket and read me the passage that triggered the beginning of my perception: "The Egyptian shall not be an abomination to you, for you have been a sojourner in his land. The sons born to him in the third generation will have access the assembly of Yahweh."

This is in the Old Testament, in Deuteronomy XXIII-8 and 9.

If the Jews allowed the Egyptians to become their *alter egos*, the descendants of a single popular origin, it was because, despite their differences of opinion, they were brothers. Together they served the same ideal of God, whether he was called Ptah or Yahweh. This ideal is also found in admirable form in Lamartine. A friend of mine sent me his *Méditations poétiques* to ponder over at my convalescent bedside. In the first, there is this extract that I treasure in my heart:

> *But perhaps beyond the bounds of its sphere,*
> *Places where the real sun shines on other two,*
> *If I could leave my body in the earth,*
> *What I have dreamed of for so long would appear before my very eyes.*
> *There I would get drunk at the source to which I aspire*
> *There I would find hope and love again,*
> *And that ideal good to which every soul aspires,*
> *And one that has no name on earth.*

The Egyptians and the Jews had begun an action that Jews and Christians should have perpetuated through Jesus. I had had plenty of time to see before my accident, then to read during my convalescence, and suddenly I understood the sequence of this monotheism transmitted in its entirety from Osiris to Moses, then from Moses to Jesus, just as it was from Ateta (Thoth-Hermes) to Akhenaten, from Akhenaten to Pythagoras, from Pythagoras to Galileo. *The Christianity of Pisces is the logical continuation of the Jewish religion of Aries, just as the latter is the logical continuation of the religion of Osiris the Bull!* Not just the continuation, but the continuation of humanity's most ancient monotheism.

A whole hypocritical world has refused to admit this Truth, despite tentative attempts to lift the veil. They have all failed, and for good reason! I found my astonishment in a book by Raymond Weill on *Literary Transmissions from Egypt to Israel:*

"How is it that such an obvious and simple fact has not been perceived and noted for a long time? Like other gaps in observation of the same order, this one seems to be due to the fact that the Egyptological effort, applied for a long time to the translation and explanation of the texts, then aimed to collect and record their testimonies rather than to discuss them, with the intention of direct historical use, and as if under the influence of a very strong feeling of reserve which prevented research from turning to the considerations of documentary criticism. In field of comparisons between Egyptian wisdom and that of the biblical books, Chabas is undoubtedly the first of all. In 1857, studying the Ptahhotep of the Prisse papyrus, and noting the analogy that the book presents in general with Proverbs, he then records, step by step, the numerous correspondences that can be found between the Egyptian on the one hand and, on the biblical side, mainly Proverbs, but also Job, Isaiah, Psalms, Ecclesiastes and Wisdom; What does he conclude? - We should not be surprised to find in the text that I have just translated maxims that Scripture repeated later, without needing to borrow them from Egyptian wisdom. It is, however, rather interesting to see the Egyptian philosopher promise the respectful son a long existence on earth, in terms almost identical to those that the finger of God engraved on the stone tablets of the Decalogue... Careful analysis and undisguised surprise reveal a flash of genius in the precursor, still too ill-equipped to follow the facts, reduced to defending himself against the facts, and observing them with care because he has a very clear idea of the phenomenon they reflect".

The truth, as we can see, is closely held; it would be extracted if Chabas did not hold to his central point of view of the obvious independence of the elaboration of ideas in the two peoples. And it is this principle, unfortunately, that now prevails. Another Egyptologist of the same period, a German, Brugsch, speaking of the morals and wisdom treatises of the Egyptians, will only say:

"These numerous examples teach us that universal charity is by no means an acquisition of our modern times.

Raymond Weill, for his part, takes up his admirable descriptive chronological table of "similarities":

"Wiedemann's incidental remarks in 1903 and Erman's in 1906 may be considered to have been the seeds of the brief, substantial and very remarkable memoir in which Gunkel, in 1909, attempted for the first time to draw up a table of Egyptian correspondences to the Old Testament. He reviews the myths and legends, the hymns to the gods and the love songs, acknowledging that since Erman, the Egyptians' love poetry has begun to be sought as an explanation for that of the Bible; at the same time, he observes that the exhortation to enjoy material life, which the author of the Wisdom of Solomon puts into the mouth of the godless, is reproduced from an old familiar theme in Egyptian poetry.

On this excellent path, Gunkel found it easy to enrich his notes; in 1912 he brought to the attention of the general public the analogies between the hymns to the gods in Egypt and the hymns in the Psalms. Generally speaking, however, and as it stands at this moment, the question seems to have reached all the development possible in the conditions of documentary information, and in fact, we hardly see it advance until the hour of the dazzling surprise that was to come with the revelation of the Egyptian book of Amenemope, published in 1923."

Be that as it may, from 1924 onwards, this papyrus took and kept the place of a central object in the table of correspondences between the wisdom literature of Israel and Egypt. The parallels between the Proverbs and the Egyptian book are once again recorded in detail by Gressmann, in a useful and clear work whose brevity is regrettable, given the intention, expressed for the first time, of presenting the sapiental wisdom of Israel, generally speaking, in its relationship with universal literature. This book is directly related to Gunkel's excellent essay of 1909, extending and often repeating it, particularly with regard to the satire of the professions in Egyptian literature and in Sirach; Job, too, is very well characterised.

At the height of the Roman era, in the Judeo-Greek book of Wisdom, a transposition of Egyptian themes appeared, quite different in spirit from those that had found their way into the Israelite compositions of earlier centuries. This time, the Epicurean thesis of life and death is no longer presented as recommendable, but for the purpose of highlighting its odious and impious character, and so that it can be followed by refutations from the point of view of belief in immortality and divine sanctions. As we can see, this is exactly the outline of the compound in which the old materialist thesis had been wrapped up in Egypt, from the time of the new empire, by innovators enamoured of religious seriousness and orthodoxy; It is a complex form of which some appearances can be seen in later Egyptian documents, and which emerges in full light in the Judeo-Alexandrian Wisdom, with a strength and frankness that are very significant when we bear in mind that at this very moment Israel, under the influences of the Egyptian and Greco-Oriental world in which it was immersed, was coming to accept the necessity of eternal life with its punishments and rewards.

This is what I saw and understood in my bed of pain: the de facto collusion, spiritually speaking, between all Hebraic, Christian and even Greek theologies, but based on a single monotheism: that immersed with Ahâ-Men-Ptah, transmitted by its survivors to Ath-Kâ-Ptah.

Hence, during my twenty-six months of convalescence, I studied the texts of the Divine-Mathematical Combinations day and night. I only slept two or three hours a night, not wanting to take sleeping pills so as not to lower my level of understanding of the texts, which were still abstract but which were rapidly becoming clearer.

It was only a glimmer, still a long way from the beacon illuminating the door. I still didn't feel in control of my strength, either literally or figuratively. My physical weakness necessitated a long convalescence, and above all a readaptation of the deficient muscles at every moment. My will was still focused on this essentially laborious function. Reading ancient texts was a way of relaxing, but it also allowed me to memorise what I needed to retain in my subconscious.

Everything proved my weakness at the time, and no one was willing to put a price on my skin. Deep down, I was terrified by how little I represented, while at the same time everything was working out, not just to spare me, but to give me a firm foothold in a new world.

With each passing second, new forces penetrated me, some opposing my desires, others my will, breaking the slightest resistance to what else was to be done.

An absolute conviction had penetrated me: in order to enter the Holy of Holies of Osiris at Denderah, to become a "resident" in my own right, even if only symbolically, given my condition, I had to force my will a little more towards the possibility of returning to Egypt. Before that, however, I had to spend a whole year in Morocco to perfect my convalescence, but this was an opportunity to increase my knowledge of the journey of the survivors of Ahâ-Men-Ptah, a subject I developed at length in *Les Survivants de l'Atlantide*. It was only after this long period of patience, physical endurance and study on the very terrain of the 'Sacred Way of the Rock Engravings' that I was able to go to those who were still able to provide me with the link between what I already knew and what I still lacked. To go back to the origin of divine humanity and its terrestrial universe, I had to demonstrate in advance that the One God no longer held any secrets for me, in terms of the Law he had established to enable me to scrutinise the destiny of creatures in the future, and thus become not the equal of the Creator, but his true earthly image.

I was already interpreting the Divine-Mathematical Combinations interpenetrating each other in my intellect, which was then obsessed with re-educating the left limbs of my body. But from then on, the inescapable power of the Beneficial Breaths was exerted in an action that was as slow as it was salutary. The absurdity of any other element in this kind of resurrection was permanently anchored in me the day the plaster cast that imprisoned my torso was removed, and at the same time gave me back my freedom of movement, which was joined by my reflexes! The two years of suffering in plaster, bedridden, had passed in an extraordinary way, beyond my control, as had my convalescence in Morocco! Not only did I have the time to make journeys reputedly impossible for an invalid, I also had the capacity to devour several hundred texts, from which everything I needed to retain was integrated into the folds of my memory: the sky, the earth, the stars, day and night were thus interwoven, methodically and logically, like the true nourishing grains of ancient Egypt. It was they who enabled the Cadets to grow so that their destined destinies could be fulfilled. And there, invisible spirit and palpable matter met to manifest in a tangible and triumphant way the primacy of the Creator over the creation of his creatures. I was ready to return to Denderah, not just to see, but above all to understand.

Of course, three extraordinary people helped me on the spot in this life. I've already mentioned the good chief physician at Luxor Hospital, now retired, but I can't reveal the identity of the other two people for the moment, who are Coptic scholars and who don't want to be thanked in any way. They are not shy or afraid, but what they know about ancient monotheism is too dangerous for their lives at the moment, and they must survive to pass on what they have when the time comes.

A combination of circumstances, due to the very favourable Mathematical-Divine Combinations at the time, intervened in my favour. I was in a state of weakness, with a feverish gleam in my eyes that gave me an air of timeless mysticism! I needed this precious help, and I got it, because these two almost divine souls realised that I could be one of those fragile sons capable, when the day came, of writing the text of original monotheism for the use of the Cadets to come. This is why I have proceeded in this unusual way to communicate all the Knowledge I have acquired: a first trilogy in popular truncated form, mostly taken as a novel. The second, more substantial, with Moses and Akhenaten, including historical and exegetical notes. The third, with Jesus and the end of the Piscean era, foreseeable from the beginning thanks to the Divine-Mathematical Combinations.

The engravings around the tombs and sarcophagi should have demonstrated the intellectual and spiritual value of this people who had fallen into oblivion because they had forgotten their origins.

The oldest monuments show the family as a whole, with the father as its head. He commanded the household and directed the work, making everyone obey him. In the paintings of the mastabas, his size, two or three times greater than that of the neighbouring figures, symbolised his primacy. But here again, this was merely an obvious symbolism, as the comfort of his wife and children was his primary concern. It was the wife who ruled the house. He brought up his children, taught them, inculcated his ideas and knowledge, established them, married them and tried to make them the continuators of his personality. In this way, the family was founded on both authority and affection. The son gladdened the hearts of his deceased elders, and was as loyal to his father as he was to Ptah and to his earthly son, the

Pharaoh. He was loved by his father, who reciprocated in kind. He also sought to earn the praise and affection of his mother, his brothers and sisters, and even his servants, his neighbours and all his compatriots. Such was the family context in the early dynasties. Each of the tombs recounts this peaceful and natural family epic that we should still envy them.

Undoubtedly, among these ancient children of God, there were always people who were more or less indelicate, thieves and brigands. Administrative reports of embezzlement by administrators bear witness to this. Other documents mention the organised looting of necropolises. But these were crimes condemned in the name of public honesty. The great boasted that they had hunted down brigands, arrested thieves and guaranteed safety for peasants and travellers. The little ones professed never to have harmed others, never to have stolen fish from the ponds of the gods, never to have cheated on the scales or their weight. Everyone hated violence: some refrained from it, others fought against it.

As for the chores, what has not been said! The Hebrews held a grudge against Egypt for building new cities. No doubt they did! However, they still had fond memories of the onions and food distributed to the workers, since they were already on strike when there was a delay in the supply of this precious commodity. A report from the time of Khoufou even tells us that the Royal Intendant was beheaded for failing in this task! How much suffering, say some moderns, is involved in erecting the Pyramids! They forget all about the Royal Intendant! Hard work and discipline, yes; but why more suffering than any other job in any other country?

These relationships, both Paschal and funerary, make it possible to retrace the actions to be observed, during one's earthly life, in order to gain access to eternal life. They should put the reader in a state of grace, to make him admit the veracity of the original function of Denderah! As I am alone to carry out this immense task, I am referring to all those who have gone before me, not least Auguste Mariette, in his description of the great temple, made no secret of the spiritual and secret value of Dendera. Maspero, for his part, turned the difficulties he had encountered on their head by narrating in his own way the questions raised by the temple of the goddess Hathor:

> "The inscriptions also show that once the secret chamber had been established, every precaution was taken to ensure that it remained

unknown not only to visitors, but also to the lower priesthood. "The door is not known to the uninitiated; if it is sought, no one will find it, except the prophets of the goddess". Like the architect, these prophets of Denderah knew how to enter a room cluttered with precious metals and objects, and they were the only ones who . They saw the opening of a corridor at a raised stone, which was not visible to the general public: they crawled into it and after a few moments arrived in the middle of the treasure. Once the block was back on its bed, the most trained eye could no longer distinguish the precise point where the passage opened out.

To conclude what I have seen and understood, I am translating one of the oldest stories in the world, dating back to the time of Ahâ-Khéops, or Khoufou, of the 4th dynasty, more than five millennia ago! It is called : *The Great King and the Magicians*.

In this account, an old prophet of one hundred and twenty years knows the number of the writing chests, made of sycamore wood, contained in the crypt of Ateta, who had himself classified there his manuscripts containing the names, the hierarchy and the qualities of everything that made up the universe in the Golden Circle. Not just the number, but the place!

At the time of Khufu, who had the Temple of Isis demolished in order to find the lost entrance to the underground passageway leading to the Golden Circle, this symbol was easy to understand. For anyone who could read the books in this library and understand them (or have them explained to him) would become as powerful as this Ateta, or Thoth, or Hermes the thrice-great: he could consider himself the real Master of the Universe. But Khufu failed in this attempt, which forced him to rebuild the temple of the good "Lady of Heaven" a third time, even more resplendent, and according to the exact plans preserved on gazelle skin, drawn by the Great Architect in the distant days of the predynastic kings. It was the only way for him to be forgiven for his blasphemy and to try to regain his entry into the Beyond of earthly life for all eternity. It just goes to show that the Blackness of Evil can become the prelude to the renewal of Good. And how seeing does not necessarily mean understanding!

16

ETERNITY BELONGS TO GOD ALONE

Mingling with the burning ashes, the torrents flowed right through the streets. And one of these torrents had raged right where the priests of Isis had gathered around the altars.
George B. Lytton (The Last Days Pompeii)

The sun's disc will no longer shine, and the clouds will make it disappear. Night will reign eternally, and people, stunned by this absence, will no longer be able to live.
Hieratic papyrus N° 1116 Ms from the Leningrad museum
(The prophetic tale)

There are prophetic accounts (not tales!) from the time of the first pharaohs. They have all been authenticated, and there is no trickery in them. Prophets did exist, and they were highly respected advisers to the Elders. The gloomy picture they painted of humanity's future was no match for that of Isaiah, Saint John... or Nostradamus! It is with the help of a very special story that I would like to conclude this brief study of my life and the work I have been doing for over fifteen years. It is called : *The Great King and the Magicians.*

Of course, the account that I am going to translate here from the original text has been reproduced many times like a bedtime story! But then again, none of the eminent Egyptologists dispute the authenticity of the original document, which dates back 5,000 years. Back then, our own ancestors lived naked in smoke-filled caves! And I don't even know if they had a fire to cook the meat, which they ate straight off the carcass, fighting amongst themselves to get the best bits. The savages could in no way have been the ones who wrote the stories prophesying what would happen millennia later. We must stop, once and for all, thinking of these ancient sages as savages, when it is we who are still savages with our insane arms race! This is the only way to understand the obscurantism into which we are sinking deeper and deeper, and which threatens to plunge our planet into absolute darkness.

You have to read it to understand it! Here, then, is a text that dates back to the dawn of time, as I have translated it, and which depicts Khufu, the Khufu of the Greeks, who took credit for the Great Pyramid and had the temple of the Lady of Heaven rebuilt for the third time, at Denderah:

Great things happened in the days when His Majesty Khufu reigned over the Two Lands. Learn this, O you who read the words written by the Scribe Râbsenir, but keep them to yourself, for it would be a curse for all your family and a great misfortune for you if you were to spread them among strangers! In this way you will learn the Wisdom of the Pharaoh, to Him be long life, strength and health! Khufu was the benefactor of the entire land stretching from the Sunset, where the Blessed Sleeping Ones rest, to his capital Men-Nefer, from where I prepare my calames to blacken these papyrus scrolls spread out on my palette. For here is the Heart of Ath-Ka-Ptah.

Now, one morning when Pharaoh's Intimate Advisers, to Him very long Life, Strength and great Health, had finished their daily deliberations and had retired as usual to attend to their many important occupations, Khufu, seized by a sudden inspiration, ordered his great Chamberlain, who never left the throne as long as His Majesty was seated there: "Run after my Intimate Advisors, even if they have already left the Palace, for I wish to speak to them again, at once! Go and bring them back! I am finished." The Grand Chamberlain waited no longer, ran outside the walls, flew to the Advisers, brought them back trembling, wondering how they had incurred the wrath of Pharaoh, to Him L.V.F.S., and what awaited them! Barely in front of His Majesty's throne, everyone threw themselves to the ground, full of fear, expecting a terrible sentence, in complete silence.

But the silence lasts, for the Pharaoh, to Him L.V.F.S., is astonished by this fear that he feels seeping through the skin of his Intimate Advisors! Khoufou can only speak in a serene, neutral and imperative voice, for his request is the conclusion of a dream that Usir, whose life is eternal, has inspired in him: to ask a Magus to reveal the Great Secret!

His Majesty, having regained full control of his voice, raised it with a hint of irritation: "What? My faithful Councillors bowing down like slaves? What have they done to deserve my wrath?"

The four Intimate Advisors and the Grand Chamberlain sat up painfully, wondering by what happy chance they had not been reproached. It was Khafriré, the royal son, who replied in the name of all, to his father the pharaoh, to Him

L.V.F.S.: *"It is unusual for Your Majesty to call back his Councillors in this way to deliberate a second time: We feared that we had in some way offended Your august Divine person, O Khoufou, to You long Life, great Vigour and eternal Health."* Then His Majesty, exasperated, spoke thus to Khafriré, his son: *"What? Is your state like that of full old age, that you cannot discern the opprobrium of an urgent request for advice? Do you have such a guilty conscience, Khafriré? Do my Councillors lie to me in some way to fear my wrath so much?..."* Khoufou, à Lui L.V.F.S., did not realise that as he had the right of life and death over all his subjects, each of them feared offend him in any way, including his sonPrince Khafriré. So he replied: *"May Your Majesty forgive me for this lapse in Your divine judgement. Nothing should have disturbed our Divine Parcels, since no subject likely to irritate you taints them."*

Holding out both arms in front of him in a sign of allegiance, followed by the three other Intimate Councillors and the Grand Chamberlain who made the same secular gesture, Prince Khafriré concluded his sentence as follows: *"We are listening attentively to the urgency that Your Majesty wishes us to hear. Like our carnal envelopes altered by good words, our ears open wide to the entrance of Your Just Voice. Speak..."*

The pharaoh, to Him L.V.F.S., spoke: *"This night, the Divine Voice made itself heard to me, in a succession of colours and obscurities. Everything was luminous, golden, dazzling, then suddenly it was total, absolute blackness, and I thought I had gone blind, even though I knew that was impossible. It happened eight times in a row, with the same alternations and the same words. What does this dream mean? You, my advisors, must have an explanation for this. Is it an evil omen or a beneficial prophecy?... answer me honestly."*

Faced with Prince Khafriré's silence, the pontiff of An du Nord, the venerated Amemkâ, the royal adviser on religious matters, spoke up: *You are the descendant of Ra, Lord of Almighty Eternity, O Khoufou. May his rays make you divine for millions and millions of lives to come! Your dream is not quite an omen, nor is it merely a prophecy. It is the royal mark of your omnipotence. Djoser, your divine ancestor, to Him be Eternal Life, who built a temple to the Sun at Sakârâ on such a grand scale before constructing a tomb for himself almost as sumptuous as the one that will become yours at the end of your earthly life, on several occasions had visions similar to the one you had tonight. The royal scribes at his court attest to this in their daily reports.*

The pharaoh, to Him L.V.F.S., nodded his head, as if approving the ancient existence of an identical dream, before asking: *"This is true, O Amenkâ, remind me therefore of the value placed by the Magi of that remote era on the dream similar to mine of my ancestor the great Ver-Ahâ Djoser, to Him be Eternal Life, eternally."* Amenkâ *replied to this request without the slightest hesitation: "The alternations of blinding light and total darkness, eight times in a row, are proof of Ra's divine influence over the whole Earth. His presence illuminates and dispenses Life; his disappearance blinds and sows Death. So the Magi recommended to the great Djoser, your ancestor, to Him be eternal Life, to order the construction of the most beautiful temple dedicated to the Sun, such as no king had ever built. This he did, O mighty Khufu, and his minute of eternity on the floor of our Second Heart lasted longer than usual..."*

The meditative silence of the pharaoh, to Him L.V.F.S., lasted only the time of a sigh, and His Majesty with the right voice said: "That is perfectly true, O Amenkâ, that we bring on the altar of the Iron-Ahâ Djoser, to Him the Eternal Life, an offering of a thousand loaves of bread, a hundred jugs of beer, ten bowls of incense, as well as the bull cut according to our ancestral rites determined by Set, to Him the eternal power thanks to the omnipotence of Ra. In the same way, place on the altar of his Khai-habi a good portion of pure meat, a pint of beer, a wafer and a bowl of incense, so that he may continue to glorify eternally the greatness of the soul of his Per-Ahâ, in the land of the Blessed Sleeping Ones."

Amemkâ replied: "May it be done in accordance with Your Majesty's will." And the pontiff bowed, before going to sit down in his usual place, on a small ebony stool, a little behind that of Prince Khafriré. It was he, the son of Khoufou, who rose to stand before His Majesty. He said in turn: u King Djoser certainly deserved to attain the eternity of celestial life as a result of the fervour with which he favoured the fulfilment of Ra's desires introduced during the nights of his omens. However, the Per-Ahâs follow one another, but their dreams are not alike. His successor, King Nebkâ, to Him be all Eternity, was possessed by the same visions as King Djoser and identical to those of Your Majesty. But his Magician told him that this alternation of great light and total darkness was the sign of the great universal balance, which was the sign that this Majesty would be the greatest King with the Right Voice since the beginning of time, which is what Nebkâ was during his long earthly life. He dispensed Justice with such fairness that at the moment of the Ultimate Judgement, his entry into the Beyond of Terrestrial Life elicited nothing but praise!"

The Pharaoh, to Him L.V.P.S., approved and asked: "Can you give me an example of this light that illuminated him?" Khafriré nodded: "His Justice was such that it was said to perform prodigies! One day, King Nebkâ, to Him be Eternal Life, was going to the temple of Ptah in the beautiful capital whose White Walls shine with your presence today. Now, unlike you, every time he went to the temple of Ptah, King Nebkâ, Eternal Life befriended his chief of protocol, the Khaï-habi Oubaousir, so that he could clear the way for the royal retinue during the religious ceremony dedicated to Ptah. However, Oubaousir's wife was treacherous, for in the royal retinue there was a vassal who, from the moment she first caught sight of him, made her forget where in the world her home was. For every time Ubausir joined the king for a long ceremony in the temple, she sent her maid, each time with new gifts in the form of clothes. And the wealthy vassal would leave his court garb to dress in festive garb and go to visit Ubausir's wife at his vast estate on the banks of the great river Hapy. The two of would thus spend hours of drunken sensual pleasure on the bed of a small kiosk located on the peninsula that completed the garden in front of the river. Afterwards, they both bathed so that no trace of their exertions remained. One day, when the vassal had not thanked the gardener as was his wont, the gardener went to see his master, the Khaï-habi, to tell him all about the affair. Ubousir then asked him to bring him his gold-encrusted ebony case, where he kept his collection of ancient recipes for cursing the Evil One. And he designed a wax crocodile, seven inches long according to the ritual, so that the curse would be effective. Ubaousir knew that it wasn't enough to drown a lucky man like this vassal; even in the great river, he would be able to rise to the surface with a beautiful fish between his teeth!... So he read with conviction from the crocodile the formula written on the sacred grimoire, adding: "And Divine Oumbou, as soon as the vassal who has betrayed his oath bathes near my kiosk, drag him to the bottom of the great river and keep him there until I claim him from you. Do as I ask, in the name of Khoum!"

Then he gave the wax crocodile to the gardener and said to him: "As soon as the vassal, to wash away the result of his misdeed, has immersed himself in the waters of the great river, throw this crocodile after him. "This happened the very next day, when the vassal, absent Oubaousir, rushed to bathe before setting off again. And the seven-inch wax crocodile changed into a seven-cubit crocodile, which immediately took the vassal underwater. During this time Oubaousir spoke to King Nebkâ, to Him be Eternal Life: "May it please Your Majesty to come and see the prodigy that has taken place in my house, because of the horrible conduct of your vassal with my wife."

So the King followed Ubulusir home and watched him speak to the waters of the great river, "Bring the vassal out of the water, O Ubulusir!" And the seven cubit crocodile sprang from the water, holding the vassal half-smothered. His Majesty Nebkâ, to Him a very very long Life in Eternity, was in no way frightened at this sight. His Righteous Voice only quivered a little to say to the crocodile: "This carnal envelope no longer has a Divine Parcel, it is yours, keep it!" The seven-cubed crocodile immediately dived with its prey to the bottom of the great river, and no one knew what became of either of them. As for King Nebkâ, whose voice was just for all eternity, he had Ubaousir's wife taken to the north side of the royal mound, where she was burnt alive before her ashes were thrown into the river. Thus the glow of the flames regenerated the blackness of the feelings that had animated this woman, the sad human representative of the species that the Per-Ahâ, to Him long Life, Strength and great Health, had given birth. "This, O Mighty Bull who reigns over Thy Sons as over those of the Two Lands, is the meaning of the light and darkness of thy dream."

The meditative silence of the Pharaoh, to Him L.V.F.S., lasted no longer than for the previous narration. Khufu only sighed for a breath before agreeing with himself that Nebka's righteousness was no more valuable than Djoser's nobility in relation to His Majesty Khufu, that is to say himself. However, he said: "This is true, Khafriré; let an offering of a thousand loaves of bread, a hundred jugs of beer, ten bowls of incense and a bull ritually cut according to the principles of the Great Ptah who protected Usir during the reign of King Nebkâ, eternal life to Him, be placed on the altar of Per-Ahâ Nebkâ, eternal life to Him! In the same way, place on the altar of his Khaï-habi, Oubaousir, a good portion of pure meat, a pint of beer, a wafer and a bowl of incense."

Khafriré replied: "May it be done in accordance with the will of Your Majesty." The prince bowed to his father the pharaoh, to Him L.V.F.S., before returning to sit beside the pontiff Amenkâ. The third Intimate Advisor, who had already risen, approached Khufu. He was a noble descendant of the Zamankhou family, whose own father had been the Kaï-habi of the great Snefru, long life to Him in Eternity, into which he had entered only a few years ago, mourned by the many wives and concubines who had endowed him with a flourishing progeny, from which Khufu, to Him L.V.S.F., just happened to come, and who had at that moment taken the sceptre from the hands of the sleeping king.

So Zamankhou, Khufu's Intimate Advisor, chose to illuminate his king's dream with the one that Snefru had experienced in the company of his father, the Kaï-habi. And so he began to speak: "This is one of the prodigies experienced by your father, the great Snefru, to Him be eternal Life, following a dream identical to yours, O Mighty Bull who reigns over the Two Lands". That morning, His Majesty sent for my father, the Kaï-habi, to ask him to explain his dream. After a moment's reflection, Zamankhou understood the meaning of the vision, and explained it to Snefru: "You are sad, great king of the Earth, for your heart is heavy with all the sins committed by the Cadets, your subjects. Everything is getting darker and darker if you don't do something about it. To enlighten yourself, you must set out on a cruise on the great river, and he who inspired your dream will then illuminate you with his splendour to show you the Truth." The pharaoh, to Him be the Eternal Glory, pouted, for a trip on Hapy with imprisoned rowers did not appeal to him. As if he had perceived his Master's train of thought, Zamankhou added: "You shall order her to be armed with beautiful girls from your royal harem, and not with prisoners. Your heart will lighten at the sight of them, and the countryside along the banks of the great river will seem more beautiful to you! So bring twenty oars of ebony wood inlaid with gold, with blades made from the heart of sycamore wood, to be under the protection of the divine Isis. And then order the arrival of the twenty most beautiful new arrivals to your harem, those with beautiful bodies, beautiful hair, and no children yet, dressed only in the fine fishnet above their nakedness. And something will happen to put an end to your dark thoughts and protect you in the ineffable light." And so it was, when the time came for the cruise. The beautiful girls of the harem rowed in cadence, propped up on their benches, their muscles stretching their pretty skins under the effort; and His Majesty's heart rejoiced to see them come and go as they moved, singing at the top of their voices to give themselves the strength to pull on the oars. Her Majesty's heart was close to singing likewise, when suddenly one of the woods, having missed the water, rebounded and, passing over the hair of the oarswoman on the previous bench, swept away the malachite fish that had been planted there. In despair, the girl fell silent and stopped rowing. The other beautiful girls also stopped.

His Majesty, who had been following the scene, approached the rower who had first stopped her sporting activities and asked her why she had stopped rowing, as he had not seen the malachite fish disappear. She explained why to King Snefru. His Majesty told her not to cry and to start rowing again because he would give her another one just as beautiful. The beautiful girl replied that what she wanted was not another malachite fish, but to find the one she had lost!

It was then that the pharaoh, to Him L.V.F.S., dispatched two of the fastest steeds so that my father Zamankhou could reach him without delay, because his heart, which had been close to becoming lighter according to what had been predicted, was now becoming heavy to the point of sinking! My father made haste to reach Snefru before the disaster. He recited the words of the ancient grimoires to drive back the waters of the great river. And the twelve cubits of thick water rose further than the normal twelve cubits of the rest of the water, to empty the place where the malachite fish of the beautiful daughter of the royal harem had fallen. Zamankhou went down to pick it up on dry land and handed it to Snefru before reciting the end of the grimoire's formula so that the water of the river Hapy would return to its normal course. His Majesty returned the malachite fish to the beautiful oarswoman, who then went back to work, as did her other companions. It was a memorable day for all, but it ended that night in the royal bedroom for the beautiful young bearer of the malachite fish, whose pretty hair shone with light. Of all the good things that followed, the most important was the birth of the splendour of today's Two Countries: His Majesty Khoufou! The dazzling light had triumphed over the dark abyss of the waters, to ensure the radiant glory of the Second Heart!

The pharaoh, to Him L.V.F.S. this time, meditated longer, for he knew this divine sign of his birth, and he suddenly felt the need to go to the harem himself. But he caught a furious glance from his son Khafriré, and preferred to temporise by listening to his fourth and final Intimate Advisor. And as this one was the most secretive and the least prolific with words, he thought it would not be a bad idea. So he said to Zamankhou, who was standing motionless waiting for the goodwill of his royal person: "You have spoken very well of His Majesty Snefru, to him the Eternity of the Blessed Eternal Peace of the Righteous! Take to his altar an offering worthy of his virility, place two thousand loaves of bread, five hundred jugs of beer, ten bowls of incense, a black bull ritually cut according to the precepts dear to Uzir, as well as a white bull cut according to the traditional rites of the sons of our venerated Seth. In this way, he will draw additional eternal strength from which I will be able to benefit. As for your father, the Kai-habi, have a bowl of incense brought to his private altar, on behalf of my Majesty, and surround it with the wafers and pints of beer that you deem appropriate. Go! I said."

Zamankhou bowed respectfully and returned to his seat, while the last Intimate Advisor, the great seer Senenpthah, approached his king, who watched him advance with an increasingly scrutinising eye. Senenpthah came from faraway Upper Egypt, from Thebaid, which Khufu had not yet had the opportunity to visit. In his treaty of peace and brotherhood with this important region, his governor had included the friendly presence of an adviser. Was he a spy or an adviser? And so that Senenpthah could not read his thoughts, His Majesty hastened to ask him: "And you, what do you think of my omen and of what your fellow Councillors have said about it?..."

The great seer, who was not fooled by either Khoufou's thoughts or hidden intentions, replied: "To answer you, O great King of the Two Lands, I will call upon my double Dadoukhourou". His Majesty was astonished: "Why this double whose name means; who knows the past and the future? You have never told me about him and you have never brought him before me..." Senenpthah replied sadly: "The time had not yet come, O you Almighty holder of the sceptre of the Two Lands. In view of your dream of last night, it is time to call upon him, for the dark future it portends worries me." Pharaoh, in Lui L.V.F.S., grew even darker at this sentence. He said: "Why speak here of darkness, when I have also seen the Light? It can't be dark! But so be it: introduce me quickly to this Dadoukhourou. Send for him, you who are my Advisor, so that I may know everything." Senenpthah replied without smiling: "He is in me, O great Khoufou, I ask him about the past or the future, and he answers me, and I transmit his answer by my voice." Khufu was surprised but did not show it; he asked, "Why does he not also speak of the present?" Senenpthah replied: "Because the past has passed, and everyone can tell their own perception of it from behind the mirror of time, Dadoukhourou knows the truth of past Good and Evil. Your three other Advisors have described your dream according to past omens, each in their own way, thus presenting you with three different and acceptable facets of your vision. It's impossible to talk about it in the present tense, because the very second I speak, the future becomes the past without the present remaining! Even after you've heard my words, you won't be able to use them in the present, but only prepare the future with..."

Pharaoh, in Lui L.V.F.S., *frowned with an unusual effort at comprehension, before asking again: "What do you intend to teach me again about my dream, Senepthah? Speak frankly. The great seer straightened up a little more, to say in a slightly contemptuous tone: "Until now, Your Majesty's Advisors have spoken of the prodigies performed by your more or less distant Ancestors in connection with symbolic dreams apparently identical to yours of this night. They are known through the written acts of royal Scribes, but the symbolism of certain facts, such as the transformation of the wax crocodile into a real one, or the cutting of the waters of the Great River into two parts to fish out the malachite of the harem girl, cannot be guaranteed to be true in this concrete way. I'm not saying that there is trickery, but that the truth has been transformed to explain a prophetic past that has come true, such as your birth. And this is what I propose to you: to make known to Your Majesty, Dadoukhourou, my inner double, whom you do not know, even though he is eternally in the present to speak to you only about the future!"*

Pharaoh, to Him L.V.P.S., *asked again, "How is this possible, Senenpthah?" The great seer replied, shrugging his shoulders: "I don't know exactly. What I can tell you is that he entered me at the same time as my Divine Parcel, and that he is now over 120 years old. But he was already alive at the time of the Great Cataclysm, when the Sun was advancing instead of retreating in Leo. He fought with the ox Hapy and often goes with me to the great river to spread new strength. Above all, he assisted Ateta the thrice-blessed, in his work of saving the survivors of the chosen people, by helping this pharaoh, to Him the Eternal Life at the right hand of Ptah, to reintroduce the march of Time, the pursuit of Life, and the Knowledge of the Creator's Eternity!"*

Khoufou *sighed aloud in spite of himself. The story of Ateta, whose Eternity was assured, reminded him in the same way of that of King Mena, also Eternal Life to the Unifier, builder of the Temple of Men-Nefer, of course, but also of the Golden Circle of the An-du-Sud, built on the very tomb of Mena. Ah, the Year of the South, where there were mountains and mountains of gold and jewels! On reaching this immeasurable wealth that shone before his eyes, worse than the dazzle he had experienced in his nocturnal dream, Pharaoh, at Lui L.V.F.S., was suddenly certain that it was the knowledge of the Golden Circle that had been announced to him!... So he closed his eyelids for a moment to regain control of himself and reveal nothing of his feelings to the great seer. In a more neutral voice, Khoufou said: "Atêta, eternal glory to his thrice-great name, was the great renovator of all our sacred literature! Didn't he write all the texts himself? Senepthah replied: "Not only did he know how to sew heads back on shoulders and speak to the stars, but he wrote the forty-two books himself before locking them up in their writing chests, which he took down to the crypt reserved for that purpose in the Golden Circle protected by Isis!"*

At these words Khoufou could not help but flinch, and he asked his next question without looking at Senenpthah: "Can you not make a copy for my tomb, which I will take with me to the Beyond of earthly life?" He said to His Majesty: "I cannot ask Dadoukhourou about the past, he will not answer me. But I can ask him about the future." The pharaoh, at Lui L.V.F.S., barely restrained a movement of spite. He said: "I don't care about the future. Ask him about the past. Senenpthah shook his head: "He won't answer. At his advanced age, he is sheltered from requests of this kind. He is only preparing to be bandaged and returned to his Creator. But there still an opportunity to ask him about it." His Majesty said, "Quickly, tell me which one." The great seer replied: "I will lie down on the ground and order Dadoukhourou to put me to sleep and use my body to answer your questions. Ask him about the kings of the future who will try to penetrate the Golden Circle to seize the great original treasure. He might then tell you about the location of the book chests and how to obtain a copy for your tomb. Khoufou agreed: "That is good, Senenpthah, so ask your Dadoukhourou to put you to sleep and I will speak to him." This was quickly done. When the great seer no longer had more than the rigid appearance of a carnal envelope without a soul, the Pharaoh, to Him L.V.F.S., rose on his throne and descended to the inert being lying there. Khoufou bent down and said: "What is this, Dadoukhourou, that I have never seen you before?" Another voice, much deeper, came out of Senenpthah's body to answer: "Because I am a wandering soul without a body in this life. You cannot see me, but I hear you and answer you, O King." Khoufou said again, "The great seer claims that you know how to sew heads back on." The voice replied, "I can, O King. Break a head and I will mend it!" His Majesty straightened up and ordered the great Chamberlain: "Let a prisoner be brought here before me, one of those whose sentence is pronounced, on the hour!" The Grand Chamberlain rushed to the prisons in the palace cellar with soldiers and a gaoler, and brought back a prisoner as strong as a bull, loaded with chains, who had killed two soldiers of the royal guard one drunken evening, solely with his bare hands! The soldiers forced him to prostrate himself before the pharaoh, at Lui L.V.F.S., with his head resting on an ebony stool where Senenpthah had been sitting before. And a soldier armed with a club suddenly brought it down on the prisoner's skull, smashing it as well as the stool. And Khoufou said to the still rigid body of the great seer: "It's up to you to show whether what you claim is true, Dadoukhourou: sew up that skull for me." Slowly, Senenpthah's body rose to its feet. As soon as he was on his feet, he quickly removed tools from the folds of his tunic and set about shaving the hair, cutting the skin, removing pieces of bone, mopping up the blood and putting the skins back in place. Then he turned back to Khoufou and said in the same deep voice: "The prisoner will regain consciousness and live. Now leave me in peace, O King!" His

Majesty said briskly, "Wait, Dadoukhourou. I have an important request to make to you." The deep voice answered in the standing body: "I am listening." Khoufou said, "Senenpthah claims that you know the location of the boxes of writings, those of Ateta, to Him the Eternal Eternity of the Beyond. Is this true, Dadoukhourou?" The deep voice in the motionless standing body replied, "That is correct, O King, behind the great sandstone stone that forms the entrance to the Hall of Records in the Chamber of Roles in the An-du-Sud." His Majesty then said in an emotional voice: "Can you take me there?" The deep voice replied, "I cannot, for I have no memory of the past." Khoufou continued in a saddened voice: "Then I will leave for the Hereafter without any copies of these sacred texts entering my tomb. Is there no way for me to obtain some, Dadoukhourou?" The deep voice replied: "There is, O King. Make a request in your tomb, intended for your grandchildren, because one of them will try to enter the Golden Circle, and if he doesn't get out, his retinue will find a hiding place where copies of the contents of the boxes of writings are already stored!"

Pharaoh's disappointment in Lui L.V.F.S. was great. But he did not despair of learning the secret of the entrance to the underground passage leading to the Golden Circle by questioning Dadoukhourou further. His Majesty said: "All right, I'll do that. But since you know how to read the future, answer me this: Who will penetrate the secret of the Golden Circle, now lost?" The deep voice came out of the body, still motionless and standing, to say: "It will not be until five millennia from now, when the times prescribed for a new cycle of Divine-Mathematical Combinations have come, that the Golden Circle will deliver its contents to the Cadets of that time, not before!" Khoufou said: "What will become of those who attempt to penetrate the Golden Circle, Dadoukh'ourou?" And the deep voice gave a decisive ruling: "All those who attempt to penetrate the secret before the prescribed time will perish! This is irrevocable, King."

Pharaoh, to Him L.V.F.S., was very disappointed because he had already vowed to go there himself in search of the great treasure. His Majesty said again: "Couldn't these kings redeem themselves for their curiosity, Dadoukhourou?" And the deep voice replied: "Yes, by spending the rest of their royal coffers on rebuilding a temple to Isis, even more beautiful than the one they desecrated without success! Now I rest, so that Senenpthah can recover her body." Khoufou said briskly: "Wait! wait! by the God who created you as you are, wait! Senenpthah has time." The deep voice replied, "The great seer is not pleased, he is afraid you will learn too much." His Majesty became impatient: "What do I care Senenpthah! answer me this: Which kings of the future will attempt to unlock the secret of the Golden Circle? Do you know?..." The deep voice replied: "I do know, o king, but it will do you no good for I can only answer you in the form of prophetic parables. This is what the Divine-Mathematical Combinations foretell: Three cursed princes will descend from heaven, born of the fratricidal branch of the old Lion, the death of the young! Their birth was so difficult that Isis, Nephthys and Khnum had to combine their efforts during each birth, having to enlist the help of their sistras, their sticks and their najas. This is how the three plague victims came into the world. The first child had a large belly, the second had a strong mouth and the third, although more normal, was identified by his lapis lazuli hair. These are the precise details of the three curious unborn children, who will all die in just pain, commensurate with their crimes of lèse-divinité. I rest now."

Quickly, Pharaoh, to Him L.V.F.S., said, "Give me their names first!" The deep voice said, "I rest now." Khufu prevented him from doing so by restraining him. He said: "Give me the names of the three future kings. I am your Elder, I want you to." The motionless body was speechless for a moment, and His Majesty thought he had lost touch. But the hesitant, more distant vocal gravity said, "The third, the most villainous to the Golden Circle, will come from abroad. He will be called Khambénoui the Bloodthirsty, but the first, who will start the series, will be called Rakâoui the Dark. I've finished, it's too late to secure my strips!..."

His Majesty, exasperated, did not understand the terrible meaning of these words.

Khoufou held the bending body by the tunic, but it remained in his hands. The body was melting. The material was reduced to ashes, in a small mound that the king looked at in dismay. And Senenpthah and Dadoukhourou were reduced to nothing! There was an interlude with the prisoner who came back to life, and to whom the pharaoh, to Him L.V.F.S., restored freedom, before ordering: "Let these remains be placed in an urn and carried near the altar of the temple of Ptah with a hundred bunches of shallots and a hundred bunches of garlic. They deserve nothing more for having disappeared before revealing the Truth to me... The Dark One! Who can tell me about Rakâoui the Dark One?..."

None of the three remaining Intimate Advisors could solve this enigma. And since Pharaoh, to Him be Long Life, Strength and Health, knew that he was not one of the three cursed ones, he decided to travel to far-off Sakhibou, the Thebaid, the holder, through Isis and Ateta, of such terrible secrets, but also of immense treasures! And if he failed, he would have a splendid temple rebuilt in honour of the Good Mother of Heaven, so that he could continue to reign over the Two Lands, in all earthly clarity, and therefore far from any celestial darkness.

This enigmatic and hermetic page alone would deserve a complete book, as a multitude of annotations would be necessary to try to explain each word forming the context of a sentence. I had written, precisely in a note on page 174 of *Et Dieu ressuscita à Dendérah*, that I reserved the right to write a book on the life of Khoufou at a later date.

Unfortunately, the more time goes by, the more I realise how difficult it will be to include such a work in my publications before... twenty years or so! I'll simply add here, for your understanding, an explanation of the abbreviations L.V.F.S., which were used by the ancient scribes themselves, in order to take up less space in their written texts, as it was protocol and everywhere compulsory to add the formula Long Life, Strength and Health after 'Pharaoh'. And the scribes had noticed that if they put only L.V.F.S., whose hieroglyphs are, according to the manuscripts, or :

Strength, Life, Health, for the Lover of the Sun;

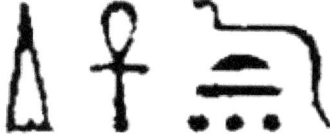

Strength, Life, provided by the Lord of Heaven.

The original symbolism is "Ankh" (Life).

Notwithstanding these considerations, here is a passage from the life of Khufu in which, by a new decree, he ordered the third reconstruction of the temple of Isis at Denderah:

> "The Sun appeared on the eastern horizon, just where hundreds of pairs of eyes were waiting for it. It seemed to sway, its gold merging before the blinking eyelids and, very quickly, it tinted the entire site of Denderah with the most vivid colours. The cloak of night had evaporated, giving way to a beautiful day that was shaping up to be very auspicious.

For the ruins of this place were about to be reborn from the sacrilege that had been committed by a cursed king - not a real Per-Ahâ - whose outrageous mysticism had, in the name of his solar idolatry, ordered the demolition of the temples of Ptah throughout the country, in the north at Men-Nefer, as here at Dendera! Twenty years of lowly dictatorship had passed, accentuating the misery of God's chosen people and adding to an already naturally stifling atmosphere. King Khufu, if he didn't mellow out late in life, seemed to be seeking Ptah's benevolence for all the evil he had done him by seeking entry to the Golden Circle and trying to monopolise its great riches. He had been cursed for it, and his reign would soon come to a pitiful end! Seeking to attract all the heavenly graces for his arrival in the Afterlife, he gave the order to re-establish freedom of worship throughout the kingdom, and even in the two lands of Ath-Kâ-Ptah and Ahâ-Men-Ptah.

The pontiff Khânepou smiled bitterly at this thought, since Amenta was the land of the Blessed Sleeping Ones, and they no doubt couldn't care less about the earthly decrees of this Sun-worshipper! But the order had arrived the day before, from His Majesty himself, to undertake the reconstruction of the Temple of Nut, the Mother Goddess of the Two Brothers, according to the original plans drawn up by the Followers of Horus long ago. It was his own son, Jedef-Ra, his youngest son and heir since the death of Prince Khafriré, who had brought the papyrus of the royal decree. He was co-regent and, as such, was present at this exceptional dawn for the prayer to purify the temple area, where the holy building would once again stand, identical to its predecessor.

Having come out of a prolonged retreat, the pontiff had welcomed this usurping crown prince and his numerous retinue, as was his duty on this occasion. The silent meditation that kept them all in external dialogue with their "kâ" resembled an external glorification of the Sun, but most of them, like An-Un, had to thank Ptah for granting them this spiritual revenge, to allow this sacred place to rise from the ashes."

Inexorably, history and the prophecies will intertwine in the inordinate length of time on earth, to be fulfilled according to the predictions. The Golden Circle will undoubtedly reappear at the propitious moment willed by the Divine-Mathematical Combinations. There is also no doubt that those who 'predict' the return of Atlantis through a new cataclysmic upheaval in 1983 or 1984 are wrong! Not because of the meaning of the prophecies themselves, but because of the interpretation they give to the sacred texts. These say that Ahâ-Men-Ptah will rise from his own ashes in a certain celestial configuration in 1983, the only possible year for this to happen. But can we not say that the original documents, all the sacred writings from the early days of Ath-Kâ-Ptah, recounting the complete history of Ahâ-Men-Ptah, will be brought to light at that time in the Golden Circle? It would be such a revelation that Atlantis would truly rise from its ashes! For Eternity alone is in the power of God... This is why I am content to record the prophetic data without divulging them.

IN CONCLUSION

FOR OUR TIME

I have seen impiety under the sun in the place of Judgement and iniquity in the place of Justice.
And I said in my heart: - God will judge the just and the unjust; then it will be the time of all.
Old Testament (Ecclesiastes, III, 1 6 -1 7)

Ask questions of past generations,
Listen to the Wisdom of their fathers;
Because we are from yesterday and know nothing.
Our days pass like shadows over the earth
But they will talk to you and teach you,
They will draw these lessons from their hearts.
Old Testament (Job, VIII, 8-1 0.)

By way of a very provisional conclusion, here are a few concrete points that will enable everyone to reflect and meditate on the need for destiny and knowledge of the future.

Among the most eminent prophets, the true visionaries of heroic times were the non-canonical Jews of the biblical centuries of the most famous Alexandrian School, i.e. between 150 BC and 150 AD. Not only did they create true non-Talmudic Jewish thought, but we owe to them the preservation of the orthodox history of the Jewish people of that time. Enoch was one of them, and perhaps the most famous, since not only Tertullian, Celsus, Eusebius and Caesarea mention him, but also Origen, St Irenaeus and Clement of Alexandria speak of his original Greek text, which subsequently disappeared. However, until 1877, Oxford had a manuscript of the Ethiopian version of Enoch, discovered in Abyssinia, on which all countries worked. Since then, a Coptic version of Enoch has been found in Egypt, in a monastery lost in Fayoum desert. It has been published by the École française du

Caire. Here is a disturbing first extract, because it combines the "Ancient One", Osiris, with the "Son of Man", Jesus:

"There I saw the Ancient of Days, whose head was like white wool, and with him another in the form of a man. His face was full of grace, like that of one of the holy angels. Then I asked one of the angels who was with me and who was explaining to me all the mysteries about the Son of Man. I asked him who he was, where he came from and why he was accompanying the Ancient of Days. He said to me, "This is the Son of Man, to whom all righteousness belongs and with whom it dwells, and who holds the key to all hidden treasures. For the Lord of spirits has chosen him and given him glory above all creatures. The Son of Man will snatch kings and mighty men from their lustful beds; he will restrain the mighty; he will break the teeth of sinners, XLVI, 1-4."

The second extract below gives even more details about Enoch's Alexandrian connections and all the hieroglyphic papyri he had in his possession. His description of the Celestial Bull is formal proof of this:

"I saw a vision in my bed. Here was a bull coming out of the earth, and the bull was white. Then a heifer came out, and with it two young calves, one black and the other red. The black struck the red... I lifted up my eyes again, and saw heaven above my head, and behold a star fell from heaven, and it stood in the midst these bulls, LXXXIV."

There is no question of dissecting the book written by Enoch, the first part of which is a visionary summary of celestial combinatorial mechanics; the second, the Apocalypse proper; and the third, his historical vision of events. I simply wish to draw readers' attention to this prophet and his true mission, for he undeniably wrote for the use of future generations.

Another prophet of the same class was Ezra. The contents of his "Fourth Book" bear witness to this. It is quoted by the same authors and Church Fathers as Enoch. It is just as important. There are several versions of this work, including the original in Aramaic. Copies in Hebrew, Armenian, Ethiopian, Syriac and Coptic have since been discovered, with no major differences. The Vulgate even published a Latin version. Like Saint John, but several centuries earlier, Ezra had seven visions which, in the original publication, are preceded by an introduction.

In his visions, Ezra uses the form of a dialogue with the angel Uriel and himself exiled to Babylon. Why did Israel, God's chosen people, become the most miserable of peoples when it was the most just? And Uriel, while prophesying, replies that while God's designs are inscrutable, the human mind is narrow-minded and blinded. After the announcement of the Messiah and the Cults that will follow, what is interesting, historically speaking, are the apocalyptic chapters XI and XII, which symbolise, enigmatically but in a real way, the Roman Empire several centuries ahead of its time:

A huge eagle (the symbol of the Roman Empire) spreads its wings over the whole earth and holds it in its talons. It has six pairs of large wings, four pairs of fins and three heads. The six pairs of large wings are six emperors. The second of them reigns so long that none of those who succeed him reaches half the number of years allotted to him.

Without any possibility of confusion, it refers to Augustus, and the six emperors in question are the six emperors of the house of Julius: Caesar, Augustus, Tiberius, Caligula, Claudius and Nero. The four fins are the four usurpers or anti-Caesars, Galba, Otto, Vitellius and Nerva, who, according to the author, should not be considered true emperors. The three heads are the Flavians, who devour the fins. The head in the middle, the largest, is Vespasian, who dies. The other two, Titus and Domitian, reign; but the head on the right devours the head on the left, an allusion to popular opinion about Domitian's fratricide, and is killed in its turn. This was the reign of the last pair of fins, Nerva. The reign of this usurper was short and full of troubles.

In this way, several dozen Jewish prophets peppered the early days with their apocalyptic visions, before the Christian prophets took their place, even though they themselves came from Judaism. John the Baptist remains the first of these. The whole world also knows about his seven visions, and you only have to read the Bible to remember them. Of course, I'll skip over all the medieval Nostradamuses to get to Saint Malachy's 111 papal mottos, from Pope Celestine II (1143) to the last one to come. The 110th being John Paul II (1978) with the motto: *De labore Solis*, already explained in various ways by several contemporaries who judiciously exploited events to do so! But logically, the only valid explanation... is the literal Latin translation that has been used for centuries: *The Work of the Sun*, because this Pope, John Paul II, is the last to precede the one at the *end of the solar era of our Christian Pisces cycle*. This, according to the Divine-Mathematical Combinations, poses enormous functional problems. The motto of the third and last pope to be enthroned in the Vatican is Malachian: *Gloria olivae*, or *The Glory of the Olive Tree*. It's too reminiscent of Golgotha and the Mount of Olives not to realise that the last pope, the one who comes after John Paul II, will suffer a fate similar to that of Christ at Golgotha, even if it's not actually a cross.

We saw in the chapter on Jesus the Christ in the Age of Pisces how many symbolic interpretations his end gave rise to and what it could still do today, if we take the Eucharistic Centenary Congress held in Lourdes during the second half of July 1981. In fact, where the Bread and Wine were advocated as the Spirit and Blood of Christ, the very Spirit of Christ intervened to ensure that John Paul II was not among the hundred thousand or so pilgrims who included a would-be assassin who would have upset the chronological order of Saint Malachy's list. For the last pope must necessarily be the pope of the end of Christianity, and that time has not yet come.

Some copy-hungry authors have pinned everything on the fact that the Mount of Olives symbolised the Jewish origin of the future last pope, who would thus be similar in form if not in substance to Christ. If this turns out to be true, it's not enough to make "six columns on the front page", because the problem with the future Holy Father will not be his birth, but *his end!* For it will be the end of the Piscean era and of the symbol represented, literally and figuratively. The third "secret" of Fatima, of which Paul VI was aware, and whose revelation was then postponed until a later date, also gave rise to several volumes of interpretations, but which will not, by any means, reflect the Truth. This end of Christianity will end like Judaism at the time of the fall of the Temple in Jerusalem, but like Hebrew monotheism, it will not be the end of Trinitarian monotheism.

Saint Malachy completes his enumeration:

In persecutione extremâ S.R.E. sedebit Petrus Rom. qui pascet oves in multis tribulationibus ; quibus transactis, civitas septicollis diruëtur, et Judex tremendus judicabit populum suum.

Finis.

In French, this means: "During the final persecution suffered by the Holy Roman Church, a Roman Peter will be seated. He will feed the sheep in the midst of the general lamentations. Once this is over, the city of the seven hills will be destroyed, and a fearsome Judge will judge the people: his own."

So let's leave all these prophecies aside and come to the *mathematical* time at the end of our era, which will determine the completion of the rest. The Denderah Zodiac shows us the Constellation of Pisces at the zenith of its path. It dominates the sky in such a blatantly obvious way that it shouldn't require much explanation. What's more, between the two aquatic vertebrates, clearly inscribed in a rectangular frame, is the hieroglyph for heavy flooding, made up of three broken sawtooth lines enclosed in a symbolic frame, as if to give it a proper name, similar to that inscribed in a cartouche, as can be seen in the following illustration.

Thus, at least six millennia ago, the Masters of Measurement and Number were already informing their pupils, the future high priests, of the state the globe would reach at the end of the Piscean cycle and the Aquarian cycle.

But let's not get ahead of ourselves, and let's take a closer look at this era which is nearing its end, and in a confusion similar to that which saw the end of Taurus and Aries. The Constellation of Pisces measures 28° in space, which means that in time it has a duration equal to 2,016 years (i.e. 28 x 72 years).

All our basic calculations have taken into account the calendrical differences that have arisen over the reigns, so the end of this period is in the year 2016. This will be the end of ONE world, not the world as the ancients bequeathed it to us, along with their knowledge. What I am going to develop throughout these lines is the nonsense of the predictions, in order to put an end to this "dreadful fear" concerning the arrival of the year 2000 and the "dreadful cataclysms" which are beginning sweep across our world in the run-up to this fateful date!...

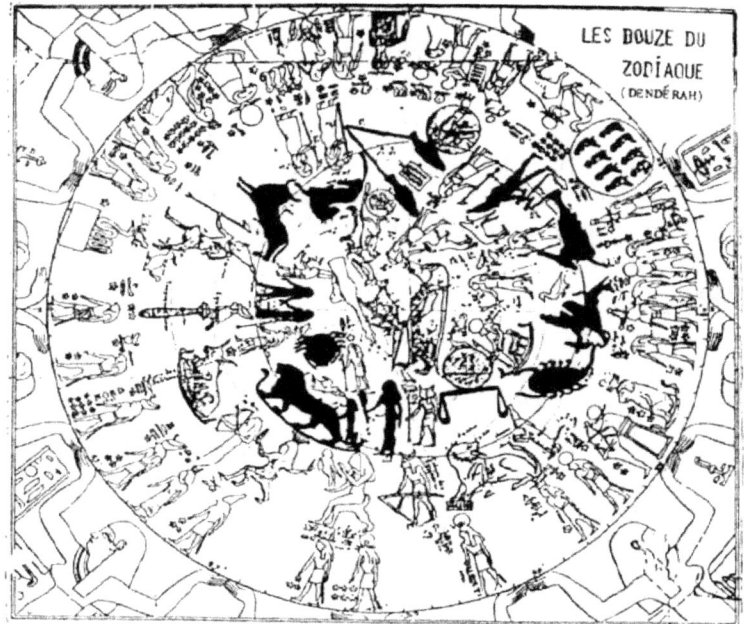

LES DOUZE DU ZODIAQUE (DENDÉRAH)

The "little prophets" of our time, desperate for copies, notoriety and above all money, are literally feeding the public with their writings and conferences on this end. A pseudo-religious sect is following suit and preparing to survive in shelters dug in carefully chosen sites! Some say it's going to happen in 1982; others say it's going to happen in 1984; others say it's not going to happen at all: it's going to happen in 1999, just as Nostradamus predicted! Well, no! Two thousand times no! The situation at the end of the Piscean Era is quite different, and what's more, it depends on man himself, as I shall demonstrate below.

In my *Astronomy according to the Egyptians*, the strict study of the Divine-Mathematical Combinations led our ancient masters to predict the astral movements from the year zero to 2016 of our era, and to develop their rhythms into "Celestial Harmonic Pulsations", as follows:

CELESTIAL HARMONIC PULSES
1ST RHYTHMIC CYCLE OF 36 YEARS:

Saturn	1 à 36	253 à 288	.../...	1765 à 1800
Venus	37 à 72	289 à 324	.../...	1801 à 1836
Jupiter	73 à 108	325 à 360	.../...	1837 à 1872
Mercure	109 à 144	361 à 396	.../...	1873 à 1908
March	145 à 180	397 à 432	.../...	1909 à 1945
Moon	181 à 216	433 à 468	.../...	1946 à 1980
Sun	217 à 252	469 à 504	.../...	1981 à 2016

2° ASTRAL CYCLES OF 5 YEARS :

(1980 was a neutral year for the development of human free will)

Sun	1981	1988	1995	2002	2009
Venus	1982	1989	1996	2003	2010
Mercure	1983	1990	1997	2004	2011
Moon	1984	1991	1998	2005	2012
Saturn	1985	1992	1999	2006	2013
Jupiter	1986	1993	2000	2007	2014
March	1987	1994	2001	2008	2015

(2016 is a neutral year for the development of human free will)

As can be seen from the table above, the statement is a striking abridgement of the entire Age of Pisces! The first calculation, for the thirty-six year periods that define the influences of the celestial rhythmic pulses, has been running the Earth since the year one of our Christian era, ending only with the year 2016 inclusive. It simply presents all the cyclical forecast elements for each of the seven Wanderers for 36 years. This numerical portion has not been chosen at random. It has been the subject of extensive research and study, with observation playing a major role in ancient Egypt. This "Second Heart of God", in which nothing could be fundamentally due to chance, had rightly noticed that the sky, too, was alive. The universe had a kind of heart with a gigantic beat, similar to that of humanity, but obviously on a different scale. The result was an inspiration of 34 years, followed and preceded by a neutral time of one year, making a total of : 1 + 34 + 1 = 36 years. This was further influenced by one of the seven Wanderers during a period of 36 solar revolutions.

This gives a complete period every 252 years (36 x 7). Thus, Saturn's influence over a period was from year one to 36, before resuming from year 253 to 288; and this until the year 1765, when Saturn began its last portion until the year 1800 to end its noxious power in our era of Pisces.

As you can see from the first table, 1980 was the last year, and therefore the neutral one, in terms of the Moon's power. And 1981 is the first year, just as neutral, under solar domination, which will bring the era to a close in 2016. What does this neutrality actually mean? It refers to the dead periods during which the inhalation and exhalation of air in the heart stop for a short time before taking on a reversed rhythm. The ancients had noticed that on a cosmic scale, these "dead times" were in some way identical, except that instead of lasting a tenth of a second before the reverse respiratory movement resumed, it remained suspended for a whole year. During these 365 days, no specific influence depended on the Fixed Ones, nor consequently on the Wandering Ones. It was humanity as a whole which, through its overall behaviour in that year, 'pre-destined', as it were, the celestial combinatorial fluctuations of its own 'future' for the next 34 years.

Each of the remarkable deeds and gestures, whether good or bad, was collated somewhere in the sky, in a sort of curve and weft which thus traced the beneficial or malefic, and at the very least highly complex, route within which the influxes of the Twelve would travel, delimiting the Divine-Mathematical Combinations. So, to take a contemporary example, with 1980 having ended the lunar cycle and 1981 having begun the solar impulse, the interested reader can examine in detail all the physical and political aspects of these two annual revolutions, in order to forecast the fluctuations to come over the next 34 years.

This brings us to the second table, which once again divides the first period into seven planetary slices, but of five years each. The last year is doubly neutral, even though it is under the tutelage of Mars in 2016. So it's perfectly clear that 1981 will be dominated by the Sun, neutralising solar influences, as the star of the day begins its 36-year journey. 1982 will be dominated by Venus, which formally contradicts those who 'predict' terrible catastrophes for that year because of the exceptional astrological configurations that will occur over our heads! And yet, cataclysms have always occurred under a serene celestial vault, free of any combinatorial complications. Without going into the sordid details of such publicity interpretations, let's remember that all the planetary clusters, century after century, have been the subject of alarming forecasts! They have all been disproved, even though the great cataclysms have never been predicted in advance by anyone.

Famous examples of these practices abound. So as not to offend any French astrologers, I will only mention a well-known German from the 15th century: the astrologer Johan Lichtenberger, who, in his book Prognosticatio, frightened his people by predicting terrible disasters at the time of 'kolossal' (sic) Saturn conjunctions: *Prognosticatio*, made his people tremble with fear by announcing terrible catastrophes at the time of the "kolossal" (*sic*) conjunctions of Saturn, Mars, Jupiter and Mercury, which intertwined in the constellation of Taurus to bring the worst calamities on earth! Nothing happened, and the 'seer' met with a bad end, as the King of Prussia decided to have his neck cut off in retaliation...

But today's 'prophets' of forecasts no longer take their readers for illiterates! Their announcements are made in such a way that, sowing confusion and even fear in people's minds, they still have a loophole that leaves a doubt in a sentence that goes unnoticed at the time, but which allows them to return to an earlier favourable proposition.

The same will be true for 1984, when nothing cataclysmic will happen. If we follow the ancient Egyptian texts, it won't be until 2016 that the next logical step in the movement of our terrestrial globe will be decided. Everything could be read in the celestial combinatorial configurations whose geometric form is applicable to all times, according to the very precise tables emanating from the Golden Circle itself- and reproduced over and over again, at random, in crypts and underground passages. The tables (A and B) will help you to better understand the hermeticism that exists between the two formulations. The first is that of the 36 decans used to define the lengths 'found' by their promoters, as well as the phonetisation generally accepted in Greek by those who used these asterisms:

LIST OF THE 36 "EGYPTIAN" DECANS

selon FIRMICUS	selon phonétique	selon SCALIGER	Planètes	Décans
SENATOR	Asicta	ASICCAN	Mars	1
SANACHER	Sentafora	SENACHER	Soleil	2
SENTACHER	Asentacer	ASENTACER	Venus	3
SUO	Asicat	ASICATH	Mercure	4
ARYO	Asou	VIROASO	Lune	5
ROMANAE	Arfi	AHARPH	Saturne	6
THESOGAR	Tesossar	THESOGAR	Jupiter	7
VER	Asue	VERASUS	Mars	8
TEPIS	Atosoae	TEPISATOSOA	Soleil	9
SOTHIS	Socius	SOTHIS	Vénus	10
SIT	Seth	SYTH	Mercure	11
THIUMIS	Thumus	THUIMIS	Lune	12
CRAUMONIS	Africis	APHRUIMIS	Saturne	13
CICK	Siccer	SITHACER	Jupiter	14
FUTILE	Futie	PHUNISIE	Mars	15
THINIS	Thinnis	THUMUS	Soleil	16
TOPHICUS	Tropicus	THOTHIPUS	Vénus	17
APHUI	Asout	APHUT	Mercure	18
SECHUI	Senichut	SERUCUTH	Lune	19
SEPISENT	Atebenus	ATERECHINIS	Saturne	20
SENTA	Atecent	ARPIEN	Jupiter	21
SENTACER	Asente	SENTACER	Mars	22
TEPISEN	Asentatir	TEPISEUTH	Soleil	23
SENTINEU	Atercen	SENCINER	Vénus	24
EREGUBO	Erghob	EREGUBO	Mercure	25
SAGON	Sagen	SAGEN	Lune	26
CHENENE	Chenem	CHENEN	Saturne	27
THEMESO	Themedo	THEMESO	Jupiter	28
EPIMU	Epremou	EPIMA	Mars	29
OMOT	Omor	HOMOTH	Soleil	30
OROTH	Orosoer	OROMOTH	Vénus	31
CRATERO	Asturo	ASTIRO	Mercure	32
TEPIS	Amapero	TEPISATRAS	Lune	33
ACHATE	Athapiat	ARCHATATRAS	Saturne	34
TEPIBUT	Tepabiu	THOTHPIBU	Jupiter	35
UIU	Atexbut	ATEMBUI	Mars	36

TABLEAU A

On the other hand, table B below shows the exact formulation of the 64 khents, or real decans.

THE GREAT HYPOTHESIS

TABLEAU DES 64 KHENTS D'ATĒTĀ

In the hypostyle hall of the great temple, the other Zodiac, around the astral engraving which is rectangular, lists the procession of Khents featuring the same total of seventy-two drawings, such as some of these:

So there are seventy-two symbols, as we know them from the papyri of the House of Life at Denderah. Eight of these are intercalated to direct the secondary influxes that do not depend on the four vital points of the universe (today we would say the four cardinal points).

The same applies to the list in Table B, where the neutralising dividers are numbers twenty *bis* and twenty *ter*, thirty *bis* and thirty *ter*, forty *bis* and forty *ter*, and fifty-five *bis* and fifty-five *ter*. Thus the 64 Khents, plus the 8 neutrals, give the 72 parts of 5 degrees each which form the 360° of the zodiacal ecliptic.

It would take too long to list here all the symbolism of the 8 times 8 celestial positions. Here again, confusion due to a lack of understanding of the texts has misled the distinguished Egyptologists who have dealt with this problem. The scribes were accused of gross errors, which is an understatement, but an excuse for the thoughtlessness of 19th century scholars. In fact, the city to which the name Hermopolis Magma was given was written in hieroglyphic:

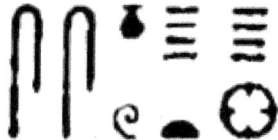

which means "Guardian of the Eight Heavenly Places", and has nothing to do with the name of an earthly city, since it symbolises the Golden Circle.

This imbroglio is explained at length in *L'Astronomie selon les Égyptiens*, which will be published in a few months' time. I really no longer feel brave enough to fight windmills, as Don Quixote, Galileo and so many others did.

Being myself at a very serious turning point in my existence, I want to see through to the end the light that will save the world, and which alone is likely, at the end of this Piscean era, to restore humanity's conscience: FAITH. And by Faith I don't mean generic Christianity, but the understanding of a Creator God who generated Sons, Messiahs, Prophets and the Humanity we all form today, whatever the colour of our skin. This is what all the philosophers and patriarchs have said for thousands of years. That's what Galileo must have said to himself when he died four years after going blind! For we forget that from the day he clumsily denied what was the simple truth, namely that it was the Earth that revolved around the Sun and not the other way round, he lost his Faith and the spark of clarity that clung to his Divine Parcel! It was not until March 1980 that the Vatican reopened the case for the rehabilitation of Galileo and assured us that he was a good man who had not lied when he said that the Earth was round and did indeed revolve around the Sun!

If it takes two centuries to be sure and say that I'm only writing the Truth, that's not my problem, because I'll have done what I had to do by passing on the torch of Denderah! But once again, will the Golden Circle remain in complete darkness before the new era wipes it off the face of the earth? Will there finally be a team with eyes wide open to understand the eternal cycle of Divine Eternity?...

NOTE NUMBER 1

CHRONOLOGICAL DATES ACCORDING TO SIRIUS

How can the ancient dating of the chronology be re-established? There are points of reference. The most commonly accepted and very valid one is provided by the Latin historian Censorinus. In his 21st chapter, he notes that just a century before he wrote his text, the first day of Thoth in the Egyptian calendar fell "on the extraordinary day of the rising of the heatwave in Egypt", the equivalent of our 19th of July in the year 139 AD.

Another major contribution to chronological compilation was the discovery, in 1865, of the text of the "Decree of Canopus". The preface states that "in year 9 of the reign of Ptolemy III Evergetes, the rising of Sothis took place on the 1st of Payni, the first day of the 10th month of the year".

The Decree was as follows:

In order that the months follow an absolute rule, in accordance with the natural order of the world, and that it no longer happens that certain solemn feasts celebrated in winter are celebrated in summer, the progress of the star advancing by one day every four years, and that other feasts among those which are now celebrated in summer are celebrated later in winter as has already happened before, and would still happen if the year remained composed of 360 days and 5 days instituted under the name of epagomena, from now on, one day will be added...

A concrete example of the chronological value of this astronomical source is the dating of the beginning of the reign of Amenhotep I, of the 18th dynasty, who was the founder of the family of which Akhenaten was the fourth reigning pharaoh - and the most controversial! Another papyrus, this one discovered by the German Egyptologist G. Ebers, reads: "In the year 9 of the reign of His Majesty Amonhotep, Health and Eternal Life to him who has the Right Voice, and more precisely on the Day of the Year of the rising of Sep'ti on the 9th day of the 3rd month of Shemou, the King...".

Calculating the precise date is crucial here, because it provides a mathematical and uncontroversial date for the beginning of the reign of Amenhetep I, and hence the very beginning of the 18th dynasty, which had only the famous Yahmes, or Amosis, as its predecessor.

The delay between the 1st day of Thoth in the year 139 of Censorinus and the 9th day of the 3rd month of Shemou, which is the 11th month of the year, is 56 days. However, as there was an extra complete "canicular" cycle, there was an additional shift of 365 days a quarter for the 1,461 years. This gives: 56 + 365 1/4 = 421 1/4 days, or a time lapse of 1,685 years, obtained by multiplying by four for the shift of one day every four years of Sothis in Space.

Starting from the year 139 AD and going back 1685 years, we obtain the date 1546 BC, the ninth year of the reign of Amenophis I. So the Pharaoh was crowned in the year 1555, an irrefutable mathematical date.

Given that, here too, all the aforementioned Egyptologists give different dates, it's food for thought! After all, even for those unfamiliar with the Ebers papyrus, the astronomical key was provided by the two "classics" known the world over: the Canopic Decree and Censorin's dating.

The calculation is very simple:

The Decree announces the first day of the rising of Sirius for the 1st Payni of the year 238 BC, and Censorin for the 1st Thot of the year 139 AD, i.e. in 377 years, a time difference of :

29 days for the month of Payni,
30 days for Epiphi
30 days for Mésori,
5 epagomenal days to return to the 1st of Thoth, i.e. 94 days' difference.

Now, 94 days' difference, at the rate of one every 4 years, gives (94 x 4) the 376 years separating 238 before from the start of 139 after.

Similarly, it is easy to calculate the start of the chronology, since Athothis re-established the hieroglyphic system on the day of the Sun-Sirius conjunction, after a two-year reign.

Starting from the 1st day of Thoth 139, backwards, by 3 x 1,461 years, we get 4,383 years. We need to subtract 139 for the date to start before Christ, i.e. the 1st day of Thoth 4,244. His reign therefore began two years earlier with the death of the Unifier Menes, in 4,246 BC.

Here, then, is the beginning of this "Chronology of Ath-Kâ-Ptah", which readers will have found in the Origins Trilogy as the three books were published:

N°	Noms HIÉROGLYPHIQUES	Noms GRECS	Durée Règne	Datation (avant J.-C.)	Fait marquant du REGNE
	I" DYNASTIE				
1		MENES	62	4308-4246	Fut l'unificateur des Deux-Clans fratricides.
2		ATHOTHIS	55	4248-4191	Restaurateur de la Hiéroglyphique. Dès 4244 lors de la conjonction Soleil-Sirius
3		ATHOTHIS II	31	4195-4160	(1)
4		HENEPHTYS	19	4160-4141	Fut la première Reine. Elle eut à combattre une très grave famine.
5		OUANEPHES	23	4141-4118	
6		OUSIRPHERES	20	4118-4098	
7		MIEVIS	26	4098-4072	Quitta sa capitale Thinis, pour aller dans le Delta.
8		SEMEMPSIS	18	4073-4054	Une peste violente tua 1/3 du peuple.
9		BINOCHIS	26	4054-4028	

1. Les différences de dates entre la fin d'un règne et le début d'un autre proviennent d'années de corégence avec le Pharaon précédent.

NOTE N° 2

THEON OF ALEXANDRIA AND SIRIUS

To understand Theon's rule of calculation for the heliacal rising of the Dog, and therefore of Sirius, we need to study its various parts in turn, and find the principle on which each of them is based. First of all, since the Greek author prescribes counting the years from Menophres to the end of Augustus, and immediately adds the years of Diocletian to make a total sum, it is obvious that all these years immediately follow one another, and so these expressions, the beginning of Menophres, the end of Augustus, the years of Diocletian, must be understood not as referring to the birth or death of these princes, but to the origin of the eras named after them. Thus, when we say the hundredth year of Nabonassar, it means the hundredth year from the time when the era of Nabonassar began.

Secondly, since the Greek author adds these various kinds of years together, it is obvious that he considers them, at least in this first calculation, to be of the same duration. Now, we know that the years of Augustus and Diocletian were years of 365 days subject to quadrennial intercalation; or, in other words, average years of this form, which the Greek author expresses as the interval elapsed from the beginning of Menophres to the end of Augustus.

We now know that the Alexandrian era of Augustus began 24 years before the Christian era, and 21 years after the reform prescribed by Julius Caesar. The first day of the Thot Vague coincided with Julian August 29. From that time onwards, the Alexandrians made their year fixed by intercalating one day every four years, according to the Julian method; and so the first day of the fixed Thoth has always been on August 29, in common years, and on August 30, in leap years. We also know that this era of Augustus lasted until the 29th of August in the year 284 A.D., when the era of Diocletian began. In order to present these elements of calculation in a way that is convenient because of its continuity, I will report here their place in Scaliger's Julian period, also including that of the Christian era:

Reform of the year by Julius Caesar: 4,669 - 1 January Fixation of the year by the Alexandrians: 4,690 - 29 August
Christian era: 4,714 - 1 January

End of the Alexandrian era of Augustus, and beginning of the era of Diocletian: 4,998 -29 August

With these data, we can first of all relate to the Christian era the unknown origin to which the Greek author gives the name of Menophres. For the sum of the years of Menophres and Augustus, which, according to him, makes 1,605 years, which he uses in this calculation as average Julian years, it suffices to subtract the years completely passed from the Christian era to the end of Augustus, i.e. 283, and the remainder, 1,322, will express the rank of the Julian year prior to the Christian era, in which the years of Menophres begin. Now, we have seen above, both from astronomical calculations and from the testimony of Censorinus, that in fact this year, 1322, is that of the first renewal of the pre-Christian Julian cycle, i.e. that the heliacal rising of Sirius in Egypt coincided with the first day of the Vague Thoth. It is therefore this first renewal of the period that Theon's rule assigns as the origin of his Menophres.

Now, since the interval between the consecutive heliacal sunrises of Sirius in Egypt must have been 365 days 1/4, i.e. precisely equal to an average Julian year, it follows that the epoch of this phenomenon was fixed in this form of year. But it was not fixed in the vague 365-day year. If we imagine two series, one of vague Egyptian years, the other of fixed Alexandrian years, both originating from the same physical day, a day on which the heliacal rising of Sirius coincides with the first of Thoth, when four complete Alexandrian years have elapsed, and the addition of the intercalary day made in the fourth will have maintained the heliacal rising of Sirius at the first of Thoth, we will count four vague years, plus one day ; and consequently the heliacal rising of Sirius will take place on the second day of Thoth in this particular form of year.

In the same way, when eight Julian years have elapsed, two of which are leap years, we will count eight wave years, plus two days, and so it will be on the third day of Thoth that the heliacal rising of Sirius will take place. From this we can see that, in general, to find out the number of days whose heliacal rising will have moved in the vague year, starting from the first of Thoth, it is sufficient to divide the number of Julian years that have passed by 4, or to take a quarter. This is also what the Greek author does, and he thus finds 1,705 : 4 or 426 using only whole numbers. Consequently, if we suppose that the two corresponding series of vague years and fixed years, which we imagined earlier, continued for 1,705 Julian years, the displacement of the heliacal sunrise in the vague years would be 426 days or a whole vague year plus 61 days, i.e. this phenomenon would have travelled once through the whole vague year, would thus have returned to the first Thoth and would already have exceeded him by 61 whole days.

However, this result can only be applied to the terrestrial parallel for which the origin of the period was originally established, i.e. for the parallel where the heliacal sunrise coincided with Thoth's first sunrise, at the time taken as the starting point; and, if we wanted to obtain the date of the phenomenon for another latitude, we would have to add or subtract a certain number of fixed days depending on the difference in latitudes. This is what the Greek author seems to do by adding 5 days to the 426 found above, which gives him a total of 431. And, as his correction is additive, we can see that he makes his calculation for a more northern parallel than the one to which the period is originally supposed to apply.

We can even say what this primitive parallel is, because by adding 5 days in this way, the Greek author definitively finds the 29th epiphi fixe, or the 23rd of July for the time of the heliacal sunrise, which corresponds fairly well to the latitude of Alexandria, since Ptolemy indicates the 28th epiphi, or the 22nd of July, for the parallel of fourteen hours which passes a little to the south of this city. Thus, without the addition of these five days, we would find the 24th epiphi instead of the 29th, in other words, the 18th of July instead of the 23rd. Now, Ptolemy assigns the 22nd epiphi to the parallel where the longest day is 13 hours 1/4, which corresponds to the latitude 23°51', and he assigns the 28th to the parallel where the longest day is 14 hours, which corresponds to the latitude 30°22': the average difference is thus 6°31' of latitude for 6 days of difference, or 1°5' per day, which gives for two days 2°10'. Adding this difference to the first latitude of 23°51', which corresponds to the 22nd epiphi, we have 26° for the latitude of the parallel where the heliacal rising of Sirius arrived on the 24th epiphi, and for which Theon's rule assumes the origin of the primitively established period. It is remarkable that this latitude, slightly more northern than that of Thebes, is precisely that of the temples of Dendera and Esne.

The preceding calculations are made on the assumption that the series of vague years continues without interruption throughout the course of the 1,705 Julian years. But this was not the actual case in Alexandria; for the year there, while retaining its form, became fixed 21 years after the Julian reform, when the first of Thoth coincided with the 29th of August. Thus, from that day until the hundredth year of Diocletian, to which our calculation applies, a certain number of years elapsed, during which Thoth no longer moved. To find out this number, we need only first take the number of years that have elapsed since the Thoth was fixed until the end of the era of Augustus, a number which, according to the dates given earlier, is 308 years; then, by adding the 100 years of Diocletian, which lead up to the period for which we are making our calculation, we will have a total of 408 years during which the Thoth no longer varied.

Now, these 408 years divided by 4 give a quotient of 102, which makes 102 days of variation of Thoth that we had over-counted in our first calculation. These must therefore be subtracted from 431 to obtain the true variation, which is then expressed by the remainder 329. This is also precisely what the Greek author does, when, after finding the 431 days of Thoth's displacement, both for the given time interval and for the change of parallel, he prescribes subtracting from them what there were then of tetraeterides, leaving aside the number 21 ; and they must be calculated according to the total number of years elapsed since the Julian reform, less 21 years, because the Alexandrian Thoth only became fixed 21 years after this reform, and thus continued to move in the solar year during these 21 years.

Having thus found 329 days for the actual displacement of the vague Thoth since Menophres, the Greek author prescribes to distribute this number starting from the first of Thoth, counting 30 days for each month, which first gives him 10 months with 29 days remaining; and thus leads him to the 29th day of the eleventh month, i.e. to the 29 epiphi of the Egyptian vague year. However, according to the reasoning on which the calculation of the days of variation is based, it seems that they should be distributed by counting the first of them as coinciding with the second of Thoth, which would lead to 30 epiphi instead of 29.

Moreover, the difference of one day is of little consequence for the date of a phenomenon subject to so many physical uncertainties, and may be that, for this reason, the Greek author confined himself to presenting the distribution from the first of Thoth as being simpler. However, he could have simplified his rule even further by distinguishing between the heliacal sunrises before and after the fixing of the Alexandrian Thoth. For the former, a quarter of the number of years elapsed since Menophres gives the total displacement of the phenomenon without the need for any correction, of tetraeterides; and for the latter, the date of the phenomenon remains fixed on the same day of epiphi on which it took place in the year of the fixation of the Thoth.

BIBLIOGRAPHY

A) AT THE TIME OF ORIGIN

TEXTS AND REVIEWS :

Description de l'Égypte. -Recueil des observations et des recherches qui ont été faites durant l'expédition de l'armée française, 1st ed. 9 vols. of text and 12 vols. of atlases and drawn documents (1809 to 1813).

Bibliothèque de l'École des Hautes Études. -Maspero: *Genre épistolaire*, 1872; Grébaut: *Hymnes à Amon-Râ, 1875;* Virey: *Papyrus Prisse, 1887;* Jéquier: *L'Hadès*, 1894. *Annales du musée Guimet.* -Lefébure: *Hypogées royaux, 1886;* Amélineau: *Gnosticisme, 1887;* Mahler: *Calendrier, 1907.*

Bibliothèque égyptologique. -Works by French Egyptologists: Leroux: two volumes, 1893; Maspero: *Mythologie*, 1894; Devéria: *Mémoires*, 1904; Chabas: *Œuvres*, 1905; de Rouge: *Œuvres,* 1909.

Archaeological Survey. -Griffith: *Hieroglyphs*, 1895; Davies: *Ptahhetep*, 1897; Crowfoot: *Meroe*, 1911.

Altertumskunde Aegyptens. -Sethe: *Horusdiener*, 1903; Schaeffer: *Mysterien des Osiris*, 1904.

Egypt Exploration Fund. -Naville: *Pithom*, 1885; Petrie: *Denderah*, 1900.

Egyptological studies. -Lefébure: *Mythe Osirien*, 1874; Révillout: *Chrestomathie*, 1880.

AUTHORS

Amelineau E.: Étude sur le papyrus de Boulacq, I.F.A.O., Cairo, 1892.

Amelineau E.: Le culte des rois prédynastiques, Journal des Savants, Paris, 1906.

Ampère J.-J.: Transmission des professions dans l'Ancienne Égypte, Paris, 1848.

Baillet A. Fonctions du Grand-Prêtre d'Amon, Paris, 1865.

Bergmann A.: Hieroglyphs Inschrifften, Munich, 1879.

Birch S.: Select Papyri of Britisch Muséum, London, 1841.

Brugsch E.: Le Livre des Rois, Berlin, 1887.

Brugsch E.: Le dictionnaire géographique ancien, Berlin, 1877.

Budge W.: Papyrus of Ani, Oxford, 1895.

Bürton J.: Excerpta hieroglyphica, London, 1825.

Capart J.: La fête de frapper les Annou, Brussels, 1901.

Chabas F.: Le papyrus Harris, Paris, 1860.

Chassinat E.: Denderah (6 vol.), I.F.A.O., Cairo, 1911.

Davis C.: The Book of the Dead, London, 1894.

Deveria Th.: Papyrus de Nebqeb, Paris, 1872.

Devilliers: Dendérah, Paris, 1812.

Ebers G.: Papyrus Ebers, London, 1875.

Einselohr A.: Avant le règne de Ramsès III, Berlin, 1872.

Erman A.; Aegypten Leben im Alterthum geschildert, Berlin, 1885.

Erman A.: Grammaire Égyptienne, Berlin, 1894.

Frazer J.-G.: Totemism, New York, 1887.

Gaillard C.: Le Bélier de Mendès, Paris, 1901.

Gardiner A.: Berlin Papyrus, London, 1908.

Gardiner A.: The Admonitions of an Egyptian Sage, London, 1909.

Gardiner A.: Hieratic Texts (pap. Anastasi and Koller), London, 1911.

Gayet A. La Civilisation pharaonique, Paris, 1907.

Golenitscheff W. Papyrus n° 1 de Saint-Pétersbourg, Saint-Pétersbourg, 1876.

Golenitscheff W.; Hieratic papyrus n0 15, St Petersburg, 1906.

Grevaut E.: Les deux yeux du disque solaire, Paris, 1879.

Grenfell B.: The Amherst Papyri, London, 1891.

Griffith: Two Papyri hierogliphs from Tanis, Oxford, 1889.

Groff W. The Egyptian names of Jacob and Joseph, London, 1885.

Groff W. Papyrus of Orbiney, London, 1888.

Guieysse P.: Hymne au Nil, Paris, 1890.

Horrack Ph. J. (de). Les Lamentations d'Isis et de Nephtys, Paris, 1866.

Horrack Ph. J. (de). Le Livre des Respirations, Paris, 1877.

Jollois J.-B.: Dendérah, Paris, 1814.

Lanzone Rod. Le domicile des Esprits, Paris, 1879.

Lauth Fr: Pharaon Meneptah, Paris, 1867.

Lenormand Fr.: Les premières civilisations, Paris, 1874.

Le Page-Renouf P.: Religion of Ancien Egypt, London, 1880.

Lieblein J.: Recherches sur la chronologie égyptienne, Paris, 1873.

Lieblein J.: Papyri hiératiques du musée de Turin, Paris, 1868.

Lieblein J.: Dictionnaire des noms hiéroglyphiques, Paris, 1871.

Lieblein Dr J.: Recherches sur la civilisation de l'ancienne Égypte, Paris, 1910.

Loret V.: Rituel des fêtes d'Osiris à Dendérah, Paris, 1895.

Loret V.: Manuel de la langue égyptienne, Paris, 1896.

Mariette A.: Description du Grand Temple de Dendérah, Paris, 1875.

Martin T.: Opinion de Manéthon sur sa chronologie, Paris, 1960.

Maspero G.: Littérature religieuse des anciens Égyptiens, Paris, 1872.

Moret A. Le rituel du culte divin, Paris, 1902.

Moret A. Rois et Dieux, Paris, 1911.

Moret A. Mystères égyptiens, Paris, 1911.

Morgan J. (de): Recherches sur les origines de l'Égypte, Paris, 1897.

Naville E.: La litanie du Soleil, Geneva, 1875.

Naville E.: La religion des anciens Égyptiens, Geneva, 1906.

Petrie W. Flinders: Religion of ancient Egypt, London, 1906.

Pierret P.: Horus sur les crocodiles, Paris, 1869.

Pierret P.: Vocabulaire hiéroglyphique, Paris, 1875.

Reinach A. J.: L'Égypte préhistorique, Paris, 1908,

Revillout E.: Chronique contemporaine de Manéthon, Paris, 1876.

Rouge Emm (de): Origines de la race égyptienne, Paris, 1895.

Sharpe S.: History of Egypt, London, 1870.

Virey P.: Religion de l'ancienne Égypte, Paris, 1909.

Young T.: Hieroglyphics, London, 1823.

B) IN THE TIME OF MOSES

TEXTS

The Holy Bible, trans. École Biblique de Jérusalem, 1955.

The Koran, trans. F. Rouhani, 1959.

The Jerusalem Talmud, trans. M. Schwab, 1960.

AUTHORS

Abecassis Armand: La Mystique du Talmud, Paris, 1977.

Aharûni Yohanan: The McMillan Bible Atlas, London, 1968.

Albright William F.: Yahveh and the Gods of Canaan, London, 1970.

Auzou Georges: Étude du livre de l'Exode, Paris, 1968.

Barrois A. G.: Manuel d'archéologie biblique (2 vols.), Paris, 1939.

Basil De Cesaree: Homélies sur l'Hexameron, Paris, 1976.

Bayle J.-B.: Saint Basile, Paris, 1958.

Beegle Dewey: Moses, servant of Yaweh, Michigan, 1972.

Bridel J.-L.: Traité sur L'Année juive ancienne, Tours, 1818.

Bright John: An history of Israel, Philadelphia, 1972

Bryant Jacques: Analyse de la mythologie ancienne, London, 1773.

Buber Martin: Moïse, Paris, 1957,

Buis Pierre: Notion d'alliance dans L'Ancien Testament, Paris, 1976.

Buxtorf A.: Moré Néboukim, Hamburg, 1674.

Cazelles Henri: Étude sur le code de L'Alliance, Paris, 1946.

Cazelles Henri: À la recherche de Moïse, Paris, 1979.

Childs Breward S.: The Birth of Moses, New York, 1965.

Choisy Maryse: Moïse, Geneva, 1966.

Clement of Alexandria: The Stromata, Paris, 1932.

Congar Yves: Le Mystère du Temple, Paris, 1958.

Coote Robert: Meaning of the name: Israel, Harvard, 1972.

Danielou Jacques: Platonisme et théologie mystique, Paris, 1964.

Denys L'Aeropagyte: La Hiérarchie céleste, Paris, 1882.

Doresse Jean: Les Livres des gnostiques d'Égypte, Paris, 1958.

Du Burr F.-M.: Cain and his Qenite sons, Paris, 1970.

Dupont-Sommer: Écrits esséniens de la mer Morte, Paris, 1959.

Duvfrnoy Claude: Moïse, Paris, 1977.

Eliade Mircea: Le Mythe de l'éternel retour, Paris, 1952.

Epsteïn Isidore: Le Judaïsme, Paris, 1970.

Feuler F.-X. Biographie universelle (in 9 volumes), Paris, 1844.

Festugiere A. J.: Les Révélations d'Hermès Trismégiste, Paris, 1952.

Flavius Joseph: Antiquités judaïques, trans. Buchon, Paris, 1841.

Fleg Edmond: Moïse, Paris, 1928.

Fohrer Georg: History of the Israelite religion, Nashville, 1972.

Frankfort H.: Les Rois et les Dieux, Paris, 1954.

Gaubert Henry: Moïse face à l'Éternel, Paris, 1965.

Glueck Nelson: Across the Jordan, Newhaven, 1940,

Grayzel Salomon: Histoire des Juifs, Paris, 1974.

Greeberg Moshe: Understanding the Exodus, New York, 1969.

Gregory of Nyssa: The Life of Moses, Paris, 1954.

Gressmann H.: Moses and his time, Gottingen, 1913.

Gugenheim G.: Le Judaïsme dans la vie quotidienne, Paris, 1978.

Guillàbert Emile: Moïse phénomène judéo-chrétien, Paris, 1976.

Gunneweg Antoine: Moses in Midian, Munich, 1964.

Hamel Edouard: Les Dix Paroles, Brussels, 1969.

Harrington Wilfrid: Nouvelle introduction à la Bible, Paris, 1971.

Herrmann Siegfried: Moses, Leiden, 1969.

HyattJ. Philip: Commentary on Exodus, London, 1971.

John of Alexandria: On the Creation of the World, Paris, 1954.

Lenormant François: Histoire ancienne de l'Orient, Paris, 1909.

Lestienne Michel: Comment la Bible a été écrite, Paris, 1976.

LODS Adolph: Israël, Paris, 1972.

Maignan (Cardinal): De l'Éden à Moïse, Paris, 1883.

Maimonides Moses: The Book of the Lost, Leiden, 1806.

Malka Victor: Le Judaïsme, Paris, 1976.

Martines de Pasqually: Traité de la réincarnation, Rennes, 1977.

Meyer Eduard: Histoire de l'Antiquité, Paris, 1912.

Michaeli Frank: Textes de l'ancien Orient, Neuchâtel, 1961.

Michaud Robert: Moïse : histoire et théologie, Paris, 1978.

Monloubou Louis: Prophète ; qui es-tu ? Paris, 1968.

Moret Alexandre: Au temps des Pharaons, Paris, 1941.

Moret Alexandre: Histoire de l'Orient ancien, Paris, 1936.

Muller Edouard: Histoire de la mystique juive, Paris, 1950.

Nehler André: Moïse et la vocation juive, Paris, 1957.

Nicholson E.: The Origin of the Exodus Tradition, London, 1976.

Noth Martin: Histoire d'Israël, Paris, 1970.

Origene: Homélies sur l'Exode, Paris, 1884.

Parroy André: Abraham et son temps, Paris, 1973.

Philo of Alexandria: The Life of Moses, Paris, 1883.

Pittazzoni Roberto: Formation of Monotheism, Turin, 1931.

RAGD Gherart: La Genèse, Geneva, 1968.

Renan Ernest: Histoire du peuple d'Israël, Paris, 1956.

Roth Cecil: Histoire du peuple juif, Paris, 1977.

Rothemberg B.: Un temple égyptien dans la Arabah, Paris, 1970.

Rowley H. H.: From Joseph to Joshua, Oxford, 1970.

Salvador Jean: Les Institutions de Moïse, Paris, 1862.

Scholem G.: Grands courants de la mystique juive, Paris, 1950.

Seale Morris: The Desert of the Bible, London, 1974.

Toussaint Gabriel: Origines de la religion d'Israël, Paris, 1931.

Vaux Robert (de): Histoire ancienne d'Israël, Paris, 1971.

Vaux Roland (de): Bible et Orient, Paris, 1967.

Velikovski Isidore: Mondes en collision, Paris, 1967.

Vigouroux François: Dictionnaire de la Bible (6 vol.), Paris, 1904.

Vincent Louis: Chanaan d'après l'exploration, Paris, 1907.

Weigall Arthur: Histoire de l'Égypte ancienne, Paris, 1935.

Weill Raymond: Séjour des Israélites au désert, Paris, 1909.

C)   IN THE TIME OF JESUS

TEXTS AND REVIEWS

The Catholic Encyclopédia (16 vols.), New York, 1917.

Dictionnaire des Antiquités gréco-romaines (9 vols.), Paris, 1877.

Dictionnaire d'archéologie chrétienne (11 vols.), Paris, 1933.

Dictionnaire de la Bible (6 vols.), Paris, 1888,

Proceedings of Biblical Archeology. Muse on.

Revue Biblique.

Revue des Études juives.

Revue de l'histoire des Religions.

AUTHORS

Bacon B. W. Story of St. Paul, Boston, 1904,

Bacon B. W. Jesus and Paul, New York, 1921.

Boissier G.: La fin du paganisme (2 vols.), Paris, 1899.

Bouche-Leclerc A.: L'Astrologie grecque, Paris, 1899.

Brassac A.; Manuel Biblique (2 vols.), Paris, 1908.

Brehier E. ; Idées Philosophiques de Philon d'Alexandrie, Paris, 1925.

Father Bruckberger R. L.: Jésus-Christ (Reprint), Paris, 1965.

Causse A. Les Dispersés d'Israël, Paris, 1929.

Dechamps V.: Christ et les Antéchrist (2 vols.), Paris, 1858.

Père Dibon: Jésus-Christ (2 vols.), Paris, 1891.

Doresse J.: Les Livres des Gnostiques d'Égypte (2 vols.), Paris, 1959.

Duchesne L.: Histoire ancienne de l'Église (4 vol.), Paris, 1906.

Mgr Dupanloup: Jésus-Christ, Paris, 1870.

Duval R.: La littérature syriaque, Paris, 1899.

De Faye E.: Origine des Églises de l'âge apostolique, Paris, 1909.

De Faye E.: Clément d'Alexandrie, Paris, 1899.

Goguel M.: Jésus de Nazareth, Paris, 1925.

Comperz Th.: Les penseurs de la Grèce (3. vol.), Paris, 1910.

Père Grandmaison L. (de) : Jésus-Christ, Paris, 1928.

Guignebert Ch.: Tertullian, Paris, 1901.

Guignebert Ch.: Le monde juif au temps de Jésus, Paris, 1933.

Herriot E.: Philon le Juif, Paris, 1898,

Klein F.: La Vie de Jésus-Christ, Paris, 1946.

Père Lamennais (de): Imitation de Jésus-Christ, Paris, 1921.

Lazarus B. Les idées religieuses de Plutarque, Paris, 1920.

Père Le Camus: La vie de Jésus-Christ, Paris, 1883.

Loisy A.: La naissance du Christianisme, Paris, 1933.

Père Maistre A.: La Passion du Christ, Paris, 1876.

Père Marin: Jésus-Christ et son règne, Paris, 1886.

Menard Jacques E.: L'évangile de vérité, Paris, 1962.

Menard Jacques E.: l'évangile selon Philippe, Paris, 1969.

Menard L.: Les Livres d'Hermès Trismégiste, Paris, 1866.

Montefiore C. G.: Judaism and St. Paul, London, 1914.

Moore G. F.: Judaism in the first Centuries (3 vols.), Cambridge, 1927.

Père Motais A. Salomon et l'Ecclésiaste (2 vols.), Paris, 1876.

Père Ollivier M.: Les amitiés de Jésus, Paris, 1895,

Oursler F.: La vie du Galiléen, Paris, 1955.

Pradines M.: Esprit de la Religion, Paris, 1945.

Père Prat F.: Jésus-Christ (2 vols.), Paris, 1933.

Püech A.: Histoire de la littérature gréco-chrétienne (3 vol.), Paris, 1928.

Radin P.: La religion primitive, Paris, 1941.

Renan E.: Origines du Christianisme, Paris, 1891.

Renan E.: Histoire du peuple d'Israël (3 vols.), Paris, 1887.

Reville J.: Le quatrième Évangile, Paris, 1901.

Rougier L.: L'origine astronomique, Cairo, 1933.

Scott W.: Corpus Hermeticum, Oxford, 1934.

Père Variot J.: Les Évangiles Apocryphes, Paris, 1878.

Venard L.: Les origines chrétiennes, Paris, 1911.

Père Vigouroux F.: Les Livres Saints (4 vols.), Paris, 1890.

Dr William F.-M.: La vie de Jésus, Mulhouse, 1934.

ON THE WORK OF ALBERT SLOSMAN

It was by applying his method of translating the texts engraved in the crypts of the Temple of Denderah that Albert Slosman discovered and delivered to the public the story of the origin European civilisation.

Cairo Progress

In the light of Albert Slosman's texts, Plutarch's fanciful account collapses! Isis, Osiris and Horus no longer appear as divinities, but as human beings.

The Courier from Egypt

The importance of Albert Slosman's ongoing research in the field of Egyptology has not yet been fully appreciated, nor has the revolution in our understanding Egyptian history.

Le Courrier de Genève

In the light of Slosman's theory, a lot of questions disappear: in particular the one about the birth of an idea that will go down in history: monotheism! It's the central element of the book!

Le Monde

The construction that is taking place before us is perhaps one of the events of our time. Historians are beginning to study the work of Albert Slosman.

Le Figaro

Drawing on texts, recent discoveries and a logical line, Slosman shows how the cradle of monotheism was formed in Egypt. A fascinating and thought-provoking book.

Le Méridional-Dimanche

OTHER TITLES

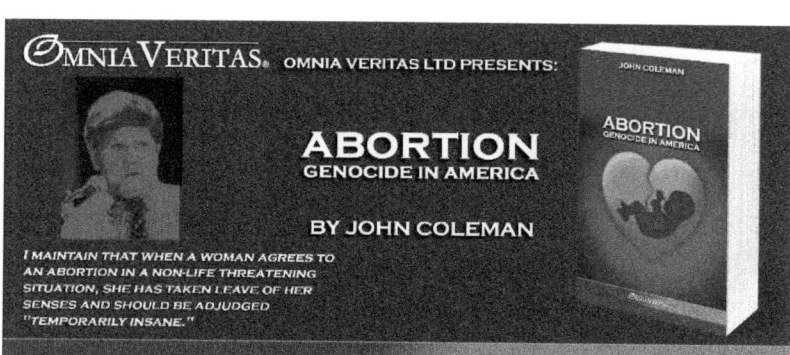

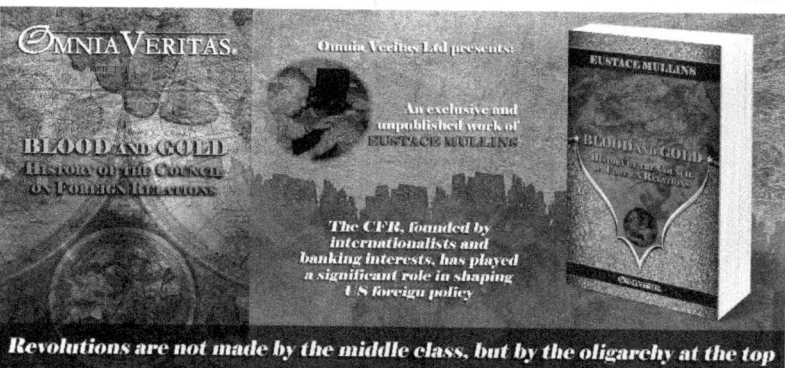

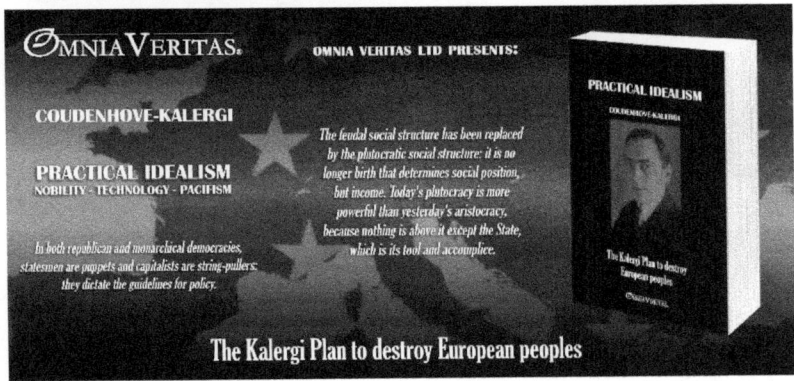

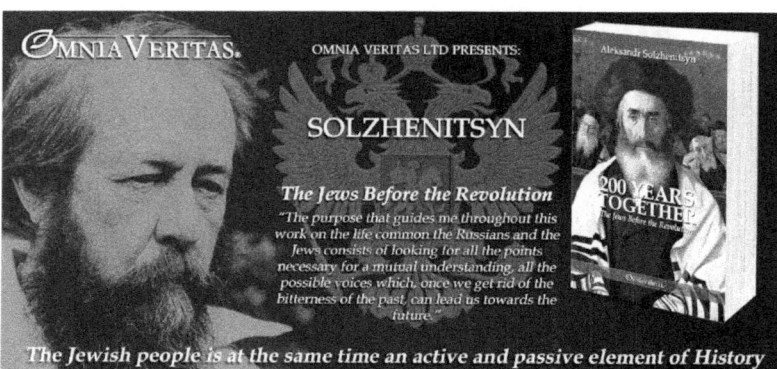
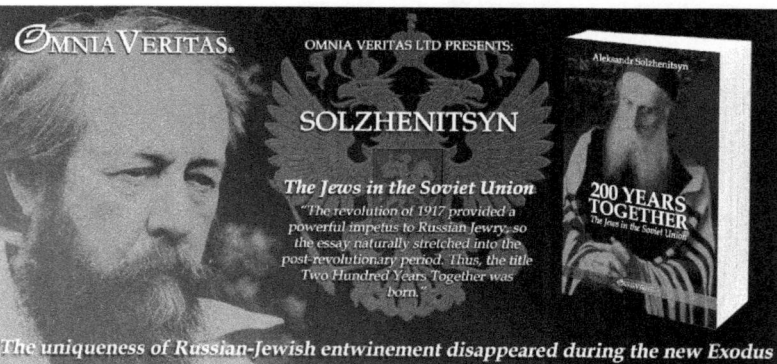

www.ingramcontent.com/pod-product-compliance
Lightning Source LLC
Chambersburg PA
CBHW051038160426
43193CB00010B/991